The Power of the Arts

The Power of the Arts

Creative Strategies for Teaching Exceptional Learners

by

Sally L. Smith
Founder/Director
The Lab School of Washington

Director, Master's Degree Program in
Special Education: Learning Disabilities
School of Education
American University

Washington, D.C.

·P·A·U·L·H·
BROOKES
PUBLISHING Cº ®

Baltimore • London • Sydney

Paul H. Brookes Publishing Co.
Post Office Box 10624
Baltimore, Maryland 21285-0624

www.brookespublishing.com

Third printing, January 2006.

Typeset by Pro-Image Corporation, York, Pennsylvania.
Manufactured in the United States of America by
The Maple Press Company, York, Pennsylvania.

All examples and case studies in this book are composites. Any similarity to actual individuals or circumstances is coincidental, and no implication should be inferred.

The song "How We Do Rap," which appears on pp. 133−134 and is excerpted on the back cover, was written by Sally L. Smith and several Lab School students and is based on a rap written by Pam Knudson.

Photography compliments of John Aaronson and Jeff Hamill.

Cover illustration by Jeff Hamill. Design by Paula Sloman.

Library of Congress Cataloging-in-Publication Data

Smith, Sally L.
   The power of the arts: creative strategies for teaching exceptional learners / by Sally L. Smith.
     p.   cm.
   Includes bibliographical references (p.) and index.
   ISBN-13: 978-1-55766-484-6
   ISBN-10: 1-55766-484-6
   1. Learning disabled children—Education—United States.   2. Arts—Study and teaching (Elementary)—United States.   3. Lab School of Washington (Washington, D.C.)   I. Title.
LC4704.825 .S65 2001
371.9′0445—dc21

                                               01-050759

British Library Cataloguing in Publication data are available from the British Library.

Contents

About the Author vii
Foreword   *Robert Rauschenberg* ix
Preface xi
Acknowledgments xix

1   The Power of the Arts with Exceptional Learners 1

2   Abilities and Disabilities, School Failures, Adult Successes 17

3   Providing Order and Focus Through the Arts 31

4   Developing a Sense of Self-Worth 41

5   The Educative Process at The Lab School of Washington 49

6   The Curriculum of The Lab School of Washington 63

7   The Lab School's Visual Arts Teachers Speak Out 87
     Woodwork: A Conversation with Dieter Zander 89
     Graphic Arts: A Conversation with Karen Hanish 92
     Plaster Art and Painting: A Conversation with Kelly McVearry 96
     Sculpture: A Conversation with Frank Cappello 99
     Architectural Design: A Conversation with Mark Jarvis 102
     Film Animation: A Conversation with Ruth Schwartz 105

8   The Lab School's Performing Arts Teachers Speak Out 111
     Drama: A Conversation with Shaun Miskell 113
     Dance: A Conversation with Stephen Johnson 117
     Elementary and Intermediate Music: A Conversation with
         Susan Mebane Carter 121
     Secondary Music: A Conversation with Sean Rozsics 125

9   Putting It All Together 129

10   A Clarion Call 139

References 143
Appendix A: Task Analyses 149
Appendix B: Lesson Plan 157
Appendix C: The Outstanding Learning Disabled Achiever Awards 161
Appendix D: The Lab School of Washington Fact Sheet 163
Index 165

About the Author

Sally L. Smith is the Founder/Director of The Lab School of Washington, a school she founded and designed in 1967 for intelligent children and adults with learning disabilities. Since 1976, she has been a professor in the School of Education at American University in charge of the Master's Degree Program in Special Education: Learning Disabilities.

Professor Smith is a national leader in the field of learning disabilities. In May, 1999, she was recognized by Birmingham-Southern College as a "Woman of Distinction." In October, 1997, she was the first recipient of the Celebrating Abilities Award for Outstanding Contributions to the Field of Learning Disabilities presented by the Learning Disabilities Association of Georgia. In May, 1995, Professor Smith was honored with the 1995 American University Faculty Award for Outstanding Scholarship, Research, and Other Professional Contributions. In February, 1993, she received the LDA Award from the Learning Disabilities Association of America, the highest honor given in her field, in recognition and appreciation of outstanding leadership in the field of learning disabilities.

She is one of the elected specialists on the Professional Advisory Board of the Learning Disabilities Association of America and was an elected member of the Professional Advisory Board of the National Center of Learning Disabilities for 6 years. The 1985 *Encyclopedia Britannica Medical and Health Annual* included a section on learning disabilities authored by Sally Smith. Since 1988, she has been a consultant on learning disabilities to the State Department Family Liaison Office and since 1990, a member of the Advisory Board of the I Have A Dream Foundation in Washington, D.C. Professor Smith served on the U.S. Task Force on the Definition of Developmental Disabilities in 1976/1977 and has been a consultant to numerous organizations and state bodies. She has testified as an expert witness before the Senate Committee on Labor and Human Resources. She was a member of the Advisory Council on the Arts in Education for the National Endowment for the Arts. She has run workshops all over the United States and Canada well as in Greece and in Switzerland for the European Council of International Schools.

It is Professor Smith's belief that everyone can learn, and she has designed teaching approaches involving all of the art forms and experiential education to teach academic skills to children and adults. In 1966, she originated the Academic Club Method, which has been overwhelmingly successful with Lab School students.

As the author of eight books and a number of articles in professional magazines, Professor Smith has mastered the art of translating difficult clinical issues into popular language. Her best known books are *No Easy Answers: The Learning Disabled Child at Home and at School* (Bantam, 1995) and *Succeeding Against the Odds: How the Learning-Disabled Can Realize Their Promise* (Tarcher/Perigee, 1993). *Succeeding Against the Odds* was the recipient of the New York Orton Dyslexia Society's 1995 Margot Marek Book Award. *Sin respuestas simples: Reconozca al niño con problemas de aprendizaje* (Editorial Plaza Mayor, Inc.), the Spanish translation of *No Easy Answers*, published in the fall of 1999. *Different Is Not Bad, Different Is the World: A Book About Disabilities*

(Sopris West, 1994), a book for young children is being used widely in inclusive class-rooms. In 1996, both *No Easy Answers* and *Different Is Not Bad,Different is the World* were selected to receive the prestigious 1996 Parents' Choice Award.

The National Public Broadcasting Corporation will be producing a series of short documentaries in early 2001 demonstrating Professor Smith's original teacher education in-service techniques and its application in The Lab School setting. The documentaries will emphasize the use of the arts, Academic Club Approach, experiential, hands-on, object-centered learning that works most effectively with Lab School students and helps build a commitment to inquiry.

Foreword

Sally probably will blush and/or be irritated at this beginning. She has celebrated, excited, educated, and inspired youth with learning disabilities and their parents as her passion and voluntary call since 1967, more than three decades ago. Her active understanding, energy, and concern has and is removing the pain and shame of a reality that is neither a handicap nor a lack but simply a difference.

It is increasingly clear that a bright new world full of ideas about how to teach students with learning differences is being fogged in and bogged down by antiquated systems of information. The stigma of "change" and the social embarrassment is the academic enemy. The hope for a fuller world lies in the recognition of many more ways to teach and learn, rather than exposure to predigested memory that insists on the flat projection of repetition. Each thing we know should begin as a dramatic reality and a surprise. It should function wisely until replaced by a more irresistible revelation but never rejected.

This is the organic forming of knowledge growing in life with the individual. How one does this is the truest form of creativity.

RAUSCHENBERG

Robert Rauschenberg

Preface

When I designed and opened The Lab School in September, 1967, I wanted the arts to be central to the curriculum. I saw the arts as statements of the human experience—disciplines that not only enlist all of the senses and elicit strong feelings but also engender rigorous activity of the mind. I wanted the arts to be thought of as serious, as part of quality education, as contributing to the maximum growth of the total human being. I wanted the arts also to be considered as important tools of remediation for children with neurologically based learning difficulties such as severe learning disabilities and attention-deficit/hyperactivity disorder (ADHD).

The Lab School of Washington, a private day school for approximately 310 students in grades K–12, was designed to meet the special needs of students with learning disabilities and, often, ADHD who cannot function effectively in typical academic environments. More than 80% of the students are funded by the District of Columbia, Maryland, and Virginia.

When most people think of the use of art in education, they think of beautiful works of art or music included in the curriculum to heighten students' sensitivity and awareness. They think of passive enjoyment, luxury often enjoyed by the wealthy. Therefore, it is not surprising that school boards often elect to cut art programs from education budgets when money has to be saved. They certainly don't see the arts as allies for exceptional learners. But they are. The arts can be organizers. They can be employed to teach reorganization and reasoning. They can provide pictures for students who cannot learn just from hearing, and they can provide sounds and movement for those who cannot learn just from seeing.

Too many children are failing in school today. New teaching methods need to be explored. Traditional approaches have failed repeatedly with exceptional learners. I learned about the devastation of failure from the youngest of my three sons. I took clues from him to determine ways that the arts could be at the base of teaching students with learning disabilities. Consequently, in 1966 I designed what I call The Integrated Arts and Academic Club Method (which later became The Lab School Approach) to use with at-risk children who were failing at school.

The Integrated Arts and Academic Club Method became the basis of the way we teach at The Lab School. It is a format that enables each child to be an intimate and active part of the history of any topic being studied. I chose the word *club* to give a sense of belonging, ownership, membership, and privilege to children who tend to feel "out" and want to be "in." I developed passwords, routines, and rituals to help students pay attention and focus, to make each student feel important, and to help the group be tightly knit. I called it *academic* because, done right, highly academic material is presented through visual, hands-on means. I chose the arts because every art demands active participation, concentration, and discipline. I also chose the arts to capture the ingenuity and imaginations of children who tend to be written off. The arts capture the boundless energy many of these children demonstrate. For others who show little energy, the arts marshal it. The arts ignite ideas that these students do not express well in words. Inspiration through the arts leads to intellectual promise and productivity.

The Integrated Arts and Academic Clubs, truly multisensory experiences, are designed to lure children into learning, to excite them intellectually, to involve their bodies and all of their senses, to tap vibrant imaginations, and to capture the joy one can feel in acquiring knowledge.

For example, 6- and 7-year-olds who do not know their alphabet, cannot read, and usually have a difficult time associating a specific sound to the correct symbol, can enter the Cave Club, rise to a standing position, and say
"We slowly rise up like Homo Erectus
We use our hands like Homo Habilis
We speak and communicate like Homo Sapiens
And count one, two, three!
Greetings Wise Elder."
By chanting this daily, the children internalize the information and are comfortable with the terms *Homo Erectus*, *Homo Habilis*, and *Homo Sapien*.

The Integrated Arts and Academic Club Method presents a classical education in an original way. The typical child without learning disabilities, who doesn't need the method because he can read, listen well, remember, and slot information into its proper order benefits nonetheless. For the child with severe learning disabilities and ADHD, this approach is a lifeboat keeping afloat a fine mind; it allows the child to build up toward long journeys into learning instead of drowning in textbooks she can't read, papers she can't write, and material that she can't remember by merely listening. The Integrated Arts and Academic Club Method keeps afloat intellectually the child whose educational life is on the line.

The Integrated Arts and Academic Club Method is a way of teaching and learning history, geography, civics, science, archeology, and literature through the use of all the art forms. It appears in the form of six Academic Clubs equivalent to first through sixth grades. They are the Cave Club, the Gods Club, the Knights and Ladies Club, the Renaissance Club, the Museum Club, and the Industrialists Club. Each club lasts a full academic year, covering Ancient History to the Middle Ages, the Renaissance, the Age of Explorers, and finally the Industrial Revolution and the American Robber Barons. A child is placed according to his or her age and level of social maturity into one Academic Club a year for 50 minutes per day. Since 1967, the elementary grades of The Lab School have had 6-week-long, theme-based Academic Clubs during the summers. For example, a Caribbean Summer at The Lab School would entice children with the chance to be in the Caribbean Secret Agents Club, the Pirates Club, the Cruise Club, the Carnival Club and Jacques Cousteau's Underwater Club.

HOW DID IT ALL BEGIN?

In the 1960s, our friends and acquaintances, whose children attended my children's birthday parties, started asking me for help with their kids. I had no formal training. My undergraduate work was in psychology and cultural anthropology, although most of my energies went into modern dance and acting. My graduate work also was in psychology and cultural anthropology under the rubric of human relations in the School of Education at New York University. Therefore, I was not prepared when friends of my friends in Washington, D.C., began to drop off their children at my home, claiming that the kids had something wrong with them and asking that I please figure out what it was and fix it.

They had learned of the success I was having teaching my own child and were hoping I might be able to use these methods to work with their children. Essentially, I was using a drumbeat with my son who has ADHD and severe learning disabilities to corral his attention. We constructed big projects made of wood or heavy cardboard because his fingers and hands could not do coloring, cutting, gluing, and puzzles. Large projects were easier to tackle than small ones. We did eurythmics and jazz dancing. Drama was a basic tool I used to teach him vocabulary, content, and narrative techniques. Regardless of his learning disabilities, he spoke well as a preschooler and, finally at age 13, started to read and hasn't stopped. He's a voracious reader today.

THE POTOMAC PROGRAM, 1966

In 1966 the Adams-Morgan Community Council, a community group in Washington, D.C., that primarily serves the needs of an economically disadvantaged population, asked me to develop a program for 100 inner-city children, ages 6–12, who were seriously lagging behind in the Adams-Morgan schools. I integrated the techniques I used with my son into a new program. Mary Averett Seelye, a friend of mine who was familiar with the activities I was employing with my son, was a member of the Adams-Morgan Community Council. She and I and a few other women had served on the D.C. Arts in Education Committee together, and she knew that I could handle the job.

The Adams-Morgan Community Council had been given the opportunity, at no charge, to hold a summer program at a beautiful independent school called the Potomac School in McLean, Virginia. They came to me because they were given a grant to pay for an innovative program, but they had no program. I warned the council that I had no formal training—only my experiences with my youngest son. Despite this, they hired me to design a 6-week program that included graphic arts, woodwork, music, dance, and drama in the mornings; films at lunch; and 15 Academic Clubs in the afternoon. Because all of the students had severe reading difficulties, I analyzed the skills that are needed for a child to be able to read, broke the skills down, and then asked each artist who was participating in the program to find ways to incorporate the skills in his or her art form without sacrificing the integrity of the art form. This meant I had to develop my own form of training for artists and Academic Club teachers.

Each child participated in four 40-minute periods each morning. Woodwork sessions helped the children learn math concepts as well as eye–hand coordination and planning skills. Music classes stressed listening skills, discrimination of one sound from another, and auditory memory. Dance and organization of thought taught the children how to organize their bodies and how to follow, assemble, and remember a set of sequences. Drama sessions emphasized sequences and language arts.

The children brought their own lunches and were given some free time for conversation, then were shown film shorts. They saw films that they could relate to their own lives, such as *The Red Balloon*, as well as short documentaries on interesting people, various occupations, and animals. Animated films also were shown. My goal was to widen their horizons, help develop their vocabularies, and increase their knowledge through film. The emphasis was on the children's discussing the main point of each film and how it applied to their own experiences in addition to comparing and contrasting films—a different form of language arts training.

The afternoons from 1:00 P.M. to 2:30 P.M. were reserved for Academic Clubs, which included the Secret Agents Club, the Smokey the Bear Club, the Storekeepers

Club, the Pirates Club, the Civil War Club, the Caveman Club, and the Knights of the Middle Ages Club. Each club had carefully structured academic objectives meshed into a dramatic framework that allowed each child to pretend to be a certain character. When assigned a character, a child took on another role and often had to do things he wouldn't attempt in a more formal learning situation. The children loved the program and asked for more. The guidance counselor from the Morgan School, from which 60 of our students came, was thrilled with the positive change of attitude and motivation to learn, explore, and question that he witnessed when the children returned to school in the fall. He was so excited by the results that he called me to ask if he, himself, could be employed in the next summer's program. The next summer he did join us, at the Friends-Morgan Summer Project!

THE SIDWELL FRIENDS PROGRAM, 1967

The Sidwell Friends School, a private school in Washington, D.C., wanted to sponsor the Sidwell Friends Program and work closely with the Morgan School faculty and with our artists. This time I designed the project so that each artist was assisted by a teacher. The rationale was that the artists could learn from the teachers about the children's development and certain behavior management techniques that could be woven into the arts or club's theme while the teacher could absorb some of the creative techniques from the artists. As in the previous summer, I had to develop my own techniques to train artists and teachers together. My techniques asked teachers to think, research, and plan activities differently from staff at traditional schools.

In 1967, the Friends-Morgan Summer Project included 125 children with serious academic difficulties, ages 6–12, mostly from the Morgan School. We offered physical education in addition to dance. Drawing and painting (stressing patterns) were offered as alternatives to woodwork. This time, there were many more Academic Clubs including the Seven Seas Club (emphasizing geography) and the American Revolutionaries Club (stressing history) as well as the Ecologist's Club, the Tarzan's Jungle Club, the Nature Detective's Club, and the Smokey the Bear Club.

The Friends-Morgan Project was given a grant of less than $28,000 to fund the whole program. A research group, paid for by a grant from a major foundation in New York, was given $60,000 to evaluate the program. They met with our staff and taught us some useful methods of reporting. Then came the crash. The research group wanted me to change my methods so they could use their existing tools of measurement. I pointed out that this was a new program, and it needed new methods of measurement. The instruments of evaluation needed to be changed to work with an innovative program, not the program changed to meet the evaluation. The research director threatened that if I did not change my methods, the evaluation would show that children from Morgan School who stayed on the streets learned as much or more than the children who came to the Friends-Morgan Project. And, indeed, the report did reflect just that.

All of us witnessed the exhilarating feeling of "I can do it" that each child in our program experienced. It was impossible to evaluate the problem-solving abilities that grew, the critical thinking that took place, the oral language skills that developed, the organization skills that were gained, and, most of all, the sense of self-worth these children attained. Their experiences were organic; they became part of their being. What they learned went deep into their bones because they learned it through all of their senses and understood what they were doing.

The child who made a stringed musical instrument out of wood didn't just learn how to make a musical instrument. He studied pictures of similar instruments and decided on shape and length and texture. He learned to plan what he was doing and keep to his plan and make adjustments when necessary. He had to measure the wood to achieve the proper dimensions and then sand and stain it. Then he had to feel the vibrations of the instrument on his neck and relate those vibrations to the strings on the instrument, which had to be built in such a way that the frets the student put on the neck of the instrument achieved specific sounds. This child not only went away with a tangible reward for his labors, but his mind had been opened to a way to learn—a process that could be adapted to other situations. My staff and I were and continue to be committed to the belief that we cannot just educate students for this year and next year; we must teach them how to approach future unknowns.

A BRUSH WITH THE OFFICE OF EDUCATION

Two years later, in 1969, we made a series of 16-millimeter films on The Integrated Arts and Academic Club Method. The Bureau of Education for the Handicapped bought 32 copies of each of these films, which were rented by people all over the country. All of the Friends-Morgan Project teachers who were interviewed for these films felt that they had grown as teachers; they discovered that the adults who guide the activities are always learners who, despite popular belief, do not need to know all the answers. They found that even in large groups it was possible to identify the strengths of each individual and to encourage each member to contribute the things that she liked and could do best.

FINDING A SCHOOL FOR MY SON

The Friends-Morgan Project was a great professional success for me, the children, and the staff; but my youngest son failed first grade. How were we to school him? He was too capable verbally and too sophisticated in his comprehension and usage of ideas to be placed in a special education environment. And, even though he did not feel good about himself, he was not emotionally disturbed; therfore, it did not make sense to place him in an environment with children with mental illness. He was hyperactive, impulsive, and distractible with a very short attention span, and he had severe learning disabilities. Today, we recognize these characteristics as ADHD. His brain was damaged with a substrate of severe learning disabilities. He could not see the difference between a straight line and angle, but there was nothing wrong with his eyes. He could not hear the difference between the word "advertisement" and "adbertizement." He did not know the days of the week, could not count to 100, did not know his alphabet, and could not repeat other sequences. His thinking, problem-solving abilities, and vocabulary were ahead of his age group. Repeating a grade even twice would not do the job. He still would not receive the highly specialized help he needed. I tried to find schools, private or public, that would open a special program for children who were intelligent but had severe learning disabilities. Some of the schools were willing to talk about it and plan it over a period of years. My child needed a school in September.

In 1967, Gladys Stern, the assistant head of Georgetown Day School, a private school in Washington, D.C., introduced me to Dr. Kenneth Oldman, the head of the Kingsbury Center, a testing and tutoring agency. I brought him to see the Friends-Morgan Project, and I outlined a possible school program to him. He sympathized with me because he knew of several children who were being tutored who desperately needed a special school; however, he didn't have the space or the money for a new program.

By Labor Day 1967, I was still searching for a school when a telegram appeared under my door from Kenneth Oldman asking me to call him immediately. He had been offered the building next door to the Kingsbury Center and asked me if I would open the school. I agreed, provided that he understood that I had no formal training for the job and he would make provisions for at least one of the artists from the Friends-Morgan Project to be on board. With this understanding, I spent all night writing the program, and the next morning, I asked the artist who taught woodwork and sculpture to join me on the project. Then, because I wanted classes to begin in 20 days, I started raising money and hiring staff. Our school opened on September 25, 1967, with four students. The future had begun.

I named it The Lab School because of my deep respect for John Dewey whose Lab School of the University of Chicago was known for pioneering work, innovating, trying new methods, centering all attention on children, and using all of their senses in active learning.

The Lab School remained as part of the remedial center for 15 years. It became its own private nonprofit (501[c][3]) organization in 1982 and was renamed The Lab School of Washington. The program, staff, and students remained the same.

In 1975 I was asked on 3 days' notice to teach the graduate-level classes on learning disabilities at American University in Washington, D.C. The following year I became Associate Professor in charge of the Master's Degree Program in Special Education: Learning Disabilities, and in 1982, I became full professor and was tenured. The Integrated Arts and Academic Club Method thus has been introduced to hundreds of my graduate students as they have begun teaching children with learning disablities around the nation.

I received a grant from the National Endowment for the Arts in 1978 to offer four Saturday workshops at American University on the role of the arts in teaching academic skills. The audience was made up of policy makers in the arts and education, congressional staff assistants, educators, recreation workers, and teachers. Although they evaluated the program highly and obviously enjoyed the experience, no offers for replication came at that time.

THE HARDY CLUB PROJECT

In 1972, Hilda Wine, a general elementary school principal, wanted The Integrated Arts and Academic Club Method to be implemented in her school, the Hardy Elementary Public School, located in the District of Columbia; therefore, I designed a program for Friday afternoons from 1:15 to 2:45 P.M. Ms. Wine was thrilled, and we planned to repeat the program the following year. Unfortunately, she suddenly became ill and died late that August. The acting principal decided to discontinue the program, despite petitions from both parents and students. Children without disabilities loved this way of learning, and their parents were thrilled with the enthusiasm the program had generated. After this experience, we knew that even though efforts to use Lab School techniques in general schools were not always successful, we were gaining many supporters.

By 1980, the Lab School's reputation had grown considerably and was beginning to appeal to other schools. Therefore, we began the Urban League-Lab School

Summer Project for children from the inner city. That summer—and in the 1990s with the I Have A Dream Project at Johnson Junior High in Anacostia, an inner-city ward of Washington, D.C.—we learned that The Lab School Approach works as effectively and even faster with children from the inner city than with children who have neurological impairments. A visual-concrete method of teaching seemed to fit well with the way many of these children naturally learned.

NORTH CAROLINA PROJECT

The next outreach, which occurred in the 1980s, was initiated by Mary Averett Seeyle of the American Association of University Women (AAUW) along with a North Carolina representative of the AAUW who was a member of the Charlotte, North Carolina, School Board. The North Carolina representative received a grant from the National Endowment for the Arts to bring The Integrated Arts and Academic Club Method to the Gunn School in Charlotte, an elementary school of 550 children. Lab School staff were flown to Charlotte to immerse Gunn School teachers in The Lab School Approach over a 3-day period.

The principal, staff, AAUW members, and school board members received The Lab School Approach with unbelievable enthusiasm. The next step was for the Gunn School to receive a sizeable grant from the North Carolina Education Department in order to implement the Lab School Approach. This grant was never bestowed; however, I recently learned that some of the teachers trained during those 3 days are still teaching using The Lab School Approach in various area schools and in a summer program.

MEDIA

Passionate interest in The Integrated Arts and Academic Club Method was aroused in a totally unexpected way in 1988. In April, 1988, a CBS television magazine show called *West 57th* featured The Lab School in a 14-minute segment. The telephones of The Lab School rang off the walls for 10 days. Parents, teachers, and administrators were brought in to answer more than 700 telephone calls from every state in the nation. All of them requested written material and asked us to start a school in their locale. Alas, as a nonprofit institution we had no funds for expansion and barely the funds to meet the costs of the mailings we sent out.

The very same passion that I had felt for the unmet needs of my own son 20 years before was the same passion we heard from all corners of the country. Parents were saying, "I know my child can learn in this way." Teachers were saying, "I could do this in my classroom." But no funding was forthcoming.

Along with the enthusiasm came skeptical voices from the education establishments. A state superintendent of schools asked, "Where is validation for your method? Can you prove its effectiveness statistically? Does it all depend on the personality of one leader?" The education establishment said that The Lab School must undertake a self-study, track the progress of our students, and apply to the National Diffusion Network (NDN) of the U.S. Department of Education.

The Lab School continued to gain recognition over the next decade. In 1995, The Lab School was identified by the U.S. Department of Education as an NDN Model Education Program. A panel of experts called a Program Effectiveness Panel (PEP) validated The Integrated Arts and Academic Club Method of The Lab School and acknowledged its effectiveness. The PEP encouraged The Lab School of

Washington to disseminate The Integrated Arts and Academic Club Method and materials to public and private schools around the country. They also encouraged The Lab School to apply for a 3-year grant to seek out public schools that might be interested in the approach, set up training programs for staff and supervisors, and implement the program at the end of the third year. Unfortunately, a cost-cutting Congress in 1996 cut the funds for the NDN; therefore, no new programs could be funded. Foiled again.

In 1995, The Lab School of Washington partnered with the Martin Luther King Jr. Elementary School in Anacostia, an inner-city school, to implement The Integrated Arts and Academic Club Method. The relationship we formed with the administration of the school blossomed, and by 1997 we had a second partnership with the Brent School on Capitol Hill. In 1998, both schools asked The Lab School to do staff development for them—10 workshops on their campus and a number on our own. By 1999, Stuart Hobson Middle School from Capitol Hill Northeast joined the partnership.

In 1994–1996 and in 1996–1997, The Lab School was one of only two private special education schools in the United States to receive the National Blue Ribbon Award of Excellence for both the elementary and secondary school programs. Our programs were validated once again.

On September 13, 2000, The Lab School of Washington Baltimore Campus opened in the Port Discovery Children's Museum, starting out with only 19 children, ages 7–11. It is the first authentic duplicate of our Washington program.

The Integrated Arts and Academic Club Method is ready to work in other schools. The Board of Trustees of The Lab School of Washington has approved the development of other Lab Schools in the near future to prove that our methods can work elsewhere. We are currently in the process of producing new films that teach people to run Academic Clubs, creating packets for specific clubs, developing computer software delineating these methods, and setting up an Arts and Academic Club Advisory Service to teach schools how to implement the Lab School methods. The Integrated Arts and Academic Club Method is ready to live in other schools. Why not yours?

Acknowledgments

First and foremost, I thank one of my dearest friends in the world, Elisabeth Benson Booz, for all of your wise counsel and enthusiasm regarding this book. On that beautiful island of Crete at Elounda Beach in July, 1999, it was you who made me focus and get the job well started, and it was you who took out your editing pen and gave of your professional talent. I am deeply appreciative that you took time out of your busy schedule to read, critique, and improve this book. Thank you.

To all of the artists who have worked and continue to work at The Lab School, you have my profound respect and admiration. You have been an inspiration to me, and I feel grateful to you for fulfilling my vision of The Lab School. In fact, my gratitude goes to all Lab School faculty for sharing your incredible gifts, your uniqueness, your dedication, your ingenuity, your love, and your energy with our students whose lives are on the line.

I thank artist Kelly McVearry for inundating me with valuable research materials and books. You have introduced me to important literature and different points of view.

I am profoundly grateful to the following staff members who have read this book and given excellent advice: Lois Meyer, Head of College and Career Counseling; Betsy Babbington, Head of Development and former Academic Club Leader; Neela Seldin, Coordinator of the Elementary School; Sally Seawright, Head of the Junior High School; Dr. Lindy Rosen, Head of Speech-Language Pathology; and Gina Van Weddingen, Academic Club Leader and Teacher.

Special thanks to Peter Braun for maximum support and care for our legacy. I feel very fortunate to be surrounded by such extraordinary human beings who are The Lab School of Washington's administrators. I deeply appreciate your protecting and improving "the dream" daily. I am grateful to Noel Kerns and Dick Meltzer, as well as Eve Lilley, Helen Levine, Karen Duncan, Connie Greene, Dr. Luanne Adams, Peg O'Donnell, and Roya Rassai. Thank you Don Vicks for teaching Academic Clubs the way I envisioned them taught. Thank you Jeff Hamill for doing the illustration for this book's cover and for being The Lab School's artist. Thank you Diana Meltzer for going over all the pages of the manuscript with me and for doing all of that proofing. I am appreciative.

To all of you who have served on the Board of Trustees at The Lab School of Washington, I am profoundly grateful to you for supporting the thesis that excellence in education and excellence in the arts go hand in hand. Your role in keeping the school alive and thriving can never be minimized. To Board Chair Susan Hager, your leadership in the last few years has taken us to new heights. Thank you former Chairs Fred Brennan, Pauline Schneider, Ambassador Tim Towell, the Honorable Max N. Berry, and Ann Bradford Mathias. To Sergius Gambal, James Rosenheim, Samia Farouki, Ann Simpson, Joe Schepis, Rick Nadeau, and Antoine van Agtmael—you all have made a crucial difference in The Lab School's growth and development.

Without the volunteer efforts of our parents, The Lab School would not be where it is today; special thanks to Sheila Jonas for your outstanding leadership. Many local foundations and the business community of Washington, D.C., have been exceedingly generous to our arts-based school, for which I am indebted to you.

Thank you Day School and Night School students who have shared with me your dreams. I admire your courage, resourcefulness, problem-solving abilities, and creativity.

To American University administrators and to my colleagues in the School of Education, I am grateful for the full-time opportunity since 1976 to educate teachers in my style of teaching and learning. The Lab School has employed many American University graduates who have done outstanding work in our institution. Thank you for prodding me to keep doing new research, developing new projects, and publishing and for the stimulation of superb colleagues. I appreciate your support!

I am particularly grateful to Alma Gates for taking my purple scrawl and, with hard work and care, putting it onto the computer. You were gracious under pressure, and I thank you.

To my three sons, you are my sustenance, my pleasure, my sources of fun and creativity. Thank you Randy, Nick, and Gary. I love you guys.

Finally, I am indebted to Robert Rauschenberg, internationally acclaimed artist and Master of Modern Art. You have been kind enough to give some of your greatness to Lab School students, faculty, friends, and all of the art teachers over many years with the Rauschenberg Day at The Lab School. You have, in many ways, let us know that the arts are our humanity, and there are sparks of it everywhere lighting up our lives if we will only enjoy them. Bob, thank you for being a constant source of inspiration and kindness.

*To Nicholas Lee Smith
who has the artist's eye and
who sparked so much of my creativity.
Thank you my friend and my son.*

The Power of the Arts
with Exceptional Learners

We have known since the beginning of time that the arts serve as vehicles of communication for human beings. The Lascaux Caves showed us the fears and aspirations of ancient man. Rain dances performed by Native Americans demonstrate the hopes of people and their magical spirit to make things happen. The rhythmic beats in African communities serve as warnings, celebration, and conveyors of information. Shakespeare's works tutor us all in the ways of human beings; in addition to being great literature, dramatic works teach us about psychology, sociology, anthropology, and philosophy. The art of filmmaking has brought us humor, often by exaggerating our lives and the manner in which we wish to live. The arts reach beyond the human beings who perform them and capture the spirit of the times. They become part of civilization.

Parents have always shared their artistic talents with their children, whether the talent was making baskets out of papyrus, using pottery to fashion plates, telling stories, or acting out a role in a pageant or ritual. When groups of children learned together, it was not surprising if they used sticks in the sand to portray a lesson, chanted a rhyme to learn a concept, or leapt over obstacles while counting. Painting, singing, dancing, weaving, pot making, and poetry all have been used over the ages for teaching purposes.

QUESTIONING

When Dr. Ernest Boyer was President of the Carnegie Foundation for the Advancement of Teaching, he stated that "an educated person today is someone who knows the right question to ask" (Fiske, 1991). The arts promote the asking of questions and the habit of reflection—reflecting on experiences, analyzing them, chewing them over, and sharing them with others through conversation, the written word, or an art form. We do not learn just from experience: Learning takes place when we reflect upon an experience, when we raise questions in our own minds and discuss ideas with others. Too much of today's education consists of going to a teacher who is portrayed as "an answer person" instead of letting adults and children explore together, pursuing probing questions and establishing a commitment to inquiry.

Although the art of formulating questions is particularly difficult for children with language acquisition difficulties, it must become a major instructional goal of all teachers. Throughout time, the process of making connections has allowed us to understand and solve problems. The arts exist to promote a deep understanding of relationships. The legacies of great educational visionaries underlie arts education: John Dewey, Jean Piaget, Lev Vygotsky, Reuven Feuerstein, Jerome Bruner, Howard Gardner, and Marion Diamond.

ARTS EDUCATION RESEARCH

Many studies document the role of the arts in improving basic skills (the 3 Rs). Because of the mounting evidence that links the arts to basic learning, some researchers refer to the arts as "the fourth R." The following examples illustrate how the arts help students with basic learning:

1. When compared with a control group that used only a discussion approach, the writing quality of elementary students was consistently and significantly improved by using drawing and drama techniques. Drama and drawing techniques allow the student to test, evaluate, revise, and integrate ideas before beginning to write, thus greatly improving the student's results (Moore & Caldwell, 1993).

2. On the California Achievement Tests, students who participated in a special music and poetry program made noticeable gains over the control group in language mechanics, total language, and writing (Hudspeth, 1987).

3. Drama techniques proved to be an effective approach for promoting facility in English as a second language among young children. The "drama group" exhibited considerably greater improvement than the control group in total verbal output (O'Farrell, 1993).

4. Fifth-grade remedial readers who used creative drama as a learning strategy scored consistently higher on the Metropolitan Reading Comprehension Test. The drama readers' scores also showed a steady increase over a 6-week period. The control group engaged in the same reading activities, followed by vocabulary lessons and discussion of the story (DuPont, 1992).

5. According to the College Entrance Examination Board, in 1995, students who studied the arts for more than 4 years scored 59 points higher on the verbal section and 44 points higher on the math section of the SATs than students with no experience or coursework in the arts.

6. A review of 57 studies devoted to the emotional and social development of children revealed that self-concept—as well as language acquisition, cognitive development, critical thinking ability, and social skills—is positively enhanced through the arts (Trusty & Oliva, 1994).

Researchers at the National Center for the Gifted and Talented at the University of Connecticut found that students involved in the arts were motivated to learn for the learning experience itself, not just for test results or other performance outcomes.

The United States Labor Department's report of the Secretary's Commission on Achieving Necessary Skills (SCANS; U.S. Department of Labor, 1993) cites the important role of an arts education in achieving many "core competencies" for the workplace, including gathering information, exploring options, taking risks, making choices, collaborating, participating in teamwork, exercising responsibility, refining possible solutions, and understanding social systems. The abilities to think critically and creatively, problem solve, and exercise individual responsibility and sociability are endemic to arts education. Good analytical skills, also promoted through the arts, have special value in the workplace.

Researchers in neuroscience are finding a positive correlation between music training and higher than average levels of mathematical functioning. This strong premise, derived from highly technological medical studies, holds that the neural pathways in the brain that involve the functioning of higher cognitive skills (e.g., abstract reasoning, spatial awareness, mathematical thinking) are closely related to and connected with the neural pathways that are developed through music.

THE ARTS AND INDIVIDUALS WITH DISABILITIES

In 1980, only two states included courses in the arts in their general high school curricula. Today, 28 states require some study of the arts for high school graduation; and many colleges' admissions requirements include study of some art form. In 1984, John I. Goodlad, a well-known arts educator, stated that, "The arts are not an educational option: They are basic." However, it is difficult to find statistics on ways in which the arts are being employed in schools to help exceptional learners—students who have learning disabilities, attention-deficit/hyperactivity disorder (ADHD), and language impairments. The arts are important for all students, but for those whose educational lives are on the line, experiences in the arts are crucial.

For centuries it has been apparent that the arts are basic to education. In the United States, however, it has taken traditional educators a long time to recognize that the arts should be treated as rigorous academic subjects, an essential aspect of human knowledge based on human imagination. Most professionals do not realize that art activities require constant high-level thinking and analysis, synthesis, evaluation of what has been done, and reformulation of what needs to be done. The arts are intellectual disciplines—vital activities of the mind—that provide students with the opportunity to construct their understanding of the world.

Clearly, students who have acted out historical roles, who have been exposed to great works of art throughout history, and who, consequently, have acquired a huge storehouse of information through their senses are likely to do better than peers who have studied textbooks; in essence, history has become a part of their beings. They have seen it, heard it, and lived it. The knowledge is there for a lifetime.

The arts provide all sorts of wondrous opportunities for all children. However, for exceptional students, the arts are often a savior, a respite, and a solace that give these children a chance to express themselves and feel good about themselves.

Every child can learn; it is up to us, as adults, to seek out and discover the routes by which a particular child learns. In other words, we do not say that because we tried to teach her and she didn't learn, the child must be stupid, willful, or lazy. We must look at a child's innate abilities, her skills and talents, and her unique strengths and interests. Then we have to explore until we find the combination of methods that work for her. When we discover how the child learns—perhaps by seeing and touching or by hearing and writing down what she has heard—we must then teach her to understand her own way of learning and remembering so she can explain it to others and carry that self-knowledge with her, like armor, for the rest of her life. At every opportunity, no matter how basic, we have to encourage the child to taste success and experience the feeling of "I can do it."

The experiential learning and arts-based approach of The Lab School of Washington relies upon stretching the intellect, tapping the originality and creativity of each student, and helping each student feel good about himself. The biggest battle we face is developing the nontraditional learner's and nonreader's sense of self-worth. Because of the defeat they have experienced in their schooling at a very early age, children who have difficulty reading and learning tend to feel insecure and bad about themselves.

Have you ever met a nonreader who really does not want to read? Of course not. Nonreaders want to read, but the neurology of the brain works against them and prevents them from reading. When they find they cannot read, they may claim they do not want to read because they are afraid of failure and of looking dumb to their friends. Adults with reading problems tell us that they knew something was wrong with them as early as kindergarten. They noticed they could not do what others could do with ease. They tasted defeat in kindergarten and continued to experience failure year upon year at school. They built up their defense mechanisms to keep others from seeing their inadequacies. They put on "masks" to avoid feeling hurt from teasing or from others' recognition of their failures. Some became "class clowns" to make everybody laugh and to deflect attention from their difficulties. Others became "know-it-alls," "con artists," victims to be pitied, or Good Samaritans who pleased everyone. Most of their energies from kindergarten or first grade on went into protecting themselves with their masks and not into learning.

Many nontraditional learners are visual learners who do not think in words but, rather, think in shapes, forms, sizes, and textures. Their world is a graphic world. Many nontraditional learners shine in areas of school in which instruction is not verbal or logical/mathematical. They often experience competence and mastery in some of the arts. For example, 30-year-old Otto said, "I hated school except for that one period a day in art or music. I was alive then. People could see the person I was in the summertime, at home, everywhere but at school."

PLAY AND THE ARTS IN PRESCHOOL AND KINDERGARTEN

Like the arts, play helps children understand relationships: they think, compare, analyze, generalize, and solve problems. During play, a child makes things happen. Often, he is surprised by the results and filled with the wonder and awe of it all. According to Plato, "You can discover more about a person in an hour of play than in a year of conversation."

A young child must have experiences in order to acquire information. These experiences are filed into compartments in the mind and can then be retrieved at will. Preschool learning is all about sorting things—objects, pictures, words, animals, people—and then classifying them into a mental filing system. Such learning leaves a child's mental reference library stocked with basic concepts that form the basis for abstract learning. When children play they form connections, relationships, and groupings. This mental work adds to the development of comprehension skills and depth of understanding, which helps when more and more complex subjects are encountered. Play is crucial to the physical, cognitive, social, and emotional development of preschoolers.

Art, music, drama, and dance are part of the humanities because, like literature and poetry, they articulate the human experience. Just as social studies, psychology, sociology, and philosophy peruse social ideas and critiques, drama, dance, music, and art offer the same pathway to ideas. Hands-on experiences, pretend play, and specific kinds of movement elicit discussion from very young children on all forms of weighty matters. Listening to stories being read, telling stories through words or pictures, leaping in the air to a drumbeat, holding hands in a circle while going one way and then another, passing a funny substance around a circle to guess what it is, observing bugs, and crawling through mysterious teacher-made tunnels are all childish activities, and this is exactly what children should be doing. Through these activities, children's imaginations are stirred, patterns of language are studied, and investigations into the natural world are made—all of which raise questions in children's heads. To produce the highest possible cognitive development, we need children's minds to question everything and their bodies and hands to be active. We need to develop curiosity, questioning, and awe in children. These are the minds that, in the future, are going to take us into the information-based, electronically designed new world culture.

THE ART FORMS AS LEARNING TOOLS

All art has symbolic meaning: It can be understood without words. Therefore, the arts can and should play a central role in academic learning. All of the art forms can help ignite the entire learning process. The arts capture children's excitement, interests, and passions. They are motivators. They demand student involvement. Every child can succeed in at least one art form, whether it is photography, modern dance, puppetry, sculpture, music, or computer art. The arts produce tangible results that evoke praise from audiences. They build a sense of self-worth, confidence, and self-esteem. The Lab School experience is that the arts are essential to quality education. They encompass the civilization that human beings have created on earth—the wonder, the beauty, the joy, the sorrow, the anger, and the originality of expression.

STUDIES ON THE HAND AND THE BRAIN

The arts are also excellent learning tools because the experience of making and enjoying art often is physical. An innovative book published in 1999 by Dr. Frank Wilson, a California neurologist, takes a radical view that the hand is crucial to cognitive development. Dr. Wilson contends that it is because of the unique structure of the hand and its evolution in cooperation with the brain that *Homo sapiens* have become the most intelligent, preeminent animals on the earth.

Wilson, who also has studied archaeology in depth, states that *Homo erectus's* anatomical cranial capacity increased as *Homo erectus* made the transition to *Homo sapiens*, as he was developing more sophisticated tools and as living conditions forced a social system of cooperation for survival. The author claims that *Homo sapiens* experienced a boost in brain capacity and the acquisition of speech.

We always have assumed that our brains control our hands and our visual-motor activities. Wilson claims that the movements of the hand lead to the redesign of the brain's circuitry. He states that it has been proven that the influence of manual play and object manipulation facilitate the acquisition of language and cognitive skills in young children. It is radical to think that the hand is as much at the core of the development of civilization as the brain itself. Wilson sees the hand as the launch pad of learning—the primary mover in the organization of human cognitive architecture and operations.

What are the implications of Wilson's many years of research? First, school systems that are scrapping their arts and play programs are not listening to the lessons of biology and archaeology that claim it is necessary to develop the hands and the body as well as the mind to obtain the highest range of intelligence. "Hands-on" experiences take on more meaning in light of Wilson's highly detailed research.

It is interesting that in many schools, children who use their hands effectively to build and fix complicated things often are the students who are failing classes. They fail to perform in areas that require symbolic knowledge. The Lab School experience is that students could succeed in a linguistic-based school if teachers would have the students use their hands to make things to learn about a subject and then talk about what they did afterward. For example, Riley and Beau could not learn math in the traditional way; however, by building a 5-foot dollhouse for sick children at the local hospital, making the furniture and rugs, and finishing the whole piece, they were able to complete their math curriculum. This was problem solving at its best; Riley and Beau implemented and reinforced their math skills—estimating, taking measurements, using fractions and percentiles, adding, subtracting, dividing, and multiplying—and even studied geometry!

What about children who cannot concentrate unless they are holding or fiddling with something in their hands? Do you know a child who cannot tell you her idea but can draw it brilliantly? What about the child whose hands are so developed at massage or manipulating sore areas that they heal others? Have we thought of these things as examples of intelligence?

Frequently, through the use of manipulative objects to test intelligence, a child is shown to be quite advanced in nonverbal thinking; but what about the child with eye–hand coordination difficulties or visual-motor problems who cannot show us his intelligence by working with his hands? The implications of Dr. Wilson's work are that this child has conceptual holes in his development because his hand–thought–

language nexus was disturbed. What are the implications in this case for educators, particularly special educators?

Exceptional learners need to use their hands as much as possible to develop their brain circuitry. The arts are cerebral activities that employ the body, the mind, and the spirit.

THE ARTS RESPECT DIVERSITY

The arts tend to draw people together. They foster cooperation, group work, and helpfulness. The arts promote a deeper understanding of other civilizations, religions, and cultures. Diversity is prized in the artist's world. Differences are not only okay but are welcome. Our schools, too, must learn to treasure difference. Children with learning disabilities must learn that "different is not bad" and that their differences often make them interesting and talented.

Children learn best when they are active, not passive, partners in learning. All of the art forms require active problem solving after the basic skills have been mastered. Painters must address problems of size, shape, perspective, and color and decide how best to express an idea. Modern dancers must determine the types of movement to use and the moods they convey as well as whether to use a large space or a contained space. In the arts, students are expected to find their own answers to questions, to try out their solutions, to criticize their own work constructively, and to correct their own answers if necessary. Arts-infused learning is replete with a variety of possibilities. Just as in daily life we do many of the same things in different ways, in the arts there is no "right way"—no single correct answer. Therefore, the arts give scope to divergent thinking.

Generally, children with moderate to severe learning disabilities are passive learners; they often wait for the adults around them to pour knowledge into their brains. The Lab School Approach is experiential; it uses all the senses and multiple intelligences, including active project learning. The Lab School's philosophy is that, given a highly structured environment and concrete materials to prompt the discovery of relationships, nuances, and concepts, exceptional learners will bridge the gulf between the world of literal meanings and the world of the abstract. The arts are central to the educative process. For example, when some students at The Lab School study Shakespeare, they begin their study by looking at photographs and watching films about that time period; then they carve a large Elizabethan village and the Globe Theatre out of wood. These activities prepare them to hear the flow of Shakespeare's words.

In the following examples, the practicing artists each drew on the richness of their own particular art form to teach exceptional learners the precise skills needed to further their academic learning. While the children learned a new art form and enjoyed themselves, they also picked up all kinds of information and processes useful for a lifetime of learning.

Woodwork

Working with wood requires strong visual-motor skills. As students learn to make things out of wood, they also develop skills in math, science, following directions, problem solving, organizing, sequencing, and planning. These practical skills transfer to more traditional academics by giving abstract mathematical concepts concrete applications and honing the skills necessary for learning to read.

Barnaby was particularly successful at working with wood. The wood was strong and stood up well to his clumsy handling. The teacher with whom he worked made Barnaby draw a basic design for the chair he wanted to make. The sculptor told him it did not have to be great art; however, Barnaby had to have a design, and he had to determine which materials he needed. They discussed the project. The teacher set the pattern by verbalizing the details of the project step by step. Barnaby had seen a chair that the teacher had made but wanted to make a different kind. As he proceeded step by step, Barnaby took over the verbalization and explained what he had done and what he would do next. As the chair took shape, Barnaby had to measure the chair against his own body, which served as his source of reference. Barnaby sanded and painted the chair; before he could take it home, however, he had to be able to teach another child to make a chair or explain the process clearly to another person. In this way, the experience became organic—a part of Barnaby's being.

Music

The skills students use to understand music are similar to those necessary in many traditional academic subjects. Reading readiness can be related to auditory perception, including linking sounds and symbols. Math readiness is developed as children learn about rhythm through beats per measure, syllabication, and decoding and encoding individual notes and musical phrases.

Robin loved rhythm and music. Although Robin was very bright, she was unable to read because she couldn't decode symbols. In her music class, loud sounds were represented by red poker chips and soft sounds were represented by yellow chips. When she saw two red chips and a yellow one (going from left to right), she knew this sequence meant loud-loud-soft, so she played loud sounds on the drum and soft sounds on the xylophone. As the patterns of sound became more complex and she grew more adept at "reading" the symbols (which also became more complex, including different sizes and shapes), Robin's ability to decode letters and words in the classroom also improved.

Dance

Many elements of dance also can be applied to more traditional academic fields. Teachers at The Lab School use sensory motor training, body awareness, spatial relationships, part–whole relationships, rhythm, timing, and dance sequences to encourage skills that can be applied to geography, narrative structure, and mathematical relationships.

Gregory had a wonderful way with words, but he was always stumbling, tripping, and falling. Like many children with learning disabilities, he did not automatically know how to operate in space. He confused left and right, up and down, above and below, and inside and outside. He was unable to move backwards in space. He could not visualize space, organize the space around him, or follow directions in space. Without first differentiating the parts of his own body and being able to isolate and identify his arms, legs, head, or back, he could not make his body parts work as a unified whole. Gregory's dance teacher began each exercise with Gregory standing in an appointed place marked against the wall. In this way, Gregory could be clear about his own point of departure. Similarly, his classroom teacher marked the space around his desk with masking tape on the floor. Gregory learned to plan his movements in dance class, during which he had to leap over and glide around all sorts of obstacles. He used his hands and feet separately and pretended to be a marionette. He learned to use his arms and legs as though they were pulled by imaginary strings, and he came to understand how the parts of his body worked together as a whole. As Gregory learned where his own body was in space, his use of space on paper improved in the classroom: He planned the placement of his math problems on the page, and even his handwriting showed improvement. Soon, "the upper left-hand corner" and other classroom directions took on meaning.

Drama

One of the most basic skills that is encouraged by participating in drama is reading readiness. Children develop language skills and vocabulary as well as math and problem-solving skills as they act out scenes from plays. When children act out scenes on stage, they learn to sort plot and character information by classifying and categorizing, develop a keen sense of timing, and learn decision-making skills by determining appropriate ways to portray characters.

Brian was asked to play the part of a strong king and then a weak king in his drama class. Although he knew that the characters were different, his portrayal of them did not show their differences. Brian could not isolate the prominent characteristics of each king—strength in one and weakness in the other—and, therefore, could not exaggerate those qualities in his acting to communicate their differences. Brian was unable to integrate gestures, movements, and speech. The teacher who worked with Brian began by demonstrating a strong stride and then a weak shuffle so the children could see the difference. They practiced powerful, strutting walks. To their struts, they added strong gestures and facial expressions. In time, they also gave strong oral commands. The children then learned to act the part of the feeble king by following the same method step by step. Subsequently, the children played guessing games that involved the concepts of strong and weak. First, they verbalized what they had to remember: "What will the king's walk be like? His gestures? His facial expression? His voice?" The students' increased capacity to organize and integrate effectively in drama carried over into the classroom.

Filmmaking

Filmmaking uses many of the same skills as drama, but making movies is even more complex. Focusing on the main point, making decisions, and developing sequences are all skills necessary to successful film making. Students must pay attention to detail, develop organizational skills, and learn to understand cause-and-effect relationships. These skills prepare students for reading and mathematics in addition to honing their analytical and problem-solving skills.

Alvin and May decided to make a movie—a melodrama. They began by constructing a plot for the story. The hero and heroine would be walking in the park. A villain would carry off the heroine and tie her to the railroad tracks, but the hero would come to her rescue in time. When Alvin and May actually started shooting the film in the park using three of their friends as actors, the teacher frequently reminded them to "focus and frame," to keep their camera on the main action. The constant attention to visual focus during film making increased their ability to pay more attention to visual detail in their reading program. When Alvin and May edited the film, the teacher encouraged them to organize the sequences in such a way that the action was interesting, exciting, and understandable. To fulfill these requirements, Alvin and

May had to clearly think out the main point of their film and decide what should come first, next, and last. Subsequently, they added an animated title, a list of actors, and subtitles.

This filmmaking experience demanded intense concentration and organization. Adding in music and sound effects helped Alvin and May to understand how moods should be established. The integration of sight and sound to achieve a specific dramatic effect demanded experimentation, the sorting out of experience, and the purposeful welding of one medium to another. Alvin and May were able to handle the complexity of this project with enthusiasm. Previously, both Alvin and May had experienced great difficulty handling several things at once and had become easily disorganized and confused. While making the film, they not only had fun but also discovered new strategies to help them organize and integrate. Again, they brought these strategies back to the classroom.

OTHER ART FORMS

In addition to the previously mentioned arts, students at The Lab School also participate in collage, printmaking, architecture, and puppetry. The skills developed in collage include planning, understanding part–whole relationships, and separating foreground from background. Printmaking prepares students for reading readiness by developing left–right orientation and pattern recognition. Architecture requires students to apply math skills, integrate a knowledge of social studies and history, pay attention to detail, organize, plan, and problem solve. Puppetry often is very similar to drama and filmmaking and enhances students' language arts skills, social skills, and visual-motor skills. The arts provide a starting point for many avenues of exploration. The child who is building a canoe in woodwork is provided not only with the opportunity to apply basic math skills but also with the opportunity to learn about Native American history, aerodynamics, and the elements of design. Primary and elementary school children at The Lab School spend at least half of each day in arts classes, and the arts are regularly used to teach academic content in the classroom.

THE ARTS AND CURRICULUM

Too often, schools reduce the curriculum to comply with that which is covered on tests. Instead of exploring a wide variety of subjects, classrooms become race tracks for grades with the horses demanding to know, "Will this be on the test?"

Exceptional learners are the real victims in a climate of competing assessment. The constant pressure of legislators all over this country to raise the bar and force more testing tends to produce the one-size-fits-all approach to teaching and assessment. Education seems to have little to do with children and their individualized needs and much more to do with politics, getting votes, and promising visible action. When schooling becomes all about passing tests, it becomes a passive—certainly not an intellectual—journey.

When learning comes about as a result of full participation in activities such as building dioramas; acting; reporting as a broadcaster; or creating a book, play, puppet show, or CD, then paper and pencil assessments don't necessarily capture the degree of knowledge attained. Listening to and looking at what has been accomplished often provides a truer, albeit nonstandardized, picture. Frequently self-appraisal, journals, projects, portfolios, video portfolios, and group critiques draw out knowledge that cannot be properly evaluated in a formal examination. A measure of the whole student can be better arrived at by studying the child's various products and performances in the arts than by standardized testing.

DIAGNOSTIC CLUES THROUGH THE ARTS

Not only can the arts introduce information and reinforce skills but they can be employed as diagnostic aids to test what a child has learned. The kindergartner who cannot repeat a series of three taps should be watched. She may have difficulty responding to sound or hearing a sequence of sounds, or she may hear them correctly but be unable to reproduce them. This could affect her ability to learn to read. The student who works well on one art form but not on another is providing significant data about where his strengths and talents lie. An analysis of the art form in which a child excels provides clues to the components that the child needs to learn most effectively.

Christa's dance and graphic art abilities were superior. However, she disliked music and drama and did not want to participate in them. It turned out that her auditory discrimination was poor; her hearing was fine, but she could not distinguish the differences between sounds or decipher the blending of sounds. Her language skills were well below her age level.

Martin only loved drama. He was clumsy and awkward, always tripping over his own and others' feet, and his eye–hand coordination was so poor that he could barely color, use scissors, or do jigsaw puzzles. He was always in trouble with his peers because of his clumsiness; he constantly bumped into them! Martin failed in a lot of classes because his penmanship looked like chicken scratch; however, he was a different person on stage. He was majestic, fierce, and commanding. On stage, he could mimic what he saw, and his language was very expressive. When Martin walked onto the stage, his superior language skills and auditory memory were brilliantly displayed.

A woodwork teacher observed that Eric could not hit a nail on the head with a hammer and was unable to line up his body in a position that made it possible for his eyes and hands to work together; in addition, Eric could not focus on a printed page. When the sculptor shared his observations with Eric's reading teacher, she recognized that the position of Eric's body while he was reading interfered with what he saw; he lay down on his desk with his head on the left hand. The reading teacher was able to help Eric find a position for his body that helped him focus and also felt comfortable.

Although the correlation between academics and the arts is not always immediately apparent, sometimes we see breakthroughs in completely unexpected areas. For example, at The Lab School we find an amazing number of children who have difficulty understanding concepts of time, measuring the past, using the past tense, and moving backward in space. These children often exhibit difficulty with backward steps and gestures in dance. When these children begin to meet with some success in dance, they often begin to experience some success in the classroom as well. For example, a child who learned to walk backward in dance suddenly grasped the concept of subtraction.

THE ARTS SERVE AS ORGANIZERS

Exceptional learners, particularly students with learning disabilities, often act their age in some ways and not in others. Although they look like typical students, they do not learn through the use of conventional teaching methods. Theirs is a hidden disability. Their central nervous systems are delayed in development. Their responses and behaviors are not abnormal but often are more appropriate to much younger children. They lack many of the basic skills and foundations necessary to academic learning that usually are acquired in the preschool years. Through a panoply of art forms, children with learning disabilities can learn and succeed at school and can enjoy aesthetic experiences that lead to future pleasures, either as part of an audience to an art form and/or as the artist.

Often, *disorder* prevails in children who are delayed in development; their attention as well as their growth is scattered. What these children need most from the outside world is *order*. Through the arts, children can organize their worlds, make sense of what they know, relate past experiences to present experiences, and turn muscular activity into thought and ideas into action.

Immature children—whether they have learning disabilities, sensory disabilities, are economically disadvantaged, or speak another language—have difficulty integrating several processes at one time. They pay attention to everything that goes on in every direction. Although it may seem as if they are not paying attention to anything, in fact, these children are attending to every stimulus around them. They let themselves be bombarded by every sight, sound, or movement in the room. They cannot assign priorities and cannot determine what is most important, less important, and unimportant to attend to. Immature children give equal importance to all things; they are prey to too much information at once.

Children can learn to sort out one color, one shape, one form, and one sound from another through the arts; discriminating through the hands, the body, the eyes, the ears, and all of the senses is part of artistic experience. Learning to look, learning to listen, and remembering what has been seen and heard—problem areas for individuals with learning disabilities—are emphasized in the arts. The arts help organize experience. They help make sense of the world and of the messages coming in through the senses. That is what perception is all about—making sense of the environment and organizing it to have meaning. The arts can help children with learning disabilities develop and strengthen the perceptual skills that form foundations for further learning.

Discipline underlies every artistic endeavor. There is an order to every creation, a progression of steps. People think of the arts as being very free; they are, but the process of mastering basic skills is highly structured. The student who is neurologically immature and is consumed by the disorder engendered by indiscriminate attention and overreactiveness needs experiences that have a clear beginning, middle, and end. Understanding sequences is vital for the child who can talk to you about Homer or gravity but cannot tell you the days of the week or the seasons in order, count to 20, or say the alphabet in proper sequence. What happens first, next, and last is as crucial in a woodwork or crafts project as it is in drama or dance. To complete an artistic project, organization is mandatory. The same organization is necessary for reading; while reading, it is necessary to look at the beginning, middle, and end of a word, phrase, or sentence.

A student with learning disabilities usually experiences difficulty beginning a project. He does not know how to organize himself to start, continue, and stop a project. *Teaching the student the approach to a task* is more important than the student's learning any isolated task. This is as true in the classroom as it is in the arts; the student with learning disabilities does not know *how* to learn. To make sense of the world, a very young child learns from doing. A neurologically immature child must be given the same opportunities before he can deal with abstractions.

LIMITING THE ENVIRONMENT WITHOUT LIMITING THE CHILD

The most resourceful artists, teachers, and therapists are needed to teach the child with learning disabilities who lacks the organization to deal effectively with the freedom that is usually ascribed to the expressive arts. The teacher and the way in which the art form is used must do part of the work for the child who has an immature central nervous system—the part that cannot yet concentrate and that does not discriminate and set priorities. The immature learner needs to be organized. Instead of an expanding world that includes unlimited opportunities, free choices, and as many options as possible, the child with learning disabilities needs boundaries in order to learn effectively and to create fully.

The arts teacher must *limit* the space, the time, the student's choices, the amount of materials used and work done, the number of directions given, and the amount of discussion. The lag in the student's central nervous system that produces immaturity means that the student is bombarded by too much information coming in from the senses all at once, and she cannot distinguish between that which is most important and that which must be relegated to the background. She must be guided to discern which stimuli to pay attention to and which to ignore.

Limiting the child's world to help him create does not mean limiting his ability to express himself. In fact, it means giving the child the parameters and boundaries that will allow him to organize what he wishes to express. He needs a prescribed space for his body and a time, space, and place for all things. Clear, precise directions, given one step at a time, are a must. A child who often misses the main point needs to know what the goals are. If he cannot visualize well, he must see a model or a demonstration before he starts working on his own; he needs help learning to make pictures in his mind. He needs to know what to do first, next, and last in order to understand the parts that contribute to the whole and the order of the procedure. The nontraditional learner must be given the structure that will allow him to succeed.

BUILDING CONFIDENCE THROUGH THE ARTS

Although the arts involve serious work, much laughter and camaraderie is associated with putting on a play or a dance, building something, painting, singing together, or playing in a percussion ensemble. Crises happen all the time in the arts, and they are not the end of the world. Something always can be done to salvage the situation; improvisation, use of strategies, and ingenuity are part of the process. If a child can begin to see the funny side of a bad situation, the way out of the situation becomes possible. Artists who can laugh at themselves in an easy, accepting way are important models for children who see themselves only as a source of worry to others and of despair to themselves. The use of humor can be an effective tool for discipline, for teaching, and for testing. Nothing dispels an atmosphere of tension more quickly than laughter.

Humor can be particularly helpful with regard to the rigidity of the child who is neurologically immature—the way in which he clings to the familiar and insists that there is only one way to do things. Teachers often learn to anticipate this and say to the child, "I know you're going to say it can't be done this way!" Frequently the child will laugh at this. The child's lack of flexibility makes it hard for him to make transitions. He cannot seem to shift gears from one activity to another. Teachers learn to signal changes, to give advance warnings, to almost make the shifts with the child. In music, a drumbeat can be the transition; in painting, a color can be the signal; in drama, a prop can be displayed; and in dance, a specific movement can serve as a warning of transition.

Although each art form is defined by a specific structure, there are many ways to achieve an artistic objective. A child does not need to approach an art form in only one way. In fact, most artists encourage students to seek out new, unorthodox ways to achieve a goal. A child who has failed in so many situations need never feel condemned for making a mistake. By feeling free to experiment, to make mistakes, and to learn from them, the child is given permission by the artist to make mistakes and survive. Many great works of art have emanated from mistakes. Students who have lived with school failure take their mistakes as a personal condemnation. They live in fear of mistakes. In art there are no mistakes, only opportunities. The child must be shown that amends can be made for a mistake, that things can be restored, and that sometimes an unexpected and original effect can be achieved by accident.

Artists also can make a great academic contribution in helping the exceptional learner grasp scientific principles in woodwork, see the fundamentals of geometry in straw sculpture, learn vocabulary in drama, and match the concept of intervals in music and mathematics. In fact, when teachers can explain to artists a certain concept with which a student is struggling and not learning, the artist usually can tackle that subject through an art form. This kind of collaboration can only enhance a student's learning.

The genius of the artist is needed to preserve the integrity of the specific art form while systematically teaching the child the very skills he must have in order to succeed at school. While the child concentrates on his project in the arts, the artist concentrates on the learning process, which can involve either readiness skills or pure academic material. For many children with learning disabilities, academic content including mathematical functions, grammar, syntax, and spelling can be taught and learned by students through the arts. A vowel can dance between two consonants. Computing methods can be "invented" to save a flock of sheep in a make-believe encampment in ancient Assyria.

PARENTS AND TEACHERS AS PARTNERS

At The Lab School of Washington, we are fortunate to have so many partners. Parents of students who experience great difficulty with learning need more support and more hope than other parents. This is why, for parents, coming to art exhibits and seeing beautifully framed original works done by their children is important. This is why performing artists need to "frame" drama, dance, and music performances to demonstrate each child's strengths. The child's feeling of competence breeds confidence, and parents then can enjoy their children's talent and sense of well-being.

When parents come to visit the school, it is important that they experience the readiness, the organization, and the academic skills that can be taught through the arts. They need to experience themselves how much information, discipline, and order can be gleaned through the arts. Schools need to be sure that parents of children with special needs have these experiences; they need to be introduced to the arts as life-empowering experiences.

Many exceptional learners do not express excitement with regard to academic subjects, but students like Billy come home from school brimming with joy over what went on in film animation class. "I made it happen," he tells his parents, "when I turned the little boy on the chair studying science into the diver on a special ladder with the radar on the ocean floor discovering a new food for the 22nd century that will rid the world of starvation." His creative edge comes out in this field. He feels validated by his work. He feels empowered in an arts setting that will generalize to some of his work in academic settings. Billy wonders if this might become a career goal for him. He makes sure he goes to a college that teaches filmmaking. He knows that there are a number of filmmakers who did not do well at school because of their learning disabilities and ADHD. This knowledge helps him follow his passion for filming.

One way to help children follow their passion is to develop clear precise objectives such as the following:

- The child will learn strategies in dance to distinguish his left side from his right.

- The child will be able to move and say a few words at the same time in dramatic renderings.

- The adolescent will develop claymation figures in film animation and develop a sequence of three actions for these figures.

- The adolescent will design a 17th century court setting first in miniature and then enlarged to scale.

The exceptional learner needs to be included in discussions during which goals and objectives are established for him. Goal setting is an important part of both growing up and participating in the various arts forms. Aiming for excellence with reasonable goals is part of arts education. The exceptional learner usually wants to become an active part of his own goal setting, particularly when it involves areas and activities in which he shines. The goal setting becomes part of the challenge that prods him to soar to new realms.

Whether a child is learning how to use color in oil painting, choreographing a dance for three opposing forces, or learning to follow a sequence of colored symbols to play the xylophone, the arts offer innumerable opportunities to establish small personal objectives and to achieve the larger goals of skill development and knowledge acquisition.

Abilities and Disabilities, School Failures, Adult Successes

Every teacher in a large classroom has had the experience of being puzzled by at least one child each year. "Is this child intelligent? Is this child oppositional? Is there some reason that I cannot motivate this child to learn? Can this child learn? Why is she so good at some things and so terrible in academic work? Is she lazy? Is she not trying? Is she spoiled? Why is she failing?"

The U.S. Government states that 12% of America's students have disabilities, and more than 50% of these students have learning disabilities. The U.S. Department of Education tells us that the percentage of children who have been identified with a specific learning disability is 5%. Most specialists who work in the field would double that number because so many children with learning disabilities are not identified and drop out of school as early as junior high. According to the 21st Annual Report to Congress of the Individuals with Disabilities Education Act (IDEA) of 1990 (PL 101-476), the number of children between the ages of 6 and 21 who have been identified with a specific learning disability and who are receiving services under IDEA has increased 42% in the 10-year period between 1987/1988 and 1997/1998 and now totals more than 2.7 million. The National Institute of Mental Health and the

National Institute of Child Health and Human Development (NICHD) tell us that 4%–8% of American children have attention-deficit/hyperactivity disorder (ADHD), with a preponderance of boys experiencing this central nervous system dysfunction. These statistics mean that large numbers of children who learn differently are present in every teacher's classroom, particularly when you also consider children who have language impairments or underdeveloped language or who are learning English as a second language. According to NICHD, 20% of American children with average or above-average intelligence cannot read well enough to learn from what they are reading. They have uncovered this huge figure from random samples. Among the children identified as having a specific learning disability, tests demonstrate that reading is the primary difficulty for 80%–85% of the children. At the present time, with the emphasis on inclusive classrooms, there are more students in general education classrooms who experience difficulty learning than ever before.

Exceptional learners—a population that includes students who have learning disabilities and ADHD—have vast abilities. The challenge lies in helping them to organize themselves and focus so that these abilities may shine. Many children with learning disabilities have above-average to superior intelligence. Often, they are as exceptional in their abilities as they are in their disabilities.

EXCEPTIONAL LEARNERS

Exceptional learners often are hard to reach with typical educational methods. It is very difficult for teachers to assess the cognitive functioning of children who have language impairments that may be related to learning disabilities. Often children with learning disabilities receive the information but cannot express it verbally, even though they may be able to demonstrate their knowledge through the arts. Other students do not even receive verbal information but only visually absorb the world around them. Education founded on the arts requires constant activity of the mind and higher order thinking skills such as analysis and synthesis; however, it does not have to be verbal. We have found that exceptional learners, including students with ADHD and learning disabilities, flourish in arts-based classrooms.

ATTENTION-DEFICIT/HYPERACTIVITY DISORDER

ADHD is the official medical diagnostic label for a cluster of symptoms including inattention and/or hyperactivity and impulsivity. ADHD is listed in the standard psychiatric reference work, the *Diagnostic and Statistical Manual of Mental Disorders, Fourth Edition* (DSM-IV; American Psychiatric Association, 1994), with three subtypes:

1. ADHD, predominantly inattentive type
2. ADHD, predominantly hyperactive-impulsive type
3. ADHD, combined type

Subtype 1 describes the child who has trouble focusing and pays too much attention to too many things at once. His neurological dysfunction does not allow him to automatically filter out irrelevant and unnecessary material. This child cannot set priorities.

Subtype 2 describes the child who interrupts everybody and everything and cannot keep a secret, take turns, or slow down to think. This is the child who cannot inhibit behavior and speaks before she thinks, acts before she reasons, and leaps before she looks. Her brakes don't work to slow her down, and she has trouble ending one activity and beginning another. ADHD often is accompanied by excessive movement of the body and the mouth. Random, fidgety, restless, unfocused, unthinking behavior is typical. Subtype 3 is a combination of both subtypes.

Traditional classroom work that involves sitting still in a seat for even short periods of time is hard for a child with ADHD. These students are known to become easily distracted or feel under-stimulated in classes while doing unappealing tasks. Students with ADHD seek interest-related stimulation when trying to accomplish a task. For this reason, they may have difficulty with pages of rote and boring math problems assigned by a teacher in a traditional academic environment. The high activity level associated with various art forms, project learning, and experiential learning suits children with ADHD well.

NEUROLOGICAL IMMATURITY

Children with learning disabilities and/or ADHD display evidence of immaturity and disorganization. Frequently they seem younger than they are in the way they move, plan, and talk. Their general behavior—including their distractibility and short attention spans—is similar to that of younger children. Often, their immaturity makes them more dependent on adults than their same-age peers, and it is easy for teachers and parents to infantilize them further if they do not understand the nature of their disabilities.

Learning disabilities and ADHD are often described as neurological wiring problems. It is important to remember that the erratic, inconsistent, up-and-down quality of these children is not due to a lack of effort or intelligence or to poor parenting or teaching but is the result of a neurological deficit in the brain akin to a malfunctioning telephone switchboard: The wires somehow short circuit, scrambling the incoming messages and misdirecting the outgoing messages. What confuses teachers and other adults is the fact that, often, these children do not show any outward signs of the disability: "There's nothing wrong with this student," or "He's just lazy," is a frequent rejoinder, along with "Her parents just need to discipline her, and then she will be okay." It is easy to blame the child with learning disabilities or ADHD for not trying hard enough when teachers and other adults do not understand the nature of the disability and become impatient with the child's behavior. Once the disability is understood, expectations can be more specifically child-centered than norm-centered.

EVALUATING EXCEPTIONAL LEARNERS

The value of testing is that it is diagnostic; students and teachers are able to see what students have and have not learned. Unfortunately, evaluations of exceptional learners rarely pick up on their strengths, talents, or special interests. Traditional examinations usually fail to measure the knowledge acquired by these students. Their learning disabilities usually prevent them from achieving high scores on examinations. Concentration is a huge problem. Focusing on the main points or the sets required is a common difficulty; and because language impairments beset most individuals with learning disabilities as well as those students who are economically disadvantaged or speak English as a second language, these children are easily confused by tests. Many of these students need extended time because their central nervous systems do not process information efficiently. Performance on demand is anathema to these students. During related conversations, while doing art projects, or during drama classes in which the children pretend to be characters who have the required knowledge, often they overwhelm their teachers with the amount of information they know and with their startling insights. Although these students understand the course material, they routinely fail the examinations. Some of these students can even get through law school but, despite knowledge of the material, fail the bar exam over and over.

Unfortunately, educational improvement is not accomplished through administrative or legislative mandate. Despite rising test scores, there is little or no evidence of increased student learning. A recent study by the Kentucky Office of Educational Accountability suggests that test score gains in Kentucky are a function of students' increasing skills as test takers rather than evidence of increased learning.

THE CONCRETE CHILD

In order to deal with the abstract quality of learning, all children go through a stage of making concrete relationships. Exceptional learners continue to rely on concrete relationships longer than other children. To understand materials, they need to see, touch, smell, taste, hear, feel, and "be" them. The child who relies on concrete relationships must be immersed in all of the senses to gain the necessary experience for understanding the world around him. Typical children tend to pick this up naturally. Exceptional children need to be inundated with concrete experiences and for a longer period of time than other children.

Sometimes, a child with learning disabilities is extremely literal. For example, when she hears the phrase, "The Gifts of the Nile," she believes birthday gifts spew out of the Nile River. Subtleties, nuances, and inferences escape her. For this reason, at The Lab School, we might put blue cellophane on the classroom floor with a delta at the end to represent the Nile River and let the children open gift-wrapped boxes that have been placed on the cellophane. The boxes contain items such as papyrus (a scroll), a shaduf (irrigation), and fertile soil (from flooding). The teacher then explains that these wonderful things that made life more livable and productive are like gifts.

Exceptional learners frequently have great difficulty remembering things. Concrete experiences that involve all of their senses have to be used to help them retrieve information. The scent of spices can help them remember why Columbus discovered America. Using a piece of elastic aids them in forming the shapes of continents, and origami or building kites spurs the remembering of geometric theorems.

It is not surprising that a number of heads of museums are individuals with learning disabilities who are artistic and want to display knowledge in concrete forms. The Cooper-Hewitt National Design Museum in New York City, the United States Holocaust Memorial Museum in Washington, D.C., and the Field Museum in Chicago all have employed brilliant museum directors who have learning disabilities.

Children who rely on concrete relationships need visible proof of progress, which is why gold stars, stickers, graphs, and charts are so useful. Through the use of art portfolios or videotapes, teachers can let students examine their own work. Videotapes of productions are proof of accomplishment.

Adults and children alike seem to remember information well when it has been attained through active participation, such as by acting, touching, and constructing. Thirty-year-old Jane still sings the alphabet to herself to remember it. Twenty-two-year-old Meyer remembers multiplication tables through tricks he learned when he worked as an acrobat at a circus training school. For most exceptional learners, receiving information in a concrete way helps them to file it in their brains.

William Doyle, a well-known antique dealer and auctioneer, discovered a rare profession through his concrete experiences, curiosity, and sensitivity to concrete objects. When Doyle was a child, his favorite day was Wednesday, the garbage day, when people set out large, bulky objects on the sidewalk to be picked up. For him, it was a day-long treasure hunt, and he had the collector's penchant for squirreling away his finds. Doyle was a miserable student. He experienced severe learning disabilities and ADHD. To stay in school and to have something to look forward to, Doyle apprenticed himself after school to an antiques dealer. Quickly he mastered the complex details of the trade. He told The Lab School students, "I fell in love with objects, and I became an antique dealer. And now I've become an auctioneer, and for me it's the most exciting business. It's like theatre. It's like a treasure hunt every day. I still want to succeed. I still want to do better. If I had all the complete learning abilities, I would have been successful and done a normal job, but I never would have had the life I've had today!"

Exceptional learners often request, "Let me see it" or, "Let me do it," as if they know intrinsically how they learn best. Concrete learning can be very intellectual at its base. It is mind building and concept forming. Concrete learning usually provides a solid base for future critical thinking and language development. Concrete learners look, touch, and see what a horizon is and can think back to when they saw a horizon, what colors it radiated, and what magical shapes it formed.

In his book, *The Unschooled Mind: How Children Think and How School Should Teach* (1991), Gardner suggested that two of the best structures for learning lie in museums and apprenticeships. The Lab School philosophy supports the belief that museums are very visual and concrete structures where students can see and, in some museums, touch life-size projects. Museums offer object-centered learning. So does The Lab School. With apprenticeships, students can watch someone work on a project and then do the same project themselves. They are in an intense relationship with someone they usually admire, and they want to do well in this hands-on active learning environment. The Lab School experience is that an internship during the student's junior year in an area of special interest not only motivates students to new academic heights but also gives them career awareness that often leads to career choice.

POSITIVE ATTRIBUTES OF NEGATIVE BEHAVIORS

The negative behaviors that often are seen in children with severe learning disabilities and/or ADHD frequently turn into positive attributes in adulthood. For parents, this means a light at the end of the tunnel. Teachers should carefully list the negative behaviors displayed by their students and imagine which of those behaviors might eventually contribute to the students' success. Since 1967, we have seen many positive careers take shape at The Lab School of Washington.

For example, students at The Lab School who have been called stubborn, unyielding, or willful turn these negative traits into the positive attribute of persistence in adulthood—a fierce determination, a fighting spirit, and perseverance that leads them to achieve what they want to accomplish.

Andrew, a former student at The Lab School, commented that he could not get over how so many students in college were not used to hard work. "They don't have the discipline, the stick-to-itiveness, that my dyslexic friends and I have. It sounds funny to say, but, in a sense, we were better prepared for college than they were."

One complaint teachers often voice is that their students with learning disabilities often are rigid—that they are so literal that they can only see "one way" of doing things. People remark on the intensity that these students project. As adults, this rigidity and intensity often turns into commitment, dedication, intensity of purpose, single-mindedness, and highly focused thinking—traits that are particularly positive for a student who wants to become a medical or scientific researcher.

Dr. Donald Coffey, a Distinguished Professor of Urology, Professor of Oncology, and Professor of Pharmacology and Molecular Science at Johns Hopkins University Medical School in Baltimore, Maryland, told students at The Lab School, "I have a terrible time, as you might guess, because you cannot become a professor in three different fields if you've only read three books in your life, and that's been my problem. One of the things I have trouble doing is focusing on something. And so my mind sort of jumps around. I cannot pay attention to things, but once I sort of lock in on it, I'm sort of like a bulldog. I just stay right on it until it almost becomes absurd. I'm scatterbrained about things. I get into everything. Yet I am tenacious—the bulldog—once I am involved in something." Because Coffey learned differently from most children, he was a very difficult student to teach. Sometimes he would focus intently on one project and ignore all others, whereas other times his interests were diverted by everything around him. He told the students that his best employees today often are dyslexic because they ask "Why not?" and are willing to think big, unorthodox thoughts. He announced that, in his experience, exceptional learners were the best thinkers.

Another condition that often is seen in individuals with learning disabilities is called *perseveration*. It means beyond perseverance: a mindless repetition of the same thing over and over again, a drivenness emanating from an organic condition. It means persisting beyond the reasonable point at which most people will stop. It means doggedly pursuing a single goal. As one adult in our night school said, "When I am involved in something, nothing else matters. I will proceed at all costs, not looking around me at anything else. It's like something inside me is driving me." Perhaps this is why so many high achievers with learning disabilities are extraordinarily talented to the point of perfectionism in their chosen fields.

What often appears in childhood as a refusal to do things the same way others do them is really an inability to perform the same way. Some children have to solve problems in their own, original way. They invent their own methods rather than following known sequences of procedures. Richard Avedon, a renowned fashion photographer and photojournalist who exhibits in museums and galleries around the world, was a shy child with severe learning disabilities who was uncomfortable with the children in his neighborhood; he spent many hours in a dark bedroom observing the world through a tiny strip behind a shade. Soon, he began experimenting with the family's

Kodak Box Brownie Camera. At 20 years of age, he went to a department store, Bonwit Teller, and after that, fashion photography was never again the same. He has taught all of us to look at the world from new angles, from new perspectives, with new vision.

Sam was always drawing. Teachers frequently criticized him for not paying attention and not participating in class. Sam's parents wished he would get serious about his work. They did not realize that he was, in fact, serious about anything visual. Only his science teacher regularly had him illustrate every definition, and, in response, his recall was excellent. It took Sam more than 14 years from the time he started kindergarten to graduate from high school and 7 years to graduate from college; however, he was able to go on to graduate school in architecture and is a successful practicing architect today.

Visual thinkers tend to doodle, draw, and color their way through school to the condemnation of their teachers. They tend to think in terms of lines and shapes and not in terms of words. Charles Guggenheim, four-time Academy Award winner for documentary films, even was sent away from home as a young boy until he learned to read.

Mel used to tap his foot or fingers to the rhythms in his head. His body was moving all the time. His ADHD was demonstrated by general restlessness, impulsivity, and attention span problems. Mel learned his telephone number by making it into a drumbeat rhythm. He made his multiplication facts into a musical exercise. He enjoyed syllabication because it involved breaking down sounds. Mel failed a number of courses. The people who taught him tried to teach him their way and he failed. His tutor, Peter, used his musical abilities and "rap" to teach him academics. Mel graduated, went on to college, and now makes musical instruments and plays in a band.

Many children who display negative behaviors would rather appear naughty than unintelligent. Some just want to have their way no matter what. Mischief makers— kids who get into trouble on purpose—also can show a certain resourcefulness and excellent problem-solving abilities.

Mark made himself so useful to other children that they let him do whatever he wanted. Some people would call his behavior manipulative; however, it's not surprising that Mark started out in a very competitive field, rose fast, and now is a manager of an up-and-coming rock band.

Kenneth learned almost everything through interactions with people and also with plants. He volunteered in a nursing home and in a commercial greenhouse. He charmed nearly every soul he met. Incredibly difficult to teach, his instructors continued to work with him because he tried so hard and was genuinely sweet. His peers criticized him constantly for being "Mr. Good Guy" and for "kissing up" all the time. With great difficulty (and with the help of his adult advocates), Kenneth became proficient enough in reading, writing, and mathematics to graduate from high school; however, he could not do college work. Because he was very good with plants, Kenneth printed flyers that said, "Come to Kenneth with your plant problems," and passed them out in front of a supermarket. Today, Kenneth has a $4 million business. Because certain tasks such as writing and working with figures are still quite time-consuming for Kenneth, he has hired a secretary who writes letters, an accountant who helps with the books, and a part-time lawyer who drafts all of his contracts. Because of his success, Kenneth is able to delegate many of his business's administrative tasks to others until they need his final approval.

Philip was a student in his own world whose teachers begged him to "pay attention." His negativity and rudeness were demonstrated by his long silences, constant yawning, and passive aggression. The only time he came alive was when discussions centered around selling things. He had ideas and tried them out. Anything that involved selling—setting up refreshment stands, working in the school store, working as a grocery clerk—turned Philip on. The more experience he had in selling, the more his confidence grew, his language developed, and his attention span elongated. Philip discovered that he could sell more when he maintained eye contact with people, when he smiled at them, and when he was enthusiastic. Because Philip had a passion to sell as much as he could, his behavior changed dramatically. His motivation to go to college as a business major increased with his success. Now, with a 4.0 grade point average, he just graduated from college with a degree in marketing and is managing a paint store.

Fannie Flagg, the author of film scripts and books such as *Fried Green Tomatoes at the Whistle Stop Café, Daisy Faye and the Miracle Man* and, the latest, *Welcome to the World Baby Girl,* explained that her learning disability first revealed itself in a tap-dancing class, where she experienced trouble counting out the steps. She couldn't follow the beat or remember the routines. At school, she had trouble sounding out letters and remembering sequences of instructions. Her great passion and ability for storytelling surfaced at the same time; with the help of editors who took care of her poor spelling, Fannie Flagg became a famous writer!

A number of students with dyslexia, a loose term that encompasses learning disabilties in reading, writing, and spelling, cannot write legibly and may not be able to spell beyond a third- or fourth-grade level; however, they may be able to dictate stories of great imagination or do quality reporting. Think of Robert Benton, Pulitzer Prize–winning playwright; Wendy Wasserstein, Tony Award–winning playwright; Richard Cohen, former outstanding syndicated columnist for *The Washington Post;* and Fred Friendly, celebrated broadcast journalist. None of these individuals can spell or write legibly. Children with severe writing difficulties can become writers—and outstanding ones at that!

DIFFERENT INTELLIGENCES

Each of the previously mentioned talented achievers are alternative learners; they need to be respected because, frequently, they learn by using different intelligences than the rest of us. As Harvard psychologist and educator Dr. Howard Gardner says, most schools rely on linguistic intelligence, the world of words, or mathematical/logical intelligence, the world of numbers and logic. Alternative learners frequently use visual intelligence (e.g., artists, filmmakers, architects), musical intelligence (e.g., musicians), or kinesthetic intelligence (e.g., dancers, athletes). Gardner describes those who have interpersonal intelligence (e.g., great leaders, entrepreneurs) and those who have intrapersonal intelligence (e.g., healers, psychologists, social workers). Some people learn through nature (e.g., environmentalists, zoo keepers, explorers). Surely there are even more intelligences than Gardner names that provide alternative pathways to learning. Parents and teachers need to look for these routes. Teacher training must help new teachers identify their own routes to learning so they can provide for multiple pathways to learning in our nation's schools.

DIFFERENT PERSONALITY STYLES AND BEHAVIOR

Often, children with learning disabilities exhibit other behaviors that are unrelated to learning that are difficult for teachers to understand. Sometimes, their personality styles clash with the personality styles of their teachers or with the culture of the school. We can see some of these patterns developing in play groups and in athletic teams at school. Instead of concentrating so much on children's negative behaviors, teachers and mental health personnel should spend more time in schools looking for what comes naturally to children and determining in which environments and situations students are comfortable.

Since 1967, graduates from The Lab School have displayed a variety of personality traits; some of the students have been wholly self-absorbed, whereas others have been sensitive to the needs of others. Those who were sensitive usually were good listeners in childhood; their peers tended to trust them. They were mostly nonjudgmental. Today they are likely to work in the helping professions: social services, hospitals, schools, and child care centers. The adults who were frequently teased, humiliated, and ridiculed in their childhoods seem to understand personal pain in depth and want to help others. Some adults with learning disabilities are not successful working for anyone; they feel comfortable only when working for themselves with minimal or no staff. Other adults with learning disabilities want a big staff. There are those who are not comfortable with hierarchies but feel satisfied working as a vital member of a team or in a partnership.

Egocentricity is seen a great deal among individuals with learning disabilities. For many, it is a reflection of the immaturity of the central nervous system and of late-developing emotional maturity. Parents and teachers frequently complain that children with learning disabilities are self-absorbed. Yet, sometimes we see that egocentricity translates into creative, highly successful activity. The artist, the inventor, the novel thinker, the well-known philosopher, and the popular critic often make a great contribution to our civilization.

Rob constantly was defining rules and regulations; he nitpicked about every little infraction of the rules. He became very irritated if one of his classmates broke any rules and if a teacher did not pick up on it and take action. Very responsible as a tiny child, he wanted everyone else to be equally responsible in a very orderly world. Conversely, he took pride in rescuing kittens stuck in a gutter and caring for a wounded bird. The only art form Rob enjoyed was woodwork because of its precision and because he could anticipate the outcome of his efforts. Today, Rob is a policeman who has received many commendations from his commanding officers for his bravery and efficiency.

The negative, mischievous, so-called "bad" behavior of certain children needs to be examined. Does it exhibit a lot of creative problem solving? Then it can be redirected for positive purposes. Does it demonstrate sales ability? Then a store or enterprise of some kind can let this child shine at home and at school. Does this child's behavior demonstrate leadership? Do others naturally follow her? It must not be forgotten that many successful adults were what we call "bad" children who did not follow "the rules." They led others astray. They didn't respond to group pressure, but did their own thing.

Brash children with learning disabilities who were too direct, literal, and concrete were seen as defiant and as flouting authority. For example, Pauline simply felt unsafe when the classroom structure and rules were not clear. She so craved order that she sounded as though she was dictating to teachers what they should do. Today she is a successful lieutenant in the Army where she receives the structure she requires and where there is an answer for her every question. The following personality types are common to children with learning disabilities.

THE EXPLOSIVE CHILD

Eleanor was explosive in school. She felt passionately about everything. As she matured, her passions became collecting art, artifacts, and treasures and categorizing them. Today, Eleanor works in a museum and shares her knowledge with assistants and interns who work for her.

THE LONER

Christopher tried to be as invisible as possible in school. Rarely did he speak. He loved the outdoors and natural beauty. Teachers struggled to get Christopher involved in learning. Today he is a floral designer who has won prizes for his artistry.

Teddy could not work in a group, even a group of two. Today he is an excellent photographer who works on his own and has received recognition for his poetic photographs.

THE SENSITIVE CHILD

Ned and Minna were nurturers. Starting early in school with their friends, they made those around them feel good about themselves. They were particularly effective child care workers because they cared deeply for kids and had a sense of mission to help children as others had helped them.

Many Lab School graduates reach adulthood with more self-knowledge than their peers. In order to be effective, self-advocates may have had to learn more about themselves and their learning styles than others. They anticipate people's needs and reactions. Often, they are more aware of their strengths and interests because the adults around them tried to help them build self-esteem. They seem more prepared for bumps and bruises than their peers.

THE REBEL

Gregory was punished continually at his previous school for not doing as he was told; he was tough and aggressive. His teachers were afraid that he would lead the children out of the classroom in a protest or strike and that the other students would follow him. In adulthood, Gregory's leadership was highly recognized, and he became a very effective tough head of the Teacher's Union!

Often, though not always, the rebel is a questioner, a thinker, who sees more than one way to do things. In the arts, these students often use old materials in new, innovative ways.

THE FRIENDLESS

As Susan said, "Something I do turns people off. I don't know what I do, but I don't have friends." A number of students with severe learning disabilities tend to be friendless and isolated from groups in school. These students cause their parents enormous concern because they are alone so much of the time. Many of these students end up working with the homeless, with older adults, or those who are ill—populations that desperately need assistance. A way to help students feel significant is to have them help others, and often they want to help through art, music, dance, drama, or film-making. Mother Teresa once said, "We will never know until we get to heaven how much we owe the poor for allowing us to serve them." The truth she spoke lies in human beings' basic need to do something useful and helpful for others in order to be truly fulfilled and happy. The Lab School has found that as students with severe learning disabilities acquire helping skills, they begin to discover more of their own resources and feel more related to the world because others need them. They become empowered by giving of themselves.

THE PERFECTIONIST

One of the most challenging behaviors for teachers as well as for parents is displayed by the child with a learning disability who will not dare to risk being wrong. These students often are described as perfectionists who must have all of their answers right or will not even try. They are children with learning disabilities who have tasted failure and defeat early in life and won't risk that sour, bitter taste again. They must be cajoled, excited, inspired, and lured into learning, making it as nonthreatening as possible. They have to be told there are no mistakes in art (but a lot of possibilities for them to explore). They have to see that musical compositions can all be very different and, yet, very good. For example, Patrick proclaimed, "Sean's film is totally different from mine. How can they be equally excellent?" It is interesting to see that a number of these children gain employment as adults in jobs that are very clearly defined and highly structured such as traffic controllers, accountants, and medical technologists (e.g., radiologists). They know precisely what is expected of them, and their performance ratings tend to be very high. For many of them the multiplicity of "right" pathways in the arts can be disturbing unless they are presented very specifically by the artists, as the way the arts work.

THE IMPULSIVE CHILD

Children who are very impulsive and act before they think sometimes become successful adults because they are not afraid to take risks. Mario went into venture capital work. Philip invested in a company that took off. Zeb joined a firm that was going bankrupt and helped to turn it around. Of course, there are stories of impulsive behavior that led to disasters on the job, too.

Children with poor impulse control who have weak self-esteem and poor judgment are more likely to get in trouble with the law. However, The Lab School experience is that this can be prevented through the interventions of special schooling (particularly effective special education), good counseling, speech-language therapy, occupational therapy, experiences in the arts, and strong support from family members or other adults who participate in children's lives.

When there is just failure at school and no hope for success, the impulsive student often is reckless and thinks only of the moment. When the impulsive student feels there is hope, when his work is framed on a wall or contained in a performance, his confidence grows and so does his feeling that behavior matters; therefore, he makes that huge extra special effort to not get into trouble.

THE INSATIABLE CHILD

Gerry, whose need for attention was bottomless, ate up attention from his teachers until they felt there was little left in them. (Inexperienced teachers give and give until they are drained completely.) Veteran teachers gave Gerry what they could plus a little bit more but did not let him dry them out. He loved art and drama classes, spending extra time in those rooms. Today, Gerry is a dynamic tour guide who has audience after audience paying attention to him and loving what he does. He is center stage, and his job allows him to take people around museums and pursue his passionate interest in art history.

THE DISORGANIZED CHILD

Esther was so disorganized that she couldn't find her notebook, her homework, her hair clip, her umbrella, or her gym clothes. Her parents were exhausted by the time she went to school each day because she had no sense of time and timing. Her mother referred to her as an "unmade bed" or "a walking mess." Her teachers blamed the parents for neglecting her. She spilled her food at lunch and bumped into her classmates, causing them to drop things. A victim of time and space—the hidden dimensions of learning disabilities—Esther was all over the place, in everybody's territory, not endearing herself to anyone. Esther needed to work with an occupational therapist several times each week to help her to discover her body and its parts. Her treatment program was designed to help her organize her body and her mind. Esther's special education teachers were very aware of her spatial-temporal problems. They made sure there was a time, a space, and a place for all things. They worked with Esther on strategies to help her organize her desk, her work, and herself. Through drama, she was able to work on scenes that demonstrated disorganization, then organization. Her music teacher would not let her start any lessons until she had all of her materials together and was organized. Ferociously ambitious in a family of high achievers, Esther, as she grew older, recognized her own difficulties and used technology, paid for assistance, persuaded others to help her develop systems for remembering things, and got through high school, college, and graduate school and achieved a doctorate degree in public health. In her spare time Esther plays the flute.

THE IMPOSSIBLE CAN HAPPEN

Never discount the impossible. Some of the negative behaviors that have worn out parents and teachers and that have led to school failure have helped exceptional learners demonstrate astonishing creativity and awesome talent in adult life. The constant demands for attention and the stubbornness of children with learning disabilities frequently became a fierce determination to succeed; their perseveration turned into a singlemindedness that often brought success; and their manipulative behavior frequently showed up in adulthood as originality in problem solving. Many of the children who failed at school simply failed to learn the way they were taught at school. They learned another way and when they found that path, they developed something that others loved or needed or admired. Some of the children who could not socialize well with others in school found careers that didn't demand good social skills, or along the bumpy journey of living, they developed those skills. Children with learning disabilities typically take much longer to grow up and find themselves. An experience with a poet or a sculptor, an encounter with a drama troupe, or a try at drumming can open up new worlds to these students. Developing an interest that turns into a passion can give meaning and direction to a person's life. That is why it is so important for schools to offer students a panoply of experiences in the arts—to let students dip in and try out a smorgasbord of activities to find their rightful places.

The adults who attend The Lab School's Night School have told us over and over again that general school made them feel dumb, hopeless, and totally inadequate. Only a few felt that they achieved some skill development. The rest were saddened by the waste of years trying to learn to read and write. In some cases, their math skills were good; in others, their math skills were even worse than their language arts skills. A few adults could articulate what they needed. They were able to say that their language skills were weak. They saw things visually, but nobody drew on these strengths. They felt written off as learners at an early age. Nobody took the time or energy to find out what they could do, loved to do, or were interested in doing. When we went around the room with 60 of our 90 adult students, one after another had a talent or an interest in the arts. The power of the arts could have been used to work on their readiness skills, their organization skills, their oral and written language and core courses. Their message was simple: "Don't let another generation of poor learners suffer as we have because every method possible to teach us wasn't tried. USE THE ARTS!"

Each art is a discipline. To master each step takes practice—doing the same thing over and over again, perhaps in different ways. It means relating one thing to another and integrating them to have meaning. Most of the arts demand a certain rhythm, specific timing, which helps the child whose sense of time and timing is off. Placement in space is important in all of the arts. The arts can serve to develop basic elements of reading decoding and reading comprehension.

Many people view the arts as charming, but uninhibited, expression. The arts need to be looked upon as organizers of expression, as statements of experience, as purveyors of new information. The arts need to be seen as exhibitions and performances that can and often do host academic achievement.

Providing Order and Focus
Through the Arts

My experience with my son who had learning disabilities showed me that he was thoroughly disorganized: He had difficulty focusing; could understand material presented verbally but could not repeat it back in rote fashion; and could not remember names, titles of books or movies, or supposedly simple things such as addresses and telephone numbers. Anything involving sequences such as the alphabet, numbers in order, and the days of the week, months of the year, and the seasons eluded him. I soon discovered that there were a whole host of youngsters just like my son who had the same basic problems.

When my son learned in first grade about a Navajo rain dance, his hand shot up and he compared the Navajo rain dance to Greek myths. "People have to believe in these," he said. "Maybe, also, they thought they could bring about what they wanted to have happen by doing a dance or telling a story." His first-grade teacher went up to him, shook him hard, and said, "If you know all that, why can't you read the word *cat?*" The teacher may not have realized that reading uses a different part of the brain than comparing and reasoning; however, her frustration with students like my son was very common.

Students with learning disabilities often make very astute remarks; therefore, their teachers and, sometimes, their parents cannot understand why the students have difficulty with tasks that other students perform with ease. Parents and teachers decide that the students are lazy and that they *could* read if they only *would*. My son, the same 6-year-old who had remarked so intelligently in class, hid in the bathroom or under a table during reading time. He had been able to fake reading by using picture or context clues and making inferences, but when he was faced with the barren desert of letters placed together to form a word, he ran away, claiming to have bladder trouble— one malady he did not have.

There were incredible inconsistencies between my son's advanced vocabulary, excellent reasoning, and vibrant imagination and his inability to see the difference between a straight line and an angle. He did not know that 2 plus 2 equals 4 and was not even sure whether 4 was more than or less than 2. Erratic, uneven, and unpredictable, a jumble of "can dos" and "cannot dos," traditional schooling did not work for my son.

Facts did not stick in my son's mind. However, we found that he responded with alacrity to highly dramatic stories read aloud and to stories with pictures that he could act out and then discuss. Although he was very clumsy with his hands, he enjoyed working on very big short-term projects. He loved having a project to take to his room or to take home. Drumbeats and steady hand clapping helped him get organized. This profile was similar to a number of students enrolled at The Lab School. Many other students at the school were extremely talented with their hands but had very little language with which to express themselves.

LEARNING BY DOING

Children with learning disabilities and attention-deficit/hyperactivity disorder (ADHD) experience neurologically based disorganization. The child with learning disabilities usually has difficulty beginning a project because he does not know how to break it down into meaningful chunks: first, next, and last. This is true in the arts as well as in the classroom. These children do not have the organizational skills necessary for learning.

Young children understand touch, gesture, rhythm, tone, and movement before they understand words. They babble, croon, and sing before they speak. They color, draw, and paint before they form letters. They dance and leap and act out stories before they can read. Young children use the arts—pretending, constructing, dancing, and doing—to make sense of their environment.

As a young child learns from doing, a child who is neurologically immature must be given the same opportunities before she can handle abstractions. What happens first, next, and last is crucial in a woodworking or crafts project as well as in drama or dance. The same neurological organization is necessary for reading—for looking at the beginning, middle, and end of a word, phrase, or sentence.

Through each of the art forms, a child can learn to distinguish colors, shapes, forms, and sounds; discrimination through the use of the child's hands, body, eyes, ears, and senses is part of the artistic experience. Learning to look and to listen and remembering what has been seen and heard—problem areas for students with learning disabilities—are emphasized in the arts. The arts help children organize experiences. They help make sense of the world and the messages that come in through the senses. The arts can help students with learning disablilities develop and strengthen the perceptual skills that form the foundation for further learning.

Discipline underlies every artistic endeavor. There is an order—a progression of steps—to every creation. People think of the arts as being very free; they are, but they only become so after one has mastered a set of basic skills. The student with learning disabilities or ADHD, who is consumed by indiscriminate attention and over-reactiveness, needs experiences that have a clear beginning, middle, and end. Understanding sequences is vital for the child who can talk to you about Homer or gravity but cannot tell you the order of the days of the week or the seasons, count to 20, or say the alphabet in the proper sequence. What happens first, next, and last is as crucial in a painting or crafts project as it is in drama or dance. Organizing oneself is mandatory.

Most exceptional learners can learn very sophisticated material as long as the teacher thoroughly understands it, breaks it down into simple parts, and teaches it step by step. Very elementary skills that are ordinarily introduced to much younger children can be presented to older children with learning disabilities in a sophisticated way so as to lure them into mastering these skills. When a group of 10-year-olds needed the experience of touching and discriminating among textures, a typical nursery school experience, The Lab School of Washington set up a "tactile museum" that included a wide variety of materials for touching, including Styrofoam, sponge, velvet, fur, and metal. Because no other school had a tactile museum, the students who set up the museum were very proud of their accomplishment and felt they were performing an adult activity; at the same time, their teachers were able to give them the exact experience they needed. The arts lend themselves to the imaginative use of concrete materials and experiences to teach organizational skills.

ESTABLISHING ORDER IN SPACE AND TIME

When structure is provided from the outside, children who experience disorganization are set free and given the safety to learn. Establishing a time, a space, and a place for all things is the key. This is why the woodwork shop has a pegboard with tools hanging from it, each one fitting into the thick shape of its outline. For the student who has little understanding of his body in space, there is a big masking-tape square labeled "your space" in front of a woodworking table. There are children who have no concept of their own parameters or borders; therefore, teachers have to be guided to design the arts in a way to put boundaries around the children. For many, photography and videography—looking through a camera to frame and focus—provide the necessary structure.

The arts can help build organizational skills, which can further the process of neural maturation. Too often, children who are failing in academics are placed in clinical settings or schools where they are given more academics—more attention to the reading, writing, and arithmetic they cannot do. Increasing the workload does not help, and at the same time, these children lose the opportunity to have experiences in which they can feel competent or can learn facts to build huge storehouses of information.

Students work as hard in the arts as they do in traditional classrooms; the work is just different. When doing collages, some students cannot see the difference between the foreground and the background. Collages can be used to teach just that. These are special problems, and they often arise in printmaking as well. Printmaking can be taught so that a child must print left to right and look for and recreate patterns. At The Lab School, we used potato prints to sequence a mammoth hunt. One student sequenced them perfectly, but all backwards.

Typical in exceptional learners is a lack of a sense of time. For example, the only way 8-year-old Eric understood the concept of a short amount of time was when his mother explained that the time it takes to eat one bowl of cereal is a short time, and the time it takes to eat ten bowls of cereal is a long time. In art class, Eric would begin working when three-quarters of the class was over, and then he didn't want to leave when the class ended. The teacher/artist who taught Eric found a special place for him to sit and left a picture schedule at his desk for him to study each day. The picture schedule showed Eric going to get paper, then finding his paints, and finally painting a picture. After a few months, Eric was able to draw his own schedules and manage his time better, despite the fact that his internal clock was still not working properly.

DISCOVERING RELATIONSHIPS, SEQUENCE, AND LOGIC

In addition to having difficulties with organization and focus, many exceptional learners experience difficulty with abstract concepts and social relationships. They may not be able to link cause and effect and often have trouble understanding relationships between people, predicting the consequences of their own behavior on others, and understanding the relationship of one set of behaviors to a broader pattern of behaviors.

Just as young children use only what is directly in front of them to learn and to grow, children who have neurological delays understand and learn best from direct interaction with materials and objects. Concrete materials allow them to discover relationships, draw inferences, and make abstractions on their own. Often such experiential learning is the only way these children can begin to grasp abstract concepts and higher thinking operations.

Consider the learning styles of Bennett, age 8, and Rick, age 10. Bennett understands such concepts as truth, honesty, equality, and integrity just from hearing about these concepts from his parents and teachers and from books he reads. Rick does not. Rick understands these concepts only through playing games, playing with objects, role playing, looking at pictures, watching videos, and participating in discussions. For example, when Rick's teachers were trying to explain to Rick the concept of truth, they asked him to fold a piece of paper into three equal parts. Rick saw that Harry and Carolyn each folded their papers differently from the way he folded his, but they still ended up with three equal parts. Using this model, Rick was taught that despite the fact that Socrates, Plato, and Aristotle all had different theories, they were the same in that they all were seeking the truth. Although Bennett enjoys learning about these three philosophers in this way, he does not *need* this approach to understand the concept. Rick cannot understand the concept unless he is taught experientially.

When working with children with learning disabilities, it is important to keep in mind each child's particular experience and to create an environment in which the child may learn from further experiences. Given a structured environment and materials that will prompt the discovery of relationships, nuances, and concepts, children with learning disabilities can bridge the gulf between the world of literal meanings and the world of the abstract. The child, however, cannot be told how to bridge the gulf; he has to bridge it on his own. Teachers have to provide alluring, enticing materials that will attract his attention and excite him into making connections and discovering relationships.

THEORETICAL UNDERPINNINGS

My design for the heavy use of all the art forms has been greatly influenced by the works of the Swiss psychologist Jean Piaget and the American educational theorist John Dewey. To some extent, the work of American psychologist Jerome Bruner influenced me, and I find that American educator Howard Gardner's theory of multiple intelligences confirms the work I have done since 1966.

Jean Piaget identified four stages of intellectual development in children, each stage dependent upon the preceding stage. Children can reach these stages at different ages depending on their particular rate of development. Piaget called the first stage, during which the child organizes his world through movement and sensation (typically occurring between birth and age 2 years), the *sensorimotor* stage. During the second stage, the *preoperational* stage (typically occurring between the ages of 2 and 7), a child's mental life is dominated by what *seems* to be rather than what logically must be. During the third stage, the *concrete operational* stage (typically occurring between the ages of 7 and 11), the child's thoughts are still limited to concrete experiences and cannot deal with abstractions until they are represented concretely. During the fourth stage, the *formal operations* phase (typically occurring from age 11 and up), a child can perform logical operations without objects, can infer, and can make generalizations and deductions. Piaget's four stages illustrate that educators need to teach children at their developmental levels while using materials appropriate to their chronological ages (the number of years lived). When the development of the central nervous system is delayed, a child remains in the concrete stages for a much longer period of time and must be taught concretely no matter how old she is. The child needs experience with materials to know them well. Although teaching at a higher level may seem to be age-appropriate for this child, it is an exercise in futility; perhaps this is why they clamor to see something, to touch it, to experiment with it, and to do it.

Even though 12-year-old Mark looks like a typical 12-year-old and has an impressive vocabulary, he is developmentally more similar to a child between the ages of 7 and 11. Thus, he needs to be taught in concrete ways. In learning the months of the year, Mark had to be taught through 12 boxes, each box illustrated as the month with four or five smaller boxes inside them serving as weeks and seven cards inside those serving as days. Coloring the boxes with, for example, scenes of January and holidays such as New Year's Day and Martin Luther King Day helped Mark understand the concept.

At the end of the 20th century, education experts began to see the value of teaching according to a child's developmental rather than chronological age. A 1997 article in Newsweek by Kantrowitz and Wingert pointed out that a growing number of educators are beginning to recognize that children learn best through active, hands-on teaching methods such as games and dramatic play and that because children develop at varying rates, schools have to allow for these differences.

Dewey, an early advocate of experiential education wrote, "Anything which can be called a study, whether arithmetic, history, geography or one of the natural sciences, must be derived from the materials which at the outset fall within the scope of ordinary life experience" (1939, pp. 86–87). Dewey felt that, too often, education was imposed from above, with adult standards and inappropriate subject matter beyond the reach of experience of the young learner. He pleaded with educators to let children learn by doing. Immersed in the learning process and with appropriate materials to accomplish the purpose, children discover relationships, make connections, and draw conclusions. It is important that the teacher have a clear purpose or objective so that the provided materials will lead the child into inquiry. Dewey was a great proponent of the use of the arts. In his book, *The Schooled Society*, he said, "And so the expressive impulse of the children, the art instinct, grows out of the communicating and constructive instincts.... Make the construction adequate, make it full, free, and flexible, give it a social motive, somthing to tell, and you have a work of art."

Russian psychologist Lev Vygotsky theorized that we learn first through person-to-person interactions and then individually internalize knowledge until we arrive at deep understanding. Unlike Piaget, who compares development to a ladder, Vygotsky sees development as a spiral, the mechanism he envisions for internalizing knowledge after first experiencing it with an adult mentor. The interactive classroom puts into practice the belief in the social process of idea making. Vygotsky promoted skillful questioning by teachers to guide social interactions in the classroom. No matter what the activity—creating a collage, setting up a pantomime, or developing photographs—it can be interactive.

Israeli educator Reuven Feuerstein worked with traumatized children of the Holocaust. He believed that intelligence is capable of changing and growing and that the teacher needs to guide the discovery process of learning. With stimulation and a rich learning environment, a child's intelligence can undergo some degree of change and can even alter, to some degree, the child's pattern of strengths and weaknesses.

Dr. Jerome Bruner, who also has explored the nature of intellectual growth, believes that a child can learn almost anything if it is presented in a highly organized, simple fashion. This means that the adult has to understand thoroughly the information that he or she is presenting to the student and must be attuned to the child's capacity to absorb the material and to the degree and amount of verbalization the child can understand. Bruner believes that people can teach anything that they thoroughly understand themselves. A good way to communicate a concept to young children is through an art form or some other form of concrete learning.

Harvard psychologist and educator Howard Gardner (see also Chapter 2), who is known for his theory of multiple intelligences, demonstrates that the arts can serve as "entry points," engaging curiosity and improving students' ability to learn because they draw on a whole range of intelligences and learning styles. Gardner's work promotes the integration of the arts in all classrooms.

Marian Diamond, a current pioneering California neurobiologist, describes the growth of dendrites in the brain as the development of "magic trees of the mind." Diamond's research proves that the sights and sounds of enriched school environments cause dendrites to form neural pathways of insight. The brain's interconnected neurons sprout and branch when given the appropriate sensory, mental, and physical stimulation. Her data demonstrate that the curious mind, stimulated to further inquiry, makes the cerebral cortex thicker and the brain more developed. Hands-on activities, experiential learning, and arts-based teaching fit this model.

TOTAL INVOLVEMENT

Involvement is the key to success for exceptional learners. Children who cannot read often cannot absorb information well through listening and have trouble organizing the material they do learn. Usually they struggle to convey verbally or in writing what they understand. However, these children do have their own unique ways to take in information and express it. Teachers have to involve their students in learning through the use of many different intelligences. Touching silk or seeing silkworms at work helps some students commit to memory one of China's great products. Walking on a map that has been drawn on a classroom floor helps another child to see the location of Maryland in relation to Delaware and Pennsylvania. Most children—regardless of whether they need them as primary memory tools—enjoy these activities.

To fully appreciate the value of experiential education to exceptional learners, it is important to understand how information is acquired, organized, and remembered. The information we acquire is linked to our experiences. Each new experience is compared with past experiences, sorted, categorized, and then filed in a compartment of the brain; each new experience is much like a library book that is organized on a particular shelf or a document that is stored in computer folders for future retrieval.

The process of sorting and classifying is begun in infancy when we begin to take in the world around us using our bodies as a point of reference. As preschoolers, we begin to have experiences with our environment through play. Play is the beginning of education. It is through play that children begin to develop an information base. They begin to organize the world around them, making connections and discovering relationships. They learn to separate tall from short, round from square, blue from red. Through play, a preschooler learns to compare, find similarities, and generalize. These discoveries then are classified and sorted into categories. This process is vital to the successful storage and retrieval of information at school.

THE RELEVANCE OF PRESCHOOL SKILLS

It is my firm belief that many children with learning disabilities have not acquired skills that children typically learn during the preschool years; however, while teaching these skills—basic differentiation of textures, colors, shapes, and sizes—the educator must respect the child's chronological age and use age-appropriate vocabulary and materials. Preschool learning is all about sorting objects, pictures, sounds, animals, people, and toys and observing similarities and differences among these things. This information all gets classified into a mental filing system so that, for example, when a teacher uses the words "tall" and "short," the child's mind retrieves pictures of tall and short people, tall and short animals, tall and short objects at home, and tall and short buildings. If the filing system is in good order, it will work successfully in a first-grade classroom. If the information is diffuse, the child will not be able to retrieve information at will in first grade. Connections will not be made, and relationships will not make sense.

Studying Aesop's fables in drama, making the costumes, setting the scenes, and acting out the fables help children to sort out differences and similarities in human characteristics and to determine the moral of a story. Critical thinking is used to evaluate whether the moral of the story is appropriate. Connections and relationships are made. All of these activities contribute to building necessary academic attributes: memory, comparisons, analysis, and synthesis.

Recently, a great deal of attention has been focused on the process of storing and retrieving information. A number of educational theorists believe that children with learning disabilities may lack the ability to store information in meaningful components called *schemas* and, therefore, are unable to recall information in an efficient manner. Schemas are organized structures of knowledge that assist us in understanding and recalling events and information. Early work in *schema theory* can be traced to Bartlett (1932), who claimed that memory is not just rote recall but is reconstructive. The new information we obtain interacts with our prior knowledge, allowing us to reconstruct and construe new meanings. New schemata are created while old ones are reactivated. Subscribers to current schema theory encourage active involvement on the part of the learner along with the teacher; this strategy makes the child with learning disabilities aware of schemata and of the context and interrelationships associated with them. Schema theory explains why concrete approaches in the classroom can help trigger memory. For example, some children best remember the pythagorean theory in algebra by constructing a kite using the theory.

When there is no schema, there is no "hook" on which to hang new information; therefore, the information cannot be remembered. In order to develop appropriate schemas to facilitate conceptual understanding, teachers need to provide exceptional learners with a structure that activates previous experiences. Children remember experiences that touch their lives and give them pleasure. Often, the public becomes afraid when children appear to be playing or having too much fun at school, but it is possible to have fun while participating in well-planned academic activities that are highly intellectual.

Thirteen 6- and 7-year-olds were pretending to be in a space station. The commander and her 12-person crew were exploring the vast unknown of outer space when a real event occurred. Shoemaker Levy 9, an asteroid that had fallen out of its orbit, was heading straight for Jupiter. Aboard the space station, the crew was alarmed at the possible ramifications of the event. Therefore, the commander and the crew did a detailed analysis of the events.

The Shoemaker Levy 9 had divided into six fragments, which were all given an alphabetical code (A,B,C,D,E,F). Each of the children represented a piece of the Shoemaker Levy 9. An enormous yellow ball represented Jupiter. The children lined up and intermittently spun and collided into the yellow ball. Upon contact with Jupiter the children would place a black paper on it. The black paper represented a nuclear reaction that took place (each nuclear reaction caused a "bruise-like" effect on the surface of Jupiter). In order to help the children remember the name Shoemaker Levy 9, the children pointed at their shoes and then made the form of a hammer and pointed it at the shoe. For "Le" the children made an "L" with their hand; for "VY," the children made a "V" with their hands; and for "9" they held up nine fingers. With this kinesthetic reinforcement they rarely, if ever, forgot the word. They enjoyed gesturing the name Shoemaker Levy 9, and they remembered a historic event with the correct name that most people have never learned or, hence, have forgotten. Experiences like this can lead to further exploration of the planets, the galaxies, or cosmic events.

DEVELOPING CRITICAL THINKING

Exceptional learners need to be provided with enough opportunities to evaluate whether something is working and to anticipate problems and predict outcomes. They also must learn concrete strategies for approaching tasks, acquiring information, and solving problems. They likely will need help in developing strategies for learning new material, remembering names, memorizing directions, and attending to tasks. They must be encouraged to formulate questions despite conceptual and linguistic difficulties. The arts include a large variety of activities, and learning to ask appropriate questions is part of the plan. "What do we ask?" is a favorite question that teachers use to jolt students into seeking knowledge. A commitment to inquiry leads to a lifetime of learning.

The Lab School approach uses projects, life experiences, concrete materials, and all of the art forms to create active learning to enhance sensory motor development and promote personal, academic, and intellectual development. The acquisition of preschool skills lays the foundation for solid academic learning and intellectual pursuits. Learning to discriminate one thing from another and to integrate several things at once is part of the preschool agenda. The arts provide preschool experiences in a creative way that respects the chronological ages of the children. Students who cannot read, are poor readers, or have learning disabilities and/or ADHD learn well through concrete visual activities that use the senses and multiple intelligences.

Developing a
Sense of Self-Worth

Most exceptional learners spend 6 hours in school each day, where they have difficulty performing. In most school activities, they pull the curtain down to hide their ignorance or they fall in defeat. Theirs is an empty stage with little or no applause. As Horace, a 14-year-old with learning disabilities, so aptly stated, "Most of school tells me I am not much of a person. It is in art I become a person, and the art teacher respects me."

Sixteen-year-old Mary Lee phrased her experience in another way when she said, "In almost all subjects there is a right and a wrong. But in the arts, it's hard to be wrong; there are so many rights."

DIFFICULTIES EXPERIENCED BY EXCEPTIONAL LEARNERS

Exceptional learners experience many negative consequences as a result of a lifetime of academic disappointments. These consequences include low self-esteem, identity problems, stress, and depression.

LOW SELF-ESTEEM

The biggest battle for exceptional learners is to maintain good self-esteem. Many of these students tend to feel rotten about themselves. They are smart enough to see that, while they struggle, their peers achieve easily at school.

Imagine what it feels like to learn in an environment in which you have to choose the right answer, but most of the time you end up choosing the wrong one. Any morsel of self-esteem that exists plummets to new lows. Students who cannot answer questions correctly, particularly when they are asked in front of the entire class, experience an extraordinary sense of failure. The standardized answers required by most traditional school environments put extreme pressure on students. Under this pressure, hard-to-teach learners tend to freeze, close up, panic and withdraw, or act out and exhibit behavior problems. In any case, they do not feel good about themselves.

IDENTITY PROBLEMS

Many children with learning disabilities have little sense of identity. Children without disabilities typically grow up feeling appreciated, thriving on a plethora of positive comments and smiles. Knowing that they are pleasing almost everybody around them makes them feel good about themselves and gives them energy to try new tasks. These children develop a sense of competence that turns into self-confidence. Success feeds a sense of self-worth, and a sense of self-worth fuels success. Children with learning disabilities often are mired in criticism at a very early age. "Why can't you sit still?," "Why don't you pay attention?," "Why don't you try harder?," and, "What's wrong with you?"

The emotional toll on these children is heavy. They tend to feel they are not good enough. Their shoulders sag, their gaits slow down, and they carry a heavy load of guilt, fear, and, often, anger on their backs. As 9-year-old Troy lamented, "I try and try and try, and still it's not right."

Negative feedback, reprimands, punishment, and withdrawal of affection, privileges, or goods often accompany failure to please others. Failure to please those who matter most to you leads to a pervasive feeling of not being okay, which robs a person of initiative and energy. Learning takes energy and a belief that it can happen. Seven-year-old Christopher, with sad blue eyes and a pout on his lips, glumly said to his teacher, "I'll never do it right like my brothers. I'm just stupid. But I'm not stupid in music."

Children who demonstrate some of the behaviors associated with learning disabilities and attention-deficit/hyperactivity disorder (ADHD) often are flooded with criticisms, admonitions, and punishments. When 90 adult students who attend The Lab School of Washington's Night School for learning disabilities and/or ADHD were asked what they remember most from their childhood, they tended to list memories of "feeling stupid, depressed, and not good enough." Angelo, a computer specialist, said, "It didn't help that my parents, neighbors, teachers, and coaches all preached to me to sit still, follow directions properly, and speak clearly. There was rarely anything I seemed to do right."

STRESS

Stress is prevalent among individuals with learning disabilities across the lifespan. Although parts of the disabilities often improve, other parts remain, resulting in irritation and frustration. Children who have ADHD, language problems, and/or reading and math problems must wrestle with a great deal of frustration. They may become consumed by fears of complete inadequacy, fears that their difficulties will worsen, guilt at not pleasing others, and anxiety about all of the problems they are causing the people who love them.

Teasing from siblings and classmates; criticism from relatives; reprimands and advice from well-meaning people; and criticism during athletics, religious instruction, groups such as Girl Scouts and Boy Scouts, and after-school instruction often only reinforce the sense of inadequacy that children with learning disabilities feel.

Some children handle frustration by becoming aggressive and oppositional because they prefer to be thought of as "difficult" rather than as "dumb." Others retreat into their own worlds or drift into depression.

DEPRESSION

It is not uncommon for children under severe stress to feel hopeless, alienated, alone, and depressed as well as unhappy and unsafe in their environments. They feel they must, at all times, be alert to danger—to the threat of being "done in." They turn on their alarm systems to mobilize whatever resources they have to protect themselves against more failure, more defeat, and more insult to their beings. Having to mobilize the alarm system into action on a second's notice, time and time again, is exhausting. Chronic anxiety leads to depression—to being drained beyond the ability to take necessary action.

Depression is common among children and adolescents with learning disabilities and/or ADHD. Many adults who suffered from these problems in school talk about the clinical depression they experienced, which required therapy and medication. For a child with special needs, intervention by a team of parents, teachers, tutors, speech-language pathologists, occupational therapists, and mental health counselors can draw on the child's hidden talents and strengths and build on them as part of the healing process. The arts—which engage body, mind, and spirit—often can offer the child who is experiencing depression a sense of individual or group accomplishment. The child can see tangible results: a piece of art, a performance that elicits a lot of applause, or a film.

STRATEGIES FOR BUILDING SELF-ESTEEM

Despite the difficulties experienced by exceptional learners, teachers and artists can build the self-esteem of these students by providing positive reinforcement, cultivating passion and uncovering hidden talents, finding idiosyncratic solutions, making something out of nothing, fostering a sense of group, and employing project learning.

PROVIDE POSITIVE REINFORCEMENT

Because constant negative feedback can lead to low self-esteem, The Lab School teachers are trained to comment positively on specific behaviors, efforts, and attitudes. They say things such as, "I like the way you are sitting still," "I like having your eyes looking at me," "Good for you for trying to pronounce that difficult new word," and, "Thank you for helping your neighbor." In this way, the children learn the behaviors that please others and repeat those behaviors. They realize that a particular behavior is valued. Often, good behavior is taken for granted in a school environment and, therefore, not praised. When good behaviors are exhibited by children with learning disabilities and ADHD, they must not be taken for granted. It is vital that students' efforts to meet goals are rewarded constantly with specific praise; praise not only helps the students feel better about themselves but also helps them use this same model to help others feel positive about themselves.

It is interesting that at The Lab School, the teachers/artists on staff naturally tend to point out students' positive behaviors. They spot them quickly, praise them, and repeat them. The teachers/artists tend to demonstrate vital energy and positivity, which quickly is absorbed by their students.

It also helps when exceptional learners are recognized as the family's "best" in a certain area. In one family of high achievers, the child with learning disabilities has gained great esteem in his family for his prowess in chess. Most of the time, he would win. In other families, the child with learning disabilities may be the family computer expert, the family photographer, or the family member with the best sense of direction.

CULTIVATE PASSION AND UNCOVER TALENTS

Highly successful adults who have learning disabilities and/or ADHD will tell you that they had an overpowering passion to paint, draw, photograph, design buildings or clothes, construct boats, dance, play music, act, or write! Phrases such as, "It was music that saved me, that kept me whole," "My art nurtured my soul," "Photography gave me sustenance," "My tiny ego grew when I was on stage," "I felt worthless, except when I danced," and, "I looked at those clothes and remarked to myself that I designed them—there was something I could do well," are quite common.

The most important help that parents and teachers can give is to dig deep into the secret, unseen pockets of their children and students and search for the treasures. All of us have talent in something. These talents need to be discovered, brought out, nurtured, fostered, and strengthened. It is crucial for children with learning disabilities and/or ADHD to find one talent or one skill on which to concentrate. They need to have an area of expertise in their families that is unique to themselves. Their special areas of competence will allow them to shine, to have goals, and to build confidence. The theatre of no applause can finally become an arena of success.

Some children can be encouraged by classes in an art form; for others, an apprenticeship to one person works best. Many children learn best by doing and by demonstration, not by lecture or formal instruction. Retired senior citizens are an untapped resource as mentors to children. For example, 10-year-old Maurice loved woodwork and found that Mr. Jonaly, an 80-year-old man, had a shop in his garage where they could spend many happy hours together creating boats, lamps, and chairs. Twelve-year-old Noreen became adept at making quilts by apprenticing with 85-year-old Nancy, whose relatives had taught her many decades earlier how to create beautiful quilts. In Renaissance times, mentorship was the way most artists and artisans learned. Today, many children could benefit from the renewal of these practices.

Families today are not the same as the extended families of yesteryear, in which all ages lived together and the honorable old shared their prowess with the young. In today's world, it is important for all of us—particularly for children with special needs—to establish our own extended families of friends and colleagues. Artists who have worked with older adults frequently have been surprised at how much nurturing of talent has taken place. Drama students and senior citizens at The Lab School started performing drama selections for each other and then worked together to produce an inspiring production.

FIND IDIOSYNCRATIC SOLUTIONS

The enthusiasm and energy of older adults who love their crafts often is transmitted to young learners. Although young learners can sap their parents and teachers of energy, the reverse often takes place when students work with older adults; the older people often lean on the young students. The respect and admiration they receive from the students help them to feel useful and enhance their sense of self-worth.

Celebrated architect, Hugh Newell Jacobson, told Lab School students the following: "The cry is to find something you really love to do. I did almost the only thing I really loved to do; it all came out of drawing and imagining what was inside a drawing. . . ." Robert Rauschenberg, another visual thinker who was miserable at school but succeeded in becoming a master of modern art, said, "I think if you have difficulty achieving in one area, there's a certain kind of balance that comes out and you can achieve in another, if you can find your level." Well-known artist Chuck Close creates colossal photo realist portraits composed of minute imaginative squares, which he paints one by one; these portraits hang in major museums throughout the country. Close says, "I think accomplishment is figuring out your own idiosyncratic solution. I've always had to chop things up into little bite-size pieces in order to understand them." In May 1998, when Close spent an afternoon with the students and artists at The Lab School, he said, "I've come to appreciate how virtually every aspect of my work has been driven by my learning disabilities. By taking something that seems a deficit and channeling it, I was able to turn it into something which has served me very well. We need to find a way to teach kids that doesn't pigeonhole them or categorize them, that helps them find something they can do, that they can feel good about, that makes them feel special—everyone needs to feel special. Everyone learns differently."

What I have learned from the many winners of The Lab School's Outstanding Learning Disabled Achievers Award (begun in 1985) is that they rose to the challenge to find their unique ways and unusual paths. Dr. Fred Epstein, eminent pediatric neurosurgeon, explained, "I couldn't follow sequence A to sequence B to sequence C in removing cancer from children's brains, so I made up my own way. Little did I realize that others would be following me." He went on to say, "No one really knows what is the determination that keeps us going. It is basically a fire inside of us that is sparked by a passion in doing something we really enjoy doing."

The message to parents and teachers is to lead children to what they like to do and want to do and then encourage them to seek out their own imprints—their solutions. These imprints need to be shared with others and displayed prominently for the public to see, with the child's name in clear view. Paintings can be framed, masks can be hung on walls, and sculptures and clay models can be shown on a table with a colorful or black tablecloth to highlight the objects. Child storytellers can dictate their stories to their teachers or, if they can write, put their stories on computers and turn them into beautifully bound books. Exhibitions of their books, of their illustrated poetry, of their unique versions of the alphabet need to be placed on special shelves and tables for the public to see. Walls containing their photographs and their portraits need to be more prominent in schools. Their homemade CD-ROMs, each one with its own unique cover, need to be showcased. Prominent displays of the children's artwork helps engender confidence and feelings of self-worth. As Jane Alexander, former

Chairman of the National Endowment for the Arts, said in her commencement speech at Bennington College, "I believe in the power of art to change lives. I believe in the power of art to save lives. I've seen it firsthand. The power of art lies not in the development of a skill (although that is significant in and of itself) nor in its ability to reach us emotionally, eliciting laughter or tears, shock or diffidence: the power of art is its revelation that human potential is limitless. . . ."

MAKE SOMETHING OUT OF NOTHING

Children naturally like to find feathers, leaves, rocks, stones, and nature's treasures of one kind or another. If they are encouraged to create pieces of art with their findings, the results frequently are beautiful.

An architectural design teacher in The Lab School high school wanted his class to become excited by the rebuilding of the Globe Theater. Ultimately, he wanted his students to become knowledgeable about Shakespeare. The class began by searching the Royal Shakespeare Theater on the Internet; then, the students downloaded plans, learned to read them, and built a replica of the Globe Theater.

The students collected old wooden toys, old thread spools, discarded wood scraps, popsicle sticks and little bits and pieces of things. With these items, they took the wall of a carriage house on The Lab School property (12' x 8') and made a beautiful relief sculpture—a mix of two- and three-dimensional objects—of ancient London and the Globe Theatre. They glued on various parts and then painted some places and varnished others. One of the students looked at the tower they had created, decided it needed a clock, and glued his Timex watch face to the tower! One hundred nineteen tiny Shakespeare heads were hidden in part of the Globe Theater project. The student artists' goal was for little children to be able to play a game to discover who could find the most Shakespeare heads and, in the process, to learn to recognize Shakespeare and the Globe Theater.

Making something out of nothing takes problem-solving skills in addition to some visual thinking and resourcefulness. As one of our artists at The Lab School put it, "I want my students to look at a broken table leg and see how it can be made into a tower."

FOSTER A SENSE OF GROUP

Many art forms, such as dance, drama, puppetry, and filmmaking, are collaborative by their very nature. These arts help develop skills for working with others—listening, evaluating contributions, compromising, adapting, and acting as an integral part of a team. An appreciation of what can be achieved through teamwork arises out of these activities. Through teamwork, children experience acceptance, camaraderie, and acknowledgment of their value as team members, all of which feeds self-esteem and builds an atmosphere of trust.

Many children with learning disabilities and/or ADHD experience problems working as part of a group. Part of the reason may have to do with the immaturity of the central nervous system, which produces egocentricism, and part may occur as a result of the hidden dimensions of learning disabilities—those of *time* and *space*. Many children with learning disabilities and/or ADHD have very poor timing, are constantly late, have slower reaction times than others, and cannot estimate a duration of time. Thus, in a group, others can become impatient with their delays. Many of these children also experience great difficulty following directions because they cannot distinguish left from right, front from back, near from far, behind from in front of, a circle from a square, and other spatial relationships. This spatial clumsiness also can affect group interactions adversely.

However, when teachers are alert to these difficulties and ask the children to raise the hand that is nearest the window and stomp the foot that is closest to the door—rather than specify left or right or front or back—these children can follow directions. When children are responsible for their own individual pieces of work and each one is doing her own part, they come together to help each other.

For example, when working on computers with software called Hyperstudio, children can draw and put photographs on screen as well as use the Internet, and a group can coalesce to become coaches, critics, and cohorts. Children do best when their stories are tried out first in small groups, where helpful suggestions are given that motivate the storytellers to remodel their stories. For example, a student may tell a story about a dragon with wings; when the story continues despite the fact that the dragon with wings has disappeared from the story, peer critics demand that the dragon reappear and that he use his wings. Students are so intense about their creations and often so proud of what they have developed that they want to collaborate with one another to make the project even better. Obviously the teacher must set the tone that the group wants to help each person do his level best. The teacher becomes less of an authority and more of a guide, a facilitator, and a cheerleader.

It is The Lab School's experience that children with special needs desire to bring forth the highest quality product they can, particularly when they have chosen their own theme or unique approach. When students are involved in creative problem solving, they are full participants in the learning process, and their immersion in the task gives them a role of partnership that allows them dignity and authority. Success and self-esteem are like the fabric lining the curtains that open up to new adventures.

EMPLOY PROJECT LEARNING

William H. Kilpatrick, a well-known professor at Teachers College in New York City who believed passionately in project learning, emphasized the critical value of allowing children to plan their own projects when they could. Dr. Kilpatrick wrote up the following imaginary exchange:

Question: Don't you think that the teacher should often supply the plan? Take a boy planting corn, for example; think of the waste of land and fertilizer and effort. Science has worked out better plans than a boy can make. . . .

Kilpatrick: It depends on what you seek. If you wish corn, give the boy a plan. But if you wish boy rather than corn, that is, if you wish to educate the boy to think and plan for himself, then let him make his own plan. (Kilpatrick, 1925)

Children who have learning disabilities, ADHD, and/or language impairments need some structure and some choices. Teachers should ferret out each student's true passions and interests; they should then help the students express their interests in whatever art forms excite them so that their products become wholly theirs. This approach gives them ownership of their products as well as a sense of identity and belonging—all powerful ingredients for building self-esteem.

EMPOWERING THROUGH THE ARTS

Every time that a child with special needs
hammers a nail successfully
colors or paints
creates a design
plays a role in a skit
dances a sequence
rings the bells according to a specific rhythm
makes a puppet
photographs what he intended to
films what she intended to
sculpts a piece
he or she is receiving the message of
"I can do it!"
"I can do it again!"

Feelings of mastery counteract feelings of powerlessness and build a sense of self-worth. All of the art forms provide active learning, which is an antidote to the passivity exhibited by most hard-to-teach learners. As William Butler Yeats proclaimed, "Education is not the filling of a pail but the lighting of a fire."

The Educative Process at
The Lab School of Washington

The Lab School Approach is a method of teaching all academic subjects through the arts or some variation of visual concrete methods. While teachers ensure that clear, precise, educational objectives are achieved, a student's body, mind, and all of his senses—his total being—have the opportunity to come alive. This philosophy is strikingly apparent from the wildly imaginative painted sculptures in and around The Lab School—a 6-foot pteranodon; a 12-foot, elephant-like god of Good Fortune; Ganesh, from Hindu mythology; a kelly-green 11-foot dragon made of plywood; and an 8-foot bronzed Gryphon, a mythological creature known through the ages—to the school's reception area, which is dotted with masks that stare from the walls and chairs with either webbed feet or high heel shoes.

The school's library is another repository of the work of deeply involved students. Wall decorations range from a wall-tile composition made by 5-year-old students to a sophisticated etching of the zodiac made by 14-year-old students. Four shelves are filled with books with enticing covers created by children in lower grades (ages 6–13). "Meet the Author" sessions take place frequently. Nearby are student-created literary journals, a senior class study of murals in the Washington, D.C., metropolitan area, and an annual updated Who's Who of Artists in the Washington, D.C., metropolitan area produced by the senior class and sold at the National Gallery of Art, The Phillips Collection, and other Washington, D.C., art centers.

The nearby Board Room boasts a wall covered with stunning carpet art. A visiting artist led this project—called "A Peaceable Kingdom"—created by elementary students; the students took bundles of rug remnants donated by a local store and turned them into a magical piece of art.

The stairway leading to the dance room is a constantly changing art show; one week it may be poetry and visual images, other weeks it may be Native American designs, illustrations for a book, or a showing of photographs of the construction going on at the school with blueprints and wire models of buildings.

Loud music, stomping, and counting can be heard as you near the Dance Room, where you are as likely to see six or seven teenage males doing a majestic dance with canes as you are to see 5- and 6-year-olds create sculptures of body movements by stretching out toward each other. Everywhere a visitor looks, children are engaged in activities. Students, especially those with severe learning disabilities, relish these experiences as they frequently were not involved in learning in traditional classrooms. A 10-year-old student named Damon explained, "My body was in school, but my mind wasn't. I couldn't read and write, and I didn't listen too well either. I wanted out."

The photographs on a big junior high school bulletin board demonstrate how geometry and math surround us in architecture. Science classes use arts and crafts to teach basic concepts. History, geography, civics, and general social studies rely on drama, music, and the visual arts to convey ideas and the written creations of the students. Poetry, which is like painting a canvas of words, is a particularly popular activity. Elementary grade–level walls have quilts, puppets, and three-dimensional figures on them.

PARTNERS IN LEARNING

The Lab School of Washington was founded on the love of children; the belief that children with learning disabilities can learn, albeit differently; and the idea that it takes trust, communication, and total teamwork to get the job done. Artists work in tandem with highly trained special education teachers, speech-language pathologists, occupational therapists, psychologists, and social workers. Their conversations typically center on the children themselves: their needs, their triumphs, and the life puzzles with which they present us.

Concrete visual programming is encouraged everywhere so that project learning, activity learning, and reenactments of new information take place continually. As children become partners in learning, their curiosity, sense of awe, and ability to solve problems creatively is preserved at all costs. Students do not sit quietly but work vigorously alongside their teachers. They are attentive while they are engaged in activities with an adult or with other children.

Total involvement is the key to learning through The Lab School Approach. How does total involvement occur with 310 students? What makes it possible for 90% of our students with severe learning disabilities to go on to college?

DESCRIPTION OF PERSONNEL

Central to the students' success at The Lab School is the quality of the human beings who work there. Although love, dedication, and commitment to children are vital ingredients, these things alone are not enough to give solid help to these students. Talent is necessary. The ability to be part of a team is required. Resourcefulness and creativity also cannot work alone. Analytical thinking is important to help detect how each child learns. After analysis takes place, programs must be devised that build on each child's strengths and address his or her weaknesses. All of these components work together to allow staff to perform diagnostic-prescriptive teaching, a crucial part of The Lab School Approach.

Finally, personnel have to fully understand the characteristics of learning disabilities. Learning disabilities and ADHD are so elusive that it is easy to blame the child for the very nature of his or her disability. These students often have difficulty paying attention, learning, and following directions. It is important for staff to understand that these children are not misbehaving; the behaviors they are displaying are part of their disabilities. It is common to hear teachers complain, "This child won't pay attention," "She stubbornly refuses to learn math," or, "He flouts my authority by not following instructions." Without knowing it, the faculty is blaming these young children with learning disabilities, ADHD, and language impairments for the very nature of their conditions. One reason that the curriculum flourishes as it does at The Lab School is because of the selection of personnel, their initial training, and their in-service training.

TEACHING LAB SCHOOL STAFF THROUGH SIMULATIONS

Words alone will not teach teachers what it's like not to be able to concentrate. They need to be put in a situation in which they are distracted by radios and televisions blaring, people handing out papers, and a teacher asking them to perform on demand. They need to experience how it feels when your hands don't work properly by wearing heavy gardening gloves. They need to be put through simulation exercises in which they don't know their left side from their right, forward from back, or what it's like to have little sense of time, timing, the passage of time, and being lost in space. Teachers need to experience what it's like not to be able to say what you want to say, to retrieve a well-known word, or to respond verbally to a question. Understanding of the nature of the condition has to become visceral—a part of a teacher's being, never forgotten—to be able to meet the children's needs appropriately. Reading and talking about learning disabilities and ADHD is not enough.

In addition to training faculty of The Lab School, I also teach courses at American University that simulate for teachers and artists the world of individuals with learning disabilities. I want the individuals who work with children with learning disabilities and/or ADHD to experience the children's disability firsthand, to feel overwhelmed by too much happening at once—too much noise, too much movement—in much the same way as children with learning disabilities whose filtering mechanisms in the brain fail to screen out irrelevant stimuli do. It isn't that these children are not paying attention; in fact, they are paying too much attention to distractions in their environment and, therefore, cannot focus on the person talking or the task they are trying to complete. It's not that they aren't trying. They are overloaded with too many stimuli. Simulation exercises demonstrate viscerally to teachers and artists why they must not present too much information, give too many directions, or offer too many choices at once and why simple, clear language is necessary.

TEACHING STAFF CONCRETELY

We need to teach teachers with the same methods we want them to use to teach children. If we lecture to them and give them timed review tests, we can expect them to do the same with their students. Because the populations of students about whom we are talking are concrete learners—they need to see, touch, feel, hear, smell, and "be" the objects, pictures, or symbols—we have to teach our teachers through concrete, visual, and multisensory methods in order for them to work effectively with dyslexic children and others lost in a sea of words. Different intelligences must be recognized and used. Using a parachute, hula hoops, or yo-yos during teacher training has to become as commonplace as using workbooks, study sheets, and plan books. During professional development, teachers and artists need to have their imaginations tapped and their intelligence challenged as far and as wide as possible to turn abstract learning into concrete activities. As teachers become comfortable with the use of concrete objects, they will employ them in their classrooms with students who, initially, learn only this way.

TEACHING STAFF THROUGH PROBLEM SOLVING

Activity learning, project learning, and experiential learning need to become a routine part of the curricula in teacher training colleges. New teachers should engage in problem-solving activities, brainstorming in small groups, and developing original solutions that can work. For example, teachers could be asked to imagine that they are stuck on an island surrounded by sharks in shallow water. They will find wood, poles, a lot of rope, vines, a saw, and hammer and nails on the island. How can they get off the island? One group decides that making stilts is the answer, so the group members try that activity. Another group thinks that making a reinforced boat will work, so they try to create it. A third group envisages an overhead vine causeway supported by poles.

If the groups are small, teachers cannot be passive but must be actively engaged in such activities. With their newfound knowledge about concrete learning, they will do similar activities with their students for whom activity learning is a lifeline.

TEACHING STAFF TASK ANALYSIS

Critical, high-level analytical thinking is required by teachers to unlock the deep puzzles that block effective practice and thinking in students with special needs. I have found it helpful to give graduate students yo-yos and ask them to figure out all of the component steps and skills they need to master in order to work the yo-yo effectively. Next, they must figure out how they would teach it. To teach a child with special needs how to work a yo-yo, teachers must know the particular child's interests and weaknesses and adapt each step for the child's specific disability. Teachers have to role-play each scene, then discuss the techniques they would use to build on the child's strengths and reduce his weaknesses.

Teachers need to know each of the components that make up a task, from the simplest to the most complex, so they can adapt that knowledge to each child's strengths and weaknesses to make an effective lesson plan. Having done all of these task analyses, it becomes less likely that a teacher will blame a child with special needs for not trying or for "being difficult." A good exercise that I like to conduct with my graduate students at American University is to take a combination lock and do an in-depth analysis of how to make it work. (Many students with severe learning disabilities are baffled by combination locks and have difficulty telling left from right.) To create the lesson plan for the combination lock teachers and artists have to ask themselves questions such as

- Will this child learn best by demonstration?
- Do I need to talk him through it?
- Will he learn best by hearing instructions?
- Would written instructions help or not?
- Do I need to design strategies to help distinguish left from right (i.e., go purple to 5, the other way to 10, purple to 7, and pull [this would entail putting a small piece of purple tape on top of the combination lock])?

TEACHING STAFF TO INDIVIDUALIZE INSTRUCTION

Teachers and artists need to be familiar with every reasonable existing teaching method so that instruction can be tailored to each individual child and can build on the child's strengths. For example, current brain research shows us that poor readers require phonemic awareness—the solid ability to discriminate between individual sounds and words. They also need literature-based learning, often called "whole language," to learn about language patterns, comprehension, and the beauty of words. Teachers and artists should be encouraged to identify their own strengths and weaknesses so that they become used to thinking this way; it then will become automatic for them to isolate a child's strengths and determine the methods that may work for the child. Conversely, identifying the child's weaknesses helps indicate methods that are unlikely to work.

Part of my curriculum for graduate students at American University requires each student to create diagnostic-prescriptive teaching games as a concrete way of individualizing instruction. The trainee picks an area of difficulty for a group of children, such as telling time, then builds on the strengths of the children, such as knowing their colors and how to count to 12, to develop a game that teaches the children to tell time. The game must lure, entice, and excite the children; then the children will want to play the game because it builds on what they *can* do. Even though many of the commercial materials that exist are excellent teaching tools, students with severe learning disabilities still need more. Therefore, being able to invent teaching materials is a crucial skill.

NURTURING STAFF

Because exceptional learners often feel stupid, depressed, and totally incapable, it is vital for teachers to help them feel good about themselves. Therefore, we have to nurture our teachers and artists in the same manner that we want them to nurture their students. In the classroom, concern must not center solely on academic achievements but also on the children's emotional and social development. Specific praise must be given constantly to teachers and artists in training so the habit becomes part of their way of operating in their classrooms. They can help students feel valued for efforts and small achievements as well as for big successes. Individualizing instruction and attention and giving very specific praise must be expressed in small as well as large groups.

Nurturing and deep caring must come from everyone, including the director or principal of the school and the top administrators. At The Lab School, we have been successful at keeping a big school small enough so that everyone knows each other. We have broken The Lab School of Washington Day School into four units with a coordinator in charge who needs to know all of the students, the teachers, the artists, the assistants, the graduate students, the volunteers, and the secretarial staff in that unit. Everyone needs to be known and valued.

COMFORT WITH TECHNOLOGY

Staff members must feel comfortable with new technology. They need to be given enough time to fiddle, to apprentice with experts, and to take part in collaborative projects that use the technology. Computers fit well into The Lab School Approach because they can use all of the senses and are highly visual. Computers give form to the philosophy of a highly structured environment and concrete material that will prompt the discovery of relationships, nuances, and concepts. Computers bridge the gulf between the world of literal meanings and the world of the abstract. They can be used to make connections between historical and current events and can be used by students to create multimedia demonstrations that showcase what they have learned. The mastery of turning on and activating a computer makes students feel more in charge of their lives. Computers seem to help many students become focused and organized. Artistically talented children can create new worlds with computers.

Computers can be used to make connections among curricular areas. For example, junior high students frequently study history, social studies, and humanities as distinct components of the curriculum. Using computer technology, students are able to produce complex documentaries of life during a particular historical period. Students study the history, lifestyles, and culture of a time period and then are able to develop a complete and compelling story line to support their findings. The Lab School Approach to the use of technology maintains that just as paintbrushes, pencils, and the human body can serve as mediums of expression, so can computers.

Because we want teachers and artists to be trained in the same processes they use with students, they need to be able to use computers to search the Internet and design creative web pages. They need to learn to manipulate artistic symbols into illustrative examples and *produce* professional looking *products* that allow more in-depth use of computer-based tools such as graphic design, computer animation, and video production. Teachers and artists need to create their own logos in addition to helping students create theirs. They need to be familiar with Hyperstudio software so they can teach their students to create multisensory illustrated stories and reports. Teachers need to present technology as an empowering experience for everyone including themselves.

INTERDISCIPLINARY DELIGHTS

Working as a team, teachers and artists and professionals in the related services (e.g., occupational therapy, speech-language pathology, social work, psychology) have the power to transform lives. In an arts-based school, the interconnectedness of all forms of knowledge creates the carpet upon which all players move. The dancer who asks his students to look carefully at visual details in the mirror; the artist who teaches a lesson in collage; the math teacher who asks his students to focus on the differences between addition, subtraction, multiplication, and division; and the historian who prints out symbols, flags, and weapons of a certain period in history all are working on the same task. The more that training of new teachers builds on teachers' expertise and special interests, the more these teachers can approach their areas of expertise from different angles to benefit hard-to-teach students. Interdisciplinary teaching delights children and challenges their brains in a variety of ways. Teachers need to draw on the arts to enrich their teaching. Working side by side with artists helps generate more creativity.

A COMMITMENT TO INQUIRY

Doing the same thing over and over again may develop a pathway in certain children's minds, particularly those who have limited intelligences; but for students with learning disabilities, ADHD, and speech-language impairments who have unlimited abilities, teachers and artists need to look for the keys to unlock their potential. Part of the ability to unlock potential comes quite naturally to unorthodox learners (which many artists are), but part of it comes from a deep commitment to inquiry. Picking up on the special interests of a child often means pursuing new knowledge, reading about it, exploring in museums, and studying artifacts to discover the latest information on a subject. Great artists who are great teachers, in my experience, are exceedingly curious. They are explorers. They go in gleeful pursuit of knowledge, often giving hours of their time to find the tools that turn on a child's light. My experience is that these artists enjoy thoroughly the pursuit of knowledge, particularly knowledge that is pursued in an unconventional manner.

We know that exceptional learners *can* learn if we can determine *how* they learn and then teach them accordingly. It is my firm belief that, when necessary, we also can teach them when they are not yet reading and without having them write if this, too, is an undeveloped skill. Instead, through the arts, we can fill their minds with interesting information. However, before teachers and artists can increase their students' well of knowledge, they must fill their own.

New fountains of knowledge previously unexplored—books, stories, myths, CD-ROMs, art forms, and ancient art forms—need to be pursued. As Director of The Lab School of Washington, I feel I have failed if staff do exactly the same thing year after year. New staff need to be trained in the role of seeking out knowledge; exploring unknown, untried techniques; and then sharing their experiences as part of the team. Part of my role is to stimulate staff with the introduction of new material, such as the wonders of the Minoan civilization and what the remains of the Palace of Knossos tell us about people's lives in Crete 4,000 years ago. What is the relevance of these things today? How do they fit in with other projects and subjects our children are studying? At The Lab School we have discovered remnants of a Native American civilization in our own backyard. Working with an archeologist, our students have unearthed 8,000 artifacts and thousands of flakes; perhaps the Minoan discoveries could be woven into this area of learning. Violent happenings in schools and in the country in the late 1990s provide another potential course of study for faculty: Where does all the violence come from, and how do we cope with it? Projecting 20 years beyond the millennium and imagining what a child's life will be like then might stimulate the faculty to energize the thinking of their students. Keeping everyone on their toes, including the leaders and administrators of a school, is part of the training needed to run an arts-based school.

TEACHING STAFF IN THE POWER OF THE ARTS

The very presence in the school of a number of visual and performing artists challenges the creativity of everyone who works in the school. For example, special education teachers will want to demonstrate to artists that they are using their creativity in presenting information to their students, and they want artists to see their diagnostic-prescriptive games. Sometimes, they may ask for help in making them more artistic. Speech-language pathologists share the projects they are working on themselves with their students to encourage fluency of language. Occupational therapists consult with dancers and musicians to help make the performing arts work with students who experience special coordination and balance difficulties. Following the consultation, the therapists tend to incorporate some of the art forms into their activities. Social workers, psychologists, and other related services personnel sometimes find that students with language impairments and behavioral problems do best in a project situation such as building a fish pond or creating a play house. Related services personnel find that these activities stimulate more talk and more sharing of feelings as well as excitement with the task.

For thousands of years, the arts have been the human way of documenting how we live; teachers of history, geography, and civics rely on CDs and films to convey the span of history and the breadth of human culture. Diversity is prized in environments such as The Lab School of Washington and needs to permeate all schools.

At staff workshops, artists are paired up with teachers and therapists to problem-solve and come up with activities that might engage students. Staffings (meetings concerned with a particular student) on students always include artists who may see abilities and talents that other staff members do not see. Often, teachers see arts productions and are amazed by the extraordinary performances of their students, who don't show the same promise in their classrooms.

For many years I have taught a class at American University, entitled "Overview of Exceptionalities: The Arts in Special Education." I have been teaching this class through the arts since 1982, and because it is now so large (a required course for all teachers), I am team-teaching it with a colleague. It is difficult in 15 weeks, in 2 1/2 hours a day, to convey a great deal about each exceptionality to students who want to be mainstream teachers. However, certain key points can be covered:

- Look at abilities as well as disabilities.
- Try to find at least one area of expertise in each student.
- Adapt activities to meet the strengths of each person.
- Be full of specific (not global) praise.

- Know the state and national laws that can help people with disabilities receive the accommodations and access they need.

- Be aware of the emotional tolls on students.

- Consider it part of teaching to help students with socialization skills if needed.

- Be aware that diversity enriches us all.

- Help one another to do activities in a way that empowers others.

For as many sessions of this class as possible, artists with disabilities are brought in to the classroom to demonstrate their art forms and to discuss how they have made the adaptations they need to succeed. A dancer who is deaf gets the group to dance and explains how deaf dancers at Gallaudet University can move in unison. A weaver who has cerebral palsy shows her work and talks about her life and the way she works best. A radio and TV announcer who specializes in big band music and happens to be blind shares how he can conduct certain programs through special Braille computers. These extremely competent people impress the students with what they have done with their lives. Their abilities shine through.

Following visits by artists with disabilities, student teachers working in small groups must then pick out disabilities that were not previously explored (e.g., autism, brain injury, diabetes, multiple sclerosis, fetal alcohol syndrome) and art forms not used in class (e.g., photography, wire sculpture, shadow puppetry, cooking) and develop a series of activities for the whole class to perform. They have to think through how to use a specific art form to build on a student's strengths: diagnostic-prescriptive thinking.

THE ARTIST AS EXTRAORDINARY TEACHER

An unorthodox approach, originality, resourcefulness, and the ability to create something with materials that are on hand makes an artist supremely suited to teach children who defy typical general school practices. Because they are likely to thrive on new challenges, artists who work part time or full time in a school such as The Lab School of Washington bring a freshness, a spark, a spirit to the job. This special energy is needed to work with a population that is known to consume its teachers and wear them out. Most artists I have met refuse to believe any child is unteachable. Artists rebel against conformity and survive on divergent thinking. In general schools, the children who tend not to fit in and who have special problems seem to hang out in the art rooms, regardless of whether they have talent. The same is true of drama club, another nonjudgmental environment. Depending on the actor in charge, students feel there must be something they can do to be helpful, even if their acting skills are not excellent. The artist has an inner eye—a vision, a way of operating—that embraces the child who is not "ordinary."

Arnold Toynbee, the famous historian, believed that civilization "develops" in response to a challenge of special difficulty that rouses man to unprecedented effort (as cited in Timpe, 1987). We see that same quality in the Outstanding Learning Disabled Achievers that The Lab School has honored annually since 1985 (see Appendix C for a listing). They demonstrate a commitment to the pursuit of actualization, to being the best they can be at whatever cost. In his book, *In Search of Excellence*, Thomas Peters (1982) states that the major element in success is the perception among people that they are succeeding, regardless of whether there is a meas-urable standard. Also, he states that association with past personal success leads to more persistence and higher motivation.

The more experiences of success, the more there is to build on, which is why schools have to help students develop their pockets of talents and offer them oppor-tunities to succeed. Success builds confidence, confidence allows students to dare to try new things and take some risks, which in turn brings new learning and additional opportunities for success. The Lab School of Washington is designed to offer its stu-dents, through all of the art forms, many opportunities for daily success.

ART AND THE COMMUNITY

Students need to feel part of their neighborhoods, their cities, their states, and their country. Art serves its citizens beautifully that way. Schools merely need to look for opportunities that allow students to use their talents and express them.

AFRICAN HERITAGE CELEBRATION

The Lab School began a celebration of African heritage in 1991, incorporating African dance, drama, music, and art into a performance given in February, African Heritage Month. This project gives students the opportunity to learn about and then educate the community on African history, culture, and heritage, gain self-confidence, and learn about each other. The students' activities in preparation for the African Heritage Day program reflect The Lab School's hands-on, arts-based philosophy. The Lab School's art department, geography classes, history classes, and music classes integrate components of the African culture into their curriculum and, in this way, assist in the preparations for the performance and festivities. During African Heritage Month, The Lab School comes alive with the sounds of students rehearsing African drums and chants and the sights of beautiful costumes. The students study African design patterns and then put them on fabrics and even on the ceiling of our dance/drama room. They create African art and learn and perform dance patterns from different areas of Africa. Woodworking skills are used to build sets and to teach students math concepts and the importance of accomplishing tasks in a certain sequence. African masks are studied and constructed in art classes, then used to dec-orate the school and the sets. African poetry and folk tales are recited. These activi-ties teach students about the various African nations and their history, geography, and specific cultures. The involvement of the faculty under the supervision of Stephen Johnson, Director of Dance at The Lab School, ensures that the African Heritage Day production and sets look professional and that authentic-looking costumes are created (made by Steve and a crew of volunteers all sewing late into the night!).

Since 1994, The Lab School has partnered with the Martin Luther King Jr. Elementary School, located in the inner city of Washington, D.C., to celebrate African Heritage Month. Then we were joined by the Brent School in Capitol Hill and, finally, the Stuart-Hobson Middle School of Washington, D.C. Because these three schools have partnered with The Lab School, African Heritage Day is cele-brated at a local theater with a joint performance by all four schools. Students from the participating schools work together for months in preparation for this perform-ance. After the major performance in February, the students "take their show on the road" and share it with the community through performances at district churches, schools, and nursing homes. We have discovered that the techniques we use that work well with students with learning disabilities work even better and are more quickly effective with students who are at an educational and economic disadvantage. The benefits of the African Heritage Day program for students with learning disabilities and students who are educationally or economically disadvantaged can be measured by their new knowledge, increased coordination, self-confidence, and team-building skills.

THE LAB SCHOOL ARCHAEOLOGICAL DIG

In 1992, a student at The Lab School found an interesting stone on the school grounds and showed it to a staff member who happened to be an archaeology graduate student. This staff member identified the object as a prehistoric arrowhead and took it to Dr. David Clark, Professor of Archaeology at Catholic University, who dated the object to approximately 2,500 B.C. A partnership between Dr. Clark and his archaeology students and the 310 students from The Lab School commenced.

In 1992, in true Lab School fashion, we created a curriculum in which every skill needed to conduct an archaeological dig was incorporated into various classes. For 2 1/2 weeks, intensive work on our "find" took place in every classroom at The Lab School. Even the related sciences were involved. Occupational therapists were at the dig helping students learn how to use the tools to uncover found objects. Speech-language pathologists talked with their students about "the dig" and taught key words and important phrases. To understand how people lived in 2,500 B.C., Lab School students used rocks and ancient techniques to make tools for cutting, scraping, and hunting. On Macintosh computers, HyperCard stacks were created to teach lessons in sedimentation and stone tool production. This resulted in the development of students' problem-solving skills and imaginations of what the site was like. Analysis of the artifacts was incorporated into science and math curricula, and lessons were developed for incorporating the site findings into geology, chemistry, flora and fauna studies, and soil analysis classes. Movement and role playing helped convey some archaeological information; large dioramas and all manner of craft materials were employed to convey information to students with learning disabilities.

Today, our curriculum includes the study of how residents have adapted to the area from the time of the early Native Americans through the present. The contrast of the ancient objects on the grounds of a school full of modern computers was especially helpful in teaching about the differences between the lives of prehistoric people and the students' own lives today. The difference is very concrete. In this way, the staff could teach students how to put bits of knowledge together to form a coherent picture of ancient civilization.

Since 1992, Dr. David Clark has been the outside advisor of the archaeological dig, supervising the project and conducting a dig several weeks each spring. For Lab School students, the dig is a way to use critical deductive thinking and active experimentation to study cultures that existed on the school site between 2,000 and 6,000 years ago. The dig currently covers an area of 20 square feet that is divided into quadrants marked with string. Boxes with screen bottoms are placed on tripods to sift the soil. Proper scientific procedures are followed: Students learn observation, organization, cataloguing, and systematic arrangement. Staff members discovered that archaeology helps our students learn how to look carefully at details, categorize, classify, compare, and measure. While being introduced to the vast world of archaeology and its exciting body of knowledge, our students are doing activities that help them over-come their disabilities.

The dig site was found to be very fertile with artifacts from the Late Archaic and Early Woodlands periods. Through careful examination of the type of artifacts found, archaeologists concluded that the site was a hunting encampment connected with a Potomac River base camp. They also determined that the site was inhabited by vari-ous Native Americans at different times throughout early history. In addition to more recent arrowheads, broad spears dating back 3,000 to 5,000 years have been found at the dig site. So far, more than 8,000 artifacts have been found, including several important finds, some of which date back 5,000–6,000 years. For instance, students have discovered rhyolite, a glassy volcanic rock similar to granite found only in Hagerstown, Maryland, prior to our discovery on the grounds of The Lab School.

In 1999, an exciting new discovery led to new theories. Lab school students uncovered an ancient fireplace. Dr. Clark says that the fireplace, dated to 5,500 years ago, has caused a major reevaluation of the purpose of the ancient Indian camp. Judging from the great number of faulty stone projectile points found around the fire-place, the archaeologist thinks that our site may have been a stone tool-making camp where Native Americans discarded imperfect tools. The artifacts show the full range of manufacturing from heating the stones to making large flakes to finishing the spear points and taking them back to base camp. There are still mysteries to be explored at our dig, and Lab School students are eager to help sift through the site looking for more clues. In fact, a number of our students now are interested in pursuing careers in archaeology.

Within The Lab School there are mini-museums and dioramas on every floor displaying prehistoric and historic finds from the dig. Yearly, the science faculty and art teachers are expanding archaeological displays and preparing to install panoramic photographs of the students digging at the site. A monograph on the dig is in prepa-ration. Artifacts found at the school have been displayed at the U.S. Department of Energy and featured in *National Geographic World* (1994), which displayed a photo of a Lab School student archaeologist and included the story of the site. *Scientific American* also has written about the dig. We cannot believe our good fortune in mak-ing such a "find"; it has been a schoolmarm's delight because any subject can be taught through archaeology, and the arts are key to unlocking ancient civilizations. In addi-tion, The Lab School has been named a prehistoric site!

U.S. BOTANICAL GARDENS

The more that students with learning disabilities can see their own work displayed, the more it reminds them that they can do many things. This is why we encourage our students to help beautify our neighborhood and do art projects for local concerns. When the U.S. Botanical Gardens was looking for artists to design decorative panels that would surround the reconstruction of the gardens taking place over a 3-year period, we encouraged our youngsters to submit murals. Our students created seven panels of the large mural that surrounds the gardens.

THE KREEGER MUSEUM

Recently, a nearby museum, The Kreeger Museum, had our students working along-side an internationally known sculptor as she created a site-specific, large-scale, out-door sculpture for the museum. That same museum has commissioned celebrated composer Robert Kapilow to create a symphony on the subject of *Monuments at the Millennium.* The composer visited The Lab School, and junior and senior high school students gave him their ideas about why we need monuments as well as remarks on which monuments they remember and why. This led to our using the monument theme for our summer program in 1999, entitled "A Monumental Summer at The Lab School." Students built monuments out of every media and the monument of the U.S. Capitol is being displayed in a children's museum.

There are many artistic opportunities in each community that students can enjoy and in which they can participate. It takes work on the part of school administrators, parents, and arts departments to unearth institutions that can profit from students' efforts and achievements. It is worth doing because it helps students who often feel alienated feel more related to their own community, and it boosts their sense of self when they can point to a prominently displayed piece of art and say, "We made it!"

The Curriculum of
The Lab School of Washington

The curriculum of The Lab School is a pathway to other roads, up steep hills, down deep valleys, and to fountains of knowledge where artists and teachers can lead their students to make new discoveries. Choices are given. Decisions have to be made. Curiosity is prized. Risking untried routes is valued. Use of the intellect and imagination to the fullest extent possible is a requirement of The Lab School learning adventure, which is what quality education is all about.

For exceptional learners, the intense remediation required in a school such as The Lab School is a difficult kind of journey in reading, writing, and, often, math. It demands very specific goals and objectives, taught step-by-step through a combination of methods tailored to each individual child. Constant analyses of the difficulty and appropriateness of tasks and breaking tasks down into manageable chunks—basically, diagnostic-prescriptive teaching—is the key needed on this journey.

The Lab School infuses the learning adventure and remediation journey with high energy, enthusiasm, and the wide-ranging talents of an extraordinary staff. The Lab School Day School serves approximately 310 students between the ages of 5 and 19, who have severe learning disabilities with or without attention-deficit/hyperactivty disorder (ADHD) and who demonstrate from average to superior intelligence. In the elementary school, the primary division accepts students ages 5–6 who are exceedingly immature for their ages; students ages 6–10 follow the full elementary program. The intermediate level, also part of the elementary school, teaches students ages 10–13. A junior high setting has been created for 11- to 14-year-olds, while 14- to 19-year-olds are in senior high school. Students are placed in groups at The Lab School according to their social and emotional maturity rather than by their ages and achievements. Because the work is individualized anyway, there is no ability grouping.

THEORETICAL FRAMEWORK

The arts are central to the educative process in the primary, elementary, and intermediate divisions. By spending half of the day in highly specialized individualized classrooms and the other half of the day in the arts, younger students with moderate to severe learning disabilities acquire the basic skills necessary for their academic development. At the junior high and high school levels, up to 90 minutes per day may be devoted to the arts. The theoretical framework of the school asserts that the arts, when taught in a specific way, help give students the neural organization they lack and need to develop in order to succeed at school. In *Magic Trees of the Mind*, by Marian Diamond, Ph.D., and Janet Hobson (1998), the authors have proven that enriched environments lead to increased neural branching and connectivity; they expand the brain's cortex, which increases brain power. The theoretical framework operates under the hypothesis that The Lab School's arts-based program provides an enriched environment. Also, in Lab School methodology, the arts are treated as organizers, each art having its own series of steps. The student concentrates on the product or performance, while the faculty concentrates on teaching the process, helping the student to predict sequences, breaking steps into sequences, devising strategies, and putting into clear language what has occurred. The major goals of The Lab School are to

- Provide quality education for a lifetime of learning
- Provide intensive remediation
- Teach socialization skills explicitly
- Provide sharpened tools of problem solving and critical thinking
- Pioneer new methods and techniques
- Train extraordinary teachers to go out into the community
- Disseminate and replicate Lab School methodology

OVERVIEW OF ACADEMIC PROGRAMS AT THE LAB SCHOOL

The following sections provide an overview of the reading and language arts program and the math program at The Lab School of Washington.

READING AND LANGUAGE ARTS

With very few exceptions, Lab School students arrive at school unable to read at all, reading well below grade level, or reading haltingly or very slowly. Some students with serious language impairments demonstrate difficulty comprehending what they are reading. The intense remediation we do in reading is as important as embracing our students with a quality education in all subjects. We teach reading daily in small groups of three or four students and, whenever possible, on a one-to-one level. We do not use one particular reading method. Our staff is trained to know as many reading techniques as possible so they can tailor instruction to each child's needs and not make the child learn by a method that was chosen for all students. The head of our Tutor Training Program, a reading specialist, meets with the nonreaders who have the most difficulty, and the coordinator of each division receives reports of the reading specialist's diagnostic findings. The staff can then use this information to apply different methods of reading instruction. Reading progress is monitored carefully, is discussed frequently, and is at the heart of what we do.

In addition to the direct teaching of reading, speech-language pathologists provide therapy for all but about 30 of our 310 students. Severe speech-language impairments can be heard in every classroom. Classroom teachers, reading specialists, and therapists, who meet with one another frequently, are all addressing the same problems in reading and language arts.

Academic Clubs, science, all of the art forms, and the many programs described in this chapter are taught in ways that promote reading readiness and reading. It has been my belief, as prime designer of The Lab School curriculum, that all art forms enhance neurological development, which promotes reading progress. Our reading specialists concentrate on phonemic awareness and sound-symbol training that research shows to be valid but, also, on whole language in the sense of literature-based learning.

MATH

Some Lab School students are well ahead of their age groups in math and may be learning Algebra I when they cannot read. Others are worse in math than they are in reading. It takes them years to understand 1-to-1 association, place value, and simple concepts of *more* and *less*. Other students have no rote memory and cannot remember multiplication facts, and still others do not know how to begin when tasks become more difficult, such as in long division. Fractions cause trouble for students with part–whole difficulty. Math has to be taught individually, related to each child's specific strengths and weaknesses.

Manipulatives are used with the child who thinks concretely so that she can see what she is doing as she moves blocks, rods, or other objects around. Cooking projects are used frequently to teach math. Concrete activities such as measuring the basketball court also take place. Teacher- and student-made games are constructed to help students with particular processes.

Some high school students can succeed in trigonometry and calculus at The Lab School, whereas others take years to pass Algebra I and geometry. There is no one method of teaching math—just a great deal of hands-on project learning. Woodwork, set design, and architectural design are all, in some ways, similar to applied math.

The sections that follow describe the primary, elementary, junior high, and high school programs in more detail.

THE PRIMARY PROGRAM

Designed for children between the ages of 5 and 6 who are very immature and disorganized and who have been diagnosed as being at risk for learning disabilities, the primary program concentrates on organization of movement, organization of language, and readiness in reading, writing, and math. Regular occupational therapy (sensory integration) and speech-language therapy are an important part of this program in addition to science, art, dance, eurythmics, and drama in the classroom.

In the primary program, the classroom teacher uses singing to convey messages to the class. For example, to the tune of "This Land Is Your Land," primary students sing, "This space is my space, that space is your space. From head to toe and side to side. I'll stay in my space. You stay in your space. This space belongs to only me." Neurologically immature 5- and 6-year-olds have great difficulty establishing boundaries, and this song helps.

Drama is used continually, not just to reenact stories that have been read to students but to act out feelings such as happiness, sadness, anger, and so forth. Social skills are role-played: How do I get someone's attention? How do I interrupt? How do I introduce myself? How do I join in a group of students who are playing?

Art projects, taught by an artist, may have students look at reproductions of Monet's paintings and then create their own mural in Monet's impressionist style. Students work in many different media, such as painting, printmaking, collage, and ceramics.

Dance at the primary level relies a lot on gymnastics—jumping, leaping, doing somersaults, and learning to move and to "freeze," almost making the movement into a sculpture. Because 5- and 6-year-olds who are neurologically immature demonstrate great difficulty working in groups, a theme, such as a circus with acrobats or a space voyage with astronauts on the moon, works best. The drama of the scene makes them focus. Themes also allow for a great deal of individual performance within a group setting so that it may look like more interaction takes place than actually does. In addition, the drama and the music, if used, promote more group work. Relaxation exercises often start the day. These are exercises designed to achieve focus and to calm students. Then movement exercises can begin. For example, one day students may pretend to be various creatures; sea creatures and sharks move in the same ocean, bugs crawl on the earth, and big animals such as elephants trudge along.

Eurythmics combines music and movement. Singing and playing simple instruments and rhythm and movement games give the students concrete experiences as well as a means to express themselves. Topics in the primary program—such as transportation, rain forests, frogs, or mystery books—are integrated into songs, movements, and role playing. Storytelling is an important part of the curriculum. The teacher chooses poetry and storybooks to enrich the theme of study. For example, when studying sea creatures, the teacher reads nonfiction, fiction, and poetry about sea creatures to the students. They listen to music that sounds like the sea to encourage visualization of the scene. They count sea creatures. They name them. They categorize the sea creatures as *fish* or *not fish*, then as *fish, reptiles,* or *birds.* Then the students study the basic scientific properties of fish, reptiles, and birds. In their science classes, they study vertebrates and invertebrates. They play teacher-made lotto or bingo games to facilitate their study of vertebrates and invertebrates.

The arts play a very important role in assessing very young children with special needs. The inability to clap three times is significant; it tells teachers to look out for difficulties. A child who is unable to move from side to side, switch hands continuously, or use her eyes and hands together in the arts bears watching. These are all diagnostic clues. Can students follow one, two, or three directions in art? In dance? In drama?

Singing alphabets, stomping out telephone numbers, jumping to number combinations, and painting huge circles and squares all help students in the primary program learn. Activity learning is helpful for all children, but it is mandatory for children who are neurologically immature and disorganized.

THE ELEMENTARY SCHOOL PROGRAM

At The Lab School of Washington, the elementary school consists of two parts: the elementary program for students between the ages of 6 and 10 and the intermediate program for students between the ages of 10 and 13. The students work in their homerooms for different parts of the day, starting at 8:30 A.M. and ending at 3:30 P.M. Half of each day is devoted to Academic Clubs; the other half takes place in the classroom—where the teaching of individualized reading, spelling, writing, mathematics, and group projects take place. Their science program is infused with art, and the writer's lab includes a multimedia set of activities.

All students in the elementary and intermediate programs attend an Academic Club daily and receive a minimum of two art classes each day—one visual art (e.g., graphic arts, woodwork shop) and one performing art (e.g., dance, drama, music). Each art class has a series of systematic academic objectives as hidden agendas. All art areas deal with symbols, patterns, sequences, and problem solving. The following section provides a brief overview of the art program.

ART CLASSES

At the elementary level, art class is designed to allow each child an opportunity to experiment with a wide variety of tools, media, and techniques. It is designed to emphasize the use of shape, color, line, and texture in two- and three-dimensional projects. Some assignments, such as shape tracing, clay molding, and specific drawing exercises, are used to help students develop their coordination and sense of design. Care is taken to encourage the child's natural ability to invent forms and his or her desire to experiment with materials. Projects include ceramic sculpture, printmaking, painting, collage, and drawing. Whenever possible, students are allowed to choose their subjects, within the parameters of the assigned project. This approach sometimes leads to technical problems that students are encouraged to solve through trial-and-error improvisations guided by the art teacher. The goals of art classes at the elementary level are to

- Improve visual perception and visual-motor skills
- Improve spatial relations
- Develop self-confidence
- Develop planning and organizational skills

The art class, by the way in which it is run, emphasizes that there is no one way to approach and complete an assignment or project. Students are encouraged to try any idea they have. The teacher/artist creates problems for students to solve. The following sections describe in detail some of the specific arts and their related goals in which students participate at the elementary level.

Woodwork Shop

The woodwork shop develops learning skills through a step-by-step routine of constructing three-dimensional objects. The projects—ranging from simple boxes to more complex furniture, toys, pinball games, go-carts, and musical instruments—are geared to the children's individual needs, skills, and interests. From the beginning idea and sketch to the finished product, students develop organizational and sequential skills as they work on their projects. Eye–hand coordination, math skills, vocabulary, and a regard for both safety and craftsmanship are strengthened daily. The goals of participating in woodwork shop are to

- Develop visual perception and visual-motor skills
- Develop spatial awareness
- Improve organization and planning skills
- Develop familiarity with various workshop tools and their particular uses and functions
- Improve math skills through measuring
- Develop language skills as children explain the steps necessary to complete their project
- Develop problem-solving skills
- Develop abstract reasoning as students visualize intended projects

Dance

In dance class, students learn to isolate parts of their bodies and gradually learn to put the movements together into more and more complex sequences. Modern, ethnic, and improvisational dance and movement activities are used to develop rhythm, design, and style. Upper elementary and intermediate students also learn how to cooperate with classmates to create body sculptures—an art in which students hold specific positions and support one another to form interesting shapes. Gymnastics movements also are integrated into dances. Dance emphasizes following directions, taking turns, being aware of what others are doing, and teamwork. The goals of dance are to improve

- Body awareness
- Muscle tone of the lower and upper body
- Gross motor skills
- Eye–hand coordination
- Motor planning skills
- Memory and sequencing through memorization of the sequenced dance movements
- Ability to make accurate judgment of the use of space

Drama

The drama class at the elementary level focuses on five primary units of study. Each of these units centers around a class project. The five units are language-intensive narrative (e.g., Shakespeare), nonverbal narrative (e.g., mime shows, silent movies), exclusively verbal narrative (e.g., storytelling, radio plays), dramatic construction (e.g., developing both original material and adapting folk and fairy tales), and video and film production (e.g., original short films). Each unit culminates in a class production. The study of these five aspects of theater addresses a variety of skills. All acting involves a problem-solving endeavor. Mastery of dialogue requires the development of language and memory skills. Students analyze and articulate the narrative structure of dramatic material. The rehearsal process builds cooperation, appreciation of others, and the strengthening of social skills. The use of props, such as a magic stick or cane, often frees the students to act; when students have nothing in their hands, they often have difficulty acting. The goals of drama are to

- Elicit appropriate vocal and physical responses to common situations
- Encourage language and vocabulary development
- Improve problem-solving skills
- Encourage teamwork and cooperation
- Improve comprehension skills and awareness of cause/effect relationships through structured improvisation and prepared material
- Improve memory
- Build self-confidence
- Develop listening and attending skills
- Improve gross motor planning and spatial awareness

Music

Music class is designed to stimulate and explore students' interest and abilities in music through the active use of instruments and voice. At the same time, music appreciation is enhanced through listening activities involving classical, show, international, and contemporary music. Social skills and the rebuilding of self-confidence are addressed through the design and conduct of public and school performances. The goals of music are to

- Link sound and symbol and gain practice in encoding and decoding—necessary skills for reading
- Increase auditory skills by memorizing song lyrics and by singing melodies chosen to increase pitch accuracy
- Improve gross and fine motor skills by playing percussion instruments such as a xylophone, bells, drums, cymbals, and triangles
- Increase sequencing and eye–hand coordination by reading color-coded, random ordered music charts while playing instruments

THE ACADEMIC CLUBS

The Academic Clubs are a unique, multisensory approach that I designed in 1966; they use all the arts to systematically teach history, geography, civics, and reading readiness. The Integrated Arts and Academic Club Method is used in the Elementary

School Program and is designed to lure the child, to capture his imagination and enthusiasm, to build on his love of pretend play, and to offer fun and success in learning by immersing the child in an atmosphere of a different historical period each year. Abstract ideas are presented as tangible experiences that relate directly to the children's lives. A child is placed in an Academic Club according to his age and maturity. Although 6- and 7-year-olds may start in the Cave Club for a year and then move on to the Gods Club, a 9-year-old new student might start in the Gods Club or the Knights and Ladies Club, the next club in the progression. The degree of structure, sophistication, creativity, and materials presented in each club are appropriate for specific maturational levels as well as for maintaining the historical order. Greatly infused by all of the art forms, the Academic Clubs tap the imaginations as well as the fine intellects of students and teachers to the core. The dramatic framework of each Academic Club is used to impart a vast storehouse of information. This knowledge then becomes the scaffolding that supports the students through their early reading efforts, allowing them to make connections and anticipate ideas—the foundations of reading comprehension. The goals of the Academic Clubs are to

- Equip students with the tools that will allow them to continue the process of inquiry and discovery and give them a zest for learning and a thirst for knowledge throughout their lifetime
- Provide readiness training (visual and auditory perception) using the concepts and symbols of the clubs' historical periods
- Develop socialization skills
- Improve organizational skills
- Develop fine and gross motor skills
- Improve visual and auditory memory
- Learn concepts basic to the particular period around which the particular clubs are based (e.g., survival for the caveman, mummification for the Egyptian, guilds for the craftsmen of the Middle Ages)
- Learn about a period in history, including its people, geographical environment, important historical events, and significant ideas (e.g., political, social, economic, religious)
- Involve the students so completely in a particular recreated environment that they respond both physically and mentally to that historical period

The methods used to help students respond physically and mentally to a specific period include

- Creating a physical environment that reflects a historical period
- Creating a club identity that is reinforced through a code of behavior
- Using teaching techniques and strategies that allow for a panoply of methods within a curriculum
- Devising a curriculum that remains flexible enough to meet the needs and interests of the students but that is structured enough to remain consistently committed to the objectives

- Drawing on the students' experiences and enabling them to link present to past, cause to effect, and concrete to abstract

- Involving students in those activities that will best help them acquire solid information through experimentation, role playing, dramatization, questioning, probing, exploring, finding alternatives, and discovering answers

Currently, six Academic Clubs exist at The Lab School. They include the Cave Club, the Gods Club, the Knights and Ladies Club, the Renaissance Club, the Museum Club, and the Industrialists Club.

The Cave Club

The Cave Club employs dramatization to interpret and bring to life an early era in human evolution. By delving into an ancient existence using multisensory activities and socialization skills, students discuss, experiment with, and learn archaeology, geology, science, and math.

The club begins with the "Old Stone Age," forming a foundation on which to build throughout the year. This phase encompasses prehistoric man's social and cultural aspects, shelters, food, tools, and weapons. The ensuing topic is the "New Stone Age." This era introduces the inventions of huts, canoes, superstitions, and the wheel in addition to socialization concepts.

The Cave Club compares today's lifestyle with ways of life in the distant past. It also introduces new vocabulary and new concepts that the children learn to integrate into their lives.

The Gods Club

The Gods Club uses dramatization to study Egyptian civilization and Greek and Roman mythology and culture. The year begins "in" Egypt, where students learn about the growth of societies around the Nile and the relationship of Egyptian society to nature. Egyptian life, including the study of Egyptian gods and peoples' beliefs about life and afterlife, is explored through observing ancient rituals and holidays, creating a complete mummy-making kit, building a shaduf, and putting on ancient Egyptian puppet performances. Daily Egyptian life is depicted through students' writing hieroglyphics, making art projects, and role playing activities.

During the second trimester, students learn about the changes in culture from Egyptian to Greek society. Geographic, social, political, and religious differences are explored through role-playing games. Students learn about the various Greek gods, hear and retell myths, and study *The Odyssey* by playing a teacher-created game.

In the final trimester of the year, students explore the interplay and changeover of Greek to Roman culture. Roman myths, including *Hercules* and *The Aeneid*, are the basis for exploring geographical, political, and religious aspects of the Roman Empire.

During each trimester, emphasis is placed on main events, inventions, mythology, and the development of written language. Throughout the year, students are encouraged to compare and contrast Egyptian, Greek, and Roman ideas, lifestyles, and gods. Students also explore the influence of these ancient civilizations on their own culture.

The Knights and Ladies Club

In the Knights and Ladies Club, students learn about the history and culture of Europe during the Middle Ages through drama, stories, and art. Feudalism, the caste system, and everyday life in a medieval village are dramatically recreated. The growth of central government in England is investigated as students learn about the role of a king, the Magna Carta, and the parliamentary system. Students build model towns and explore the reasons for their growth and decline by learning about invasions, technology, the crusades, the form and function of guilds, religion, and the Black Death. As students prepare to become Knights and Ladies, they create a coat of arms, armor, and weapons; train to become pages and squires; and explore life in a castle. By assuming historical roles, such as serf, peasant, merchant, page, squire, and knight, the students participate in activities that teach history and strengthen thinking skills.

The Renaissance Club

The Renaissance Club is imagined to take place in the city of Florence, Italy. Students form a Council of Florence. Every student assumes the role of an important Renaissance artist or intellectual. Emphasis is placed on geography, main events, and cultural aspects of the period. By assuming the role of a famous Renaissance person, such as Michelangelo, Leonardo da Vinci, Dante, or Galileo, students eagerly participate in activities that teach history, help strengthen thinking skills, and introduce them to an important cultural legacy. As the Councilors meet each day with their leader, Lorenzo de Medici, they study the great Greek Revival and the development of important cultural centers such as Florence, Milan, Venice, and Genoa. The roles of the church, guilds, women, scholars, and poets, as well as the works and lives of famous classical artists, are explored. Exploration of the new world is touched upon.

The Museum Club

The purpose of the Museum Club is to review major periods of history, beginning with the Stone Age and continuing on to the earliest exploration for trade routes to the New World and the beginning of American history and culture. Emphasis is placed on exploring progress in government, architecture, technology, and communications. Life in each period is examined by looking at arts and crafts, tools, religion, and housing. Replicas of artifacts from each period of history are made and displayed in a "museum." At the end of each unit of study, an exhibit "opening" is held, with each student acting as a docent and speaking to visitors on one aspect of the exhibit.

The Industrialists Club

In the Industrialists Club, student industrialists cover American history in the latter half of the 1800s and the early 1900s. The students study the "Captains of Industry"—Rockefeller, Guggenheim, DuPont, Ford, Vanderbilt, Carnegie, and Gould as well as several others—as they learn how America's mainly mercantile, agrarian society was transformed into a mass-production economy. The students also study the Civil War, the early waves of immigration, the transcontinental railroad, the gold rush, child labor laws, antitrust legislation, and geography. During the 50-minute club sessions, students hold "board meetings," manage "trust funds," which are recorded in ledgers, and keep records concerning business and personal transactions. Students also discuss the personality characteristics of the industrialists and the methods they used for acquiring their wealth as well as the incredible legacy they left for all Americans.

SCIENCE

At the elementary levels of The Lab School, science is taught mostly through the arts. With the exception of groups of the oldest students in the intermediate division, who are studying U.S. geography, each student in the elementary and intermediate programs attends science class. The class covers five basic units: space, environmental issues, invertebrates, the archaeological dig, and plants.

Students in our simulated Science Academy begin the year by exploring the universe. They blast off in a SpaceLab (created in the classroom), explore each planet in the solar system, and eventually return to land on our moon.

Next, they focus on the earth's environmental issues, relating them to planetary conditions studied "in space." Older students learn about the layers of our atmosphere. All students learn about various types of pollution and emphasize the use of the three Rs: reduce, reuse, and recycle. Students also learn about the cycle of decomposition, laying the foundation for understanding the interdependence of animal and plant kingdoms.

The unit on invertebrates includes an introduction to classification (taxonomy) as well as hands-on experience with many of the major invertebrate groups and concludes with a focus on insects and pollination.

The final unit, plants, begins with a study of the contribution of insects to plant reproduction and covers photosynthesis, plant structures, and major plant categories.

In addition to these basic units, the science classes hold a Science Museum Convention in February, during which time students are given the opportunity to identify a problem that they are interested in solving (e.g., in 2000, it was the Space Museum; in 1999, it was The Body Museum). Then, working in teams, the students brainstorm creative solutions and create projects to illustrate their solutions to specific problems.

In May, students participate in The Lab School's ongoing archaeological dig, excavating a site in the rear play area (see Chapter 5).

GEOGRAPHY

Geography class focuses on mapping skills, history, research, library use, and social skills. Using a multisensory approach that combines oral reading, role playing, music, art, and crafts, the students develop comprehension and memory skills. Students' participation in the learning process is emphasized through hands-on projects in addition to films, guest speakers, field trips, and oral reports given by each student.

The first class in geography begins with the teacher bringing in a cake. At first glance, it looks like a large whole round cake, but really it has been cut into seven pieces. The plastic plate is also cut into seven pieces, and they are put back together to look whole. For example, the teacher might say, "The Earth is a theory. See the whole cake earth. Tell me what a theory is." Then Sarah, a student in the class, excitedly states that a theory is a belief. The teacher then has the class clap the word *Pangaea* and explains the theory that there was once one continent called *Pangaea*. But the plates moved under the earth and divided it into seven sections. The cake has seven different colors of icing. A student finds the biggest slice and plate, which is red and represents Asia, the largest continent. Africa is the next largest continent, followed by North America, South America, and so forth.

The year's study of geography begins with the acquisition of map skills. Basic concepts such as the cardinal directions, hemispheres, poles, and the equator enable students to use maps to locate oceans, continents, islands, mountains, seas, countries, rivers, states, and cities. The interpretation of physical and political maps, including the use of symbolic keys, offers students insights into regional similarities and differences. A detailed study of the United States is possible using these new skills.

The location and significance of the 50 states is reinforced via association with unique facts: Idaho is associated with potatoes; the famed Kentucky Derby symbolizes the southern state for which it is named. To help the students remember the Kentucky Derby, the teacher has each student take balloons with a picture of a horse and a number on it. The students attach the balloons to a piece of straw with tape, blow them up, and let them go; the first balloon to cross an imaginary finish line wins the Kentucky Derby crown. Famous U.S. landmarks such as the Golden Gate Bridge, the St. Louis Arch, the Liberty Bell, and the Statue of Liberty are placed in geographic space as well as in historic time. Students are encouraged to share their experiences, artifacts, souvenirs, or drawings from places they have visited. In one class, Harold sang "New York, New York" wearing his Yankees cap; Martha and Al made a reproduction of Lincoln's log cabin in Illinois; and Stacey came to school dressed as a lobster and did a report on Maine. Each student in the class also calls a Congressman's office and asks for material from that state; then the class reviews the materials together.

TECHNOLOGY/THE WRITER'S LAB

In Writer's Lab, technology, art, and storytelling are woven together. Students begin this process by learning the art of storytelling. Storytelling is a highly efficacious art that needs to become more central to learning. At The Lab School, we use miniature figures of varieties of people, animals, trees, and houses to encourage students to make up stories (the same principle as having objects to which to relate in drama). After making up a story, a student acts it out with miniature figures in front of a group of peers, who become coaches, critics, and cohorts who motivate the budding authors to make sure they have a solid beginning, middle, and end. For example, the student authors often will bring in a character, such as a magical monkey, and then forget about the character; the student's peer critics make sure the magical monkey gets reincorporated into the story. After listening to suggestions from his classmates, the student dictates the story to a teacher or keys it on a Macintosh computer. The story is then illustrated and becomes a book. The book ends with the most important feature, the "About the Author" page, which contains the student's photo and a few sentences of autobiography. Two copies of each book are produced. A cover is made and the book is bound (by parent volunteers). One copy goes home with the student, and the other book resides in the most popular section of the school library. Many of our students not only author books but learn to make their own CDs using a digital camera and scanner in addition to their own art and art they download from the Internet.

One group of 10-year-olds clustered around a Macintosh computer were totally involved in a voyage to Mars. Marianne says, "I can draw the route of our trip to Mars on the screen. I can show on the screen what we need to pack." "It won't be like my trip to my grandparents," states Arthur. "Let's use the digital camera and put our photos in space suits so it looks like we're all going to Mars," shrieks Andrew. "The sounds of the trip are up to us," yell Tom and Herb. "First, let's look on the Internet to see what we can learn about Mars," Jamie says quietly.

School dragon (wood sculpture).

Water scene (carpet art).

Notecards featuring these unique works of art, created by the students of The Lab School of Washington, can be purchased at www.labschool.org/.

Hanuman (mixed media: wood objects).

Music mural (paint).

Animal kingdom (carpet art).

Dreamweaver (mixed media: wood, rope, papier-mâché).

Globe theater (mixed media).

Ganesh (mixed media: metal, found objects).

Molly suggests, "Max and I can make a diorama to plot our trip before we even put it on the computer."

Students whose poor attention spans, distractibility, impulsivity, and severe learning disabilities have driven them away from any concentrated classroom activities become totally immersed in their multimedia creation. Their world is a graphic world. Storytelling, art, and computers, combined, lure their attention, inspire their imaginations, and entice conscientious hard work. They have become active learners. Intelligent, often gifted, students who cannot read and write can produce extraordinary creations of art on the computer. The arts and technology are a natural combination.

THE JUNIOR HIGH PROGRAM

In the junior high—seventh and eighth grades—the emphasis is on organization of schoolwork, homework, and studies in general. While students continue to develop their reading, writing, and math skills and to learn as much content as possible, the focus continues to be on experiential, hands-on learning; numerous field trips related to content are made to reinforce learning.

SOCIAL STUDIES

Humanities (Seventh Grade)

The Humanities class is designed to educate students about the cultures of three diverse countries. For example, during the 1999–2000 academic year, students studied China, Ireland, and Brazil. The Humanities class includes the study of the lifestyle, traditions, and customs of each country through the use of all of the art forms. In addition, geography, history, and literature are presented and explored. Current events then follow. Teachers and students plan, produce, and display art projects that reflect the artistic style of each country. The development of study skills is incorporated into the program through notetaking, listening to lectures, participating in discussions, and watching visual presentations. Students are required to complete related class assignments utilizing their notes, maps, graphs, and charts. The Humanities program also focuses on the culinary techniques and foods of each region. The study of each country culminates with a full-scale restaurant presentation. The students are responsible for the decorations, food preparation and cooking, customer service, and business transactions. These skills and activities are practiced and reinforced through a variety of hands-on projects done in the classroom. The proceeds from each restaurant event enable the students to dine in a local restaurant that serves cuisine from the studied country.

Democracy (Eighth Grade)

The Democracy class educates students about the concept of government, emphasizing American democracy through the study of major events in American history. Information that is studied covers the colonization of America to World War II. Students are required to analyze current events and study the relationships between historical events and today's news. Students are expected to complete class assignments and tests, including a take-home essay test, utilizing their notes, maps, and graphic organizers. Specific organizational methods are taught and reinforced periodically throughout the year. Knowledge and skills are reinforced using hands-on class projects, simulations, and role-play. Through the use of classroom simulations and role-play, students become citizens of an autocracy, government leaders of a newly independent nation, Congress members enacting laws, immigrants coming through Ellis Island, and Allied Powers waging war and making peace.

Debates are conducted within the context of a classroom simulation or reenactment. For instance, some students will take on the roles of National Association for the Advancement of Colored People (NAACP) lawyers like Thurgood Marshall, and others will role play lawyers for the southern states to recreate the historic Supreme Court debate of *Brown v. the Board of Education*. Projects, charts, maps, computer-generated CDs, and field trips help enrich the material. For example, students go to the Naval Museum and reenact the constitutional debate regarding whether the United States really needed a navy.

SCIENCE

Science and art often are combined; for example, in the junior high, students have created stained glass windows as part of their study of earth science and space science.

Each glass in a large window pane is filled in with cut out black matte board that has tissue paper glued to it. Students choose an individual project such as stars, galaxies, meteors, or planets and study them in books and on the Internet. After their research, each student creates her own image; then the group decides how to put the images together.

The junior high holds a Health Expo instead of a science fair that is all about the body, nutrition, exercise, and experiments that prove that fitness is healthy. Students conduct research, interviews, and surveys and present their findings in displays, graphs, and charts using their computer skills.

Students learn about diffusion in the "Diffusion Disco." Students are confined to a small space in the room. Each student is told that he or she is a molecule and is instructed to dance to some lively disco music. After a few minutes they are asked to stop and describe how they feel. "I feel hot." "It's too crowded." "I need more space." Then, the confined space is opened. The students are told that they now have more space and the music and dancing are resumed. They spread out and take up much more space. They are then asked to react to having more space.

Following the activity students are taught that they behaved the way molecules do during the process of diffusion. The students then make up their own experiments. One person opened up a bottle of perfume in one corner of the room. Its scent was detected everywhere. Both the scent and the air are made up of molecules which continually brush against each other. When the scent is released and no longer confined in the bottle, it moves to an area where there are fewer molecules.

THE ARTS

Studio Art

The basic approach to Studio Art at the junior high level is the same as that at the elementary level. Whenever possible, students are allowed to choose their own subjects within the parameters of an assigned project. This sometimes leads to technical problems, which students are encouraged to solve through trial-and-error improvisations guided by the teacher. Care is taken to avoid inhibiting any child's inclination to invent forms or to experiment with materials. Studio Art offers creative time for each student to encounter problems and find unique solutions. Exploring color and shape through printmaking is the first project of the year, followed by drawing, more complex printmaking assignments, and beginning work on computer graphics.

The Junior High Graphics Squad is composed of junior high students with some artistic skills and poor socialization skills. As members of the Graphics Squad, students have their own logos and cards and are solidly members of the squad that makes all decisions through a group process—pure teamwork. The Junior High Graphics Squad

- Solicits business within the school
- Uses measurement, elements of design, and graphic tools to complete each job
- Takes on a variety of jobs: classroom bulletin boards, painted murals, fliers, bare hallways

Three-Dimensional Art

The students in this class are given the opportunity to experiment with a wide variety of materials to expand their skills and gain confidence in their artwork. The projects are designed to help the students understand and utilize their knowledge of the elements of design in three dimensions. Plastercraft masks are framed right on their faces. Their personal embellishments exhibit creativity and investment in the project. Working with clay is always a favorite class assignment as students build using coils of clay and then work individually on the ceramic wheel. The students are encouraged to use their ideas and personality in all of their work. They are required to try each newly assigned project and to invest their talents in these experiential learning projects.

Dance

In dance class, students gain practice in isolating parts of their bodies and putting the movements together in increasingly complex sequences. Goals for each student are to improve gross motor skills, eye–hand coordination, and motor planning skills and to increase upper- and lower-body muscle tone. Modern, ethnic, and improvisational dance and movement activities are used to develop rhythm, design, and style. Students learn how to cooperate with classmates to create imaginative, motionless body sculptures. Gymnastics movements also are integrated into dances. Props such as canes are used to promote self-confidence and mastery; in addition, the noise made by these props helps the students focus. The canes enable them to concentrate on the objects instead of feeling self-conscious.

Drama

During the course of the semester, the class is involved in a series of projects that define the curriculum. Each project is designed to target specific skills and to encourage the students to participate in the creative and highly cooperative process of dramatic production. In one project, the class develops and produces an original video presentation. Other projects include scene work from Shakespeare and the presentation of comedy scenes.

In one junior high drama class, students looked at the credits of familiar TV programs such as *ER*. Their assignment was to make up a credit sequence using each person's name, face, and body to create a video signature for themselves. In other words, they were to come up with symbols and associations that others would have of them. Color and movement were emphasized. The students explored the capabilities of a professional video-editing program called Adobe Premiere. Their imaginations fed the software and the software, in turn, fed their imaginations. The end product is exciting and looks professional. During this project, the students learned to focus on their name and to use the camera, color, and movement to make it captivating. This project required students to coordinate several things at once, a difficult task for students with learning disabilities. The students ended up with a product that made them feel proud and technically savvy, and they felt good about themselves.

Music

The junior high music program stimulates and explores musical aptitude, ability, and potential. Two sessions of music are offered each day. In one session, a heavy emphasis is placed on the instruments used in contemporary music such as the keyboard, electric guitar, electric bass, various percussion instruments, and individual instruments introduced by students taking private instruction. In the second session, emphasis is placed on vocal training and singing. In both classes, group dynamics and cooperative skill development are addressed in ensemble performances that take place both in the classroom and in front of school audiences. Culturally themed ensemble performances enliven the Humanities Restaurants (three times a year) and the African Heritage Day celebration (once a year) and help to enhance multicultural appreciation.

THE HIGH SCHOOL PROGRAM

Although the high school curriculum focuses mostly on preparation for college, it still contains a number of arts.

THE ARTS

Architectural Design

In architectural design, students study basic principles of one-, two-, and three-point perspectives as applied to architectural design and civil engineering. Graphs and measurements for interpreting three-dimensional space are studied alongside examples of scale and measurement elevation as well as model building. Students analyze and draw mechanical objects from various points of view and eventually design and build a model as a group project, study and compare it to an existing building, and analyze their design. A group of 15-year-olds took the architect's sketches of The Lab School's new Arts and Athletic Center and made a model of it that sits in the front hall of the building.

Art History

Western art of the 19th and 20th centuries is the focus of this course for high school students, which begins with the invention of the camera and continues with the impressionist movement in painting. The course surveys American and European art from 1860 up until the present day. The course utilizes slides, videos, field trips to Washington's great art galleries, and hands-on experimentation of painting techniques. Students are required to develop research skills and complete a term paper on a specific artist.

Drawing

The central goal of this high school course is to instill in students the belief that drawing is a skill that can be learned and is not something reserved for only a select, talented few. They learn that good drawing begins with not merely looking at an object but with studying it thoroughly to appreciate all of the nuances of its design and form. Before any drawing begins, still-life objects are presented in strong lighting and are analyzed and discussed. Many of the drawing lessons are conducted outdoors so that students may draw the trees or buildings with which they are familiar. They begin by reviewing previously learned skills in the areas of perspective, shading, figure drawing, and composition. Individualized programs are designed. Periodically, students are required to participate in group critiques to evaluate their progress.

Film Animation

In the film animation class, students plan and execute films using 16-millimeter film equipment. Each student learns the basic principles of film animation through a series of short exercises. He or she then plans a film, creates all the art work, including claymation characters, scenery, and props, and then films the action. The student then edits the finished footage and adds music, voices, and/or sound effects to create a completed film. Students gain competence with the use of film equipment, including the camera, tripod, lighting equipment, light meter, and film splicer.

To produce a film, students have to exercise skills in planning, organization, and sequencing. In the course of each production, many kinds of problems are confronted and solved. In addition, students work on both individual and group projects, developing interpersonal as well as technical skills.

Stage Design

The stage design course is conducted to teach students basic principles of set design and, in the process, improve skills in basic math measurement, scale, drawing, and painting. Students work closely with the drama department as consultants on stage sets. The students read and discuss the design needs of two major plays that are presented in the fall and spring of the school year. They also are called on periodically to build quick sets for the more improvisational video performances of the drama department. Visualization and improvisation are two key elements of this course. Students learn to create something out of nothing. They often scavenge set materials from unlikely sources, an activity that enhances their problem-solving ability, stretches their imaginations, and leads to true creativity. All phases of this course require that they participate, problem solve, and critique their work in a group discussion. Often, students discover design talents they never knew they had. Students make a small (tabletop) set to scale from which they work, learning scale through demonstration and experience. The final stage set is a replica of the tabletop design, which has been refined throughout the year. Students use big materials, produce large tangible results, and expend tremendous energy. Their creations are visible to them and to many appreciative audiences.

Drama

In drama classes, high school students employ a variety of theatrical disciplines that serve to focus on and strengthen various skills. For example, when the classes produce "silent movies" on videotape, students are required to organize and communicate sequential narrative material without the use of language, relying on specifically chosen physical gestures and facial expressions. During work on material by Shakespeare, the young actors exercise their vocal expressiveness. When the class produces short, original plays, students concentrate on the organization of dramatic structure to highlight the cause-and-effect relationship between a character's actions and the course of a story. The production of original films on videotape combines all of the above-mentioned elements. Organized around a regular routine of rehearsal and performance, drama class also provides students with the opportunity to develop and strengthen the social and cooperative skills that any sort of dramatic production demands.

Music

The objective of the high school music class is to directly involve students in music, increase their understanding and appreciation of music, and develop their musical skills. The focus is on ensemble performance, and all students are encouraged to participate using a variety of instruments. Throughout the year, the class explores and experiments with many different musical styles, including rock, blues, classical, rap, metal, punk, pop, country, and jazz.

Fundamentals of music such as scales and chords are introduced at the beginning of the year and are presented within the context of simple musical exercises, enabling students to easily isolate and hear their instruments in relation to the group sound. These forms are gradually expanded on as students master their primary instrument. By mixing rehearsed songs with improvisational "jam" sessions, a student gradually develops more advanced musicianship, learning to distinguish tonality, identify harmony, and play in key. Creativity is stressed at all times as students participate in the composition and arrangement of original music. Some of the resulting pieces are performed before a live audience at the class's final performance.

Music Perspectives

Taught by a talented, young musician, the music perspectives course offers students the opportunity to study and learn about music, musicians, and the history of music. Students systematically are introduced to the fundamental principles of music such as notes, scales, and chords and are familiarized with most of the traditional symphonic instruments. The course focuses primarily on American music of the 20th century and examines, in chronological fashion, many different types and styles of music. Students attempt to understand the musicians and their music in the framework of their times and become better able to understand the relationships between artists and society.

Much of the material for this course is presented through the use of videotaped documentaries, many featuring rare archival film footage. The class also spends time in the music room, where students are able to experiment directly with a variety of musical instruments. By taking a chronological approach, the students are able to analyze the evolution of different types and styles of music and better understand the relationship between these styles. Students learn to appreciate the width of the musical spectrum as they see vastly different styles coexisting and influencing each other. For example, the 1950s saw swing jazz evolve into "be-bop" at the same time that rock and roll was in its infancy. The course covers virtually all forms of music popular in this century including jazz, classical, opera, country and western, blues, rhythm and blues, bluegrass, big band, rock and roll, punk, and rap. Some emphasis is placed on locations of musical prominence—for example, New Orleans at the turn of the century when early jazz began to take root or the Mississippi Delta where many of the early blues players lived. Near the end of the course, the focus is placed on a detailed study of individual musicians. By better understanding these musicians' lives and influence, the students come to appreciate their respective contributions to the world of music.

Arts Pamphlet

The multifaceted senior art project is the production of a pamphlet called DC Area Artists. Students learn and practice time management and communication skills while learning about art and local artists. The students are responsible for the total project, which involves choosing new artists to include in the book (although the school director and the teacher give them choices), making all of the arrangements for interviewing the artists, photographing the artists, and writing articles for the book based on the interviews. Students also complete the steps necessary for updating the entries from interviews with artists in previous years. They participate in all aspects of the book production, from an analysis of the tasks involved to final printing and distribution. Students learn strategies for short- and long-range planning as they apply them to completion of the project.

During this project, students also strengthen practical communication skills such as making appointments, conducting interviews, writing business letters, and writing and editing articles. They also learn basic desktop publishing skills. Varied source materials, including newspaper articles and books, are used to give students the vocabulary and concepts necessary to understand and discuss works of art. Trips to museums, galleries, and the artists' studios are a vital and exciting component of the course. Deadline management is effectively learned through this course.

Apprenticeship Program

As part of their academic program, eleventh-grade students are given the opportunity to work outside the school at selected job sites. An arrangement is made for the student to work Monday through Friday for 3 hours in the morning or 3 hours in the afternoon. This apprenticeship helps the student learn positive work habits and taste success, which can lead to future employment. The experience helps develop skills that are necessary for academic success, and a focus on future goals increases motivation toward both learning and work.

Students are placed in apprenticeships according to their strengths and interests. Apprenticeship sites have included the Smithsonian Institute, the National Zoo, commercial businesses, the Coast Guard, graphic arts studios, bookstores, libraries, hospitals, a radio station, a theater company, a ceramics studio, a frame shop, a preschool, and a national park.

Seminars and workshops review skills and attitudes that are necessary for success in the work place. Students keep journals to record daily activities and events "on the job." They write a detailed report of their work experiences and periodically present oral job reports to ensure reflection on their internship experiences. An employer/ employee award ceremony is the culminating activity for this course.

SENIOR SEMINAR/ETHICS

Senior Seminar/Ethics explores some of the persisting questions that have challenged the minds of great thinkers and social activists throughout human history. Some of these questions include, "What are human beings really like; selfish and greedy or generous and kind?," "Why should I be a good person?," and, "In a free society, does anyone have a right to tell another person what is right or wrong?"

During the senior seminar, students discuss the works of a diverse group of philosophers, activists, musicians, poets, and so forth. Some of these include Socrates, Aristotle, John Stuart Mill, Karl Marx, Mahatma Gandhi, Abraham Heschel, Martin Luther King, Jr., and Maya Angelou. The most important work is that of the students themselves as they learn to think, process, and act upon these ideas in the context of their own lives.

Through readings, film, music, art, cartoons, and daily entries in a journal, class members integrate the thoughts of others with their own experiences as they develop a personal statement of ethics and a code of moral behavior for the class and the larger society.

SCHOOL STORE/BUSINESS

With a homemade awning, signs of sale items, and a primitive sales brochure, The Lab School student-run store opens at 11:30 A.M. daily in time for lunch. The store, which primarily sells food but also some general supplies and t-shirts, is located on the side of a multipurpose room with a kitchen behind it. Students are responsible for the day-to-day operations of The Lab School student store, which they named "The Dragon's Lair."

The student store, which operates like a class, addresses many areas that students need to function successfully in everyday life. Students learn basic math skills throughout the year as they are applied to day-to-day situations. Some of the many mathematical areas covered are money math, estimation, rounding of numbers, personal finance, bookkeeping, and the meaning of time. Learning takes place through sales and counting change as well as through teaching games and cooking. In addition, students are exposed to the different elements required to run an effective business. Students are responsible for taking inventory, placing orders, dealing with distributors, paying bills (check writing and checkbook balancing), and keeping spreadsheets on the computer. Students learn how to follow a set schedule, sign in and out when they come to work, and deal with the public as well as obtain an overall sense of what is required to be a responsible member of a work team. Advertising requires problem-solving abilities. Students produce their own sales catalog, with drawings or photographs of items for purchase, and distribute it to all divisions within the school. They also have to invent other ways to sell their products, such as posters on bulletin boards or flyers on classroom doors.

LANGUAGE

Hard-to-teach learners often have language impairments. Because they do not have proper control of their native language, learning a foreign language becomes an arduous task. Use of all art forms makes the study of a foreign language quite effective.

Spanish

The goals of the Spanish program are to build students' general language and communication skills as well as to broaden their familiarity with the Hispanic world. The approach to teaching Spanish is functional, aiming at a linguistic level needed to accomplish the daily tasks of life.

Once they have built their skills satisfactorily, students converse among themselves, using Spanish for truly communicative purposes such as soliciting and providing previously unshared information. Students compose a cumulative narrative about themselves as they learn how to speak more Spanish. Students are introduced to approximately 900 words in the Spanish curriculum.

During Spanish class, students also make handicrafts centered around the Mexican Day of the Dead, see Spanish art at the National Gallery of Art, watch Spanish movies, and prepare Hispanic foods. They listen to Spanish music and poetry, study Spanish architecture and design, and learn about the classics of Spanish dance.

The arts are central to the teaching of a foreign language, particularly because Lab School students experience great difficulty mastering their own language, so mastering another language requires every kind of multisensory assistance.

GENERAL CURRICULUM

Whether it's American literature, world history, D.C. history, or calculus being taught in high school, experiential learning takes place. Pictures are used, projects are made, activities are engaged in, and, when possible, the mind, the body, and the spirit are all awakened.

The arts are integrated into almost every subject. Staff are hired to present material to the different senses, and in-service training of teachers reinforces this. The Lab School curriculum demands that teachers keep educating themselves not only from books, but through photography, visual arts, artifacts, and the Internet.

GROUP PROJECTS AND PRODUCTIONS

Students at The Lab School of Washington have participated in a number of group projects and productions (see color insert). For example, a local department store gave us remnants of carpets. A visiting artist came in and talked to the elementary school students about making something out of these carpets. The children decided they wanted to make a huge carpet mural to cover a wall (12′ × 8′). Fifty Lab School children between the ages of 7 and 12 decided that they wanted the mural to be called, "A Peaceable Kingdom." First, they drew their animals on large pieces of brown paper. Then, to their great excitement, they were allowed to use X-acto knives to cut out the animals by tracing the brown paper with pieces of rug under it. Once the animals were cut out, the students looked at their animals and decided they needed to make a river, so they chose a blue rug and cut it to become a winding river.

Then a few of the students insisted that they needed to have one child in the carpet art with all the animals. Therefore, they drew the child on the brown paper and used the drawing to cut the carpet using the X-acto knife. Then, as a group, the students decided on placement of animals, the river, and the boy. The artist suggested that they needed a sky, a horizon. The students then affixed these carpet pieces to the wall with nails and glue, producing a magnificent scene that now decorates the Board Room of The Lab School. Many years later, students still point out and say to visitors and former students who return for a visit, "I nailed that panda in." "We took this fur off a lady's coat to give that monkey a beard. She let us do it and I glued it!" And, "See the boy shepherd with a staff, I drew him and cut him out!"

When Lab School students are learning about other cultures, they discover through hands-on experiences how new knowledge of one subject relates to another. During a study of our African Heritage, students became fascinated with African print patterns and tiled the ceiling in the dance drama room with them. One student asked if Picasso had been to Africa because he saw similarities to African sculpture in Picasso's work; therefore, a study of some of Picasso's works that appeared to be influenced by Africa took place. While studying water pollution, some students took remnants of a rug and made another wall-sized mural (8' × 25'), this time of clear water and ocean animals and of pollution and a nearby factory. They discussed the fact that the planet earth was mostly water, located sources of water, and identified ways in which humans are drying up the earth. Their work on the carpet art reinforced their studies of water and water pollution.

A reading of the *Ramayana*, a great epic poem of ancient India, led students to become intrigued by the Monkey God, Hanuman, who was able to do almost anything he desired to do. Consequently, students made a 9-foot, two-dimensional cutout sculpture of Hanuman out of marine plywood. Various students sealed, painted, and bejeweled the sculpture. The students took soda bottle caps and made jeweled belts and a hat out of them and then made armor from aluminum. Hanuman now is bolted to the roof of one of The Lab School's buildings where the students can point to it and say what part they played in its construction. They have not forgotten who Hanuman is.

For The Lab School's 25th birthday celebration, the students created an 11-foot friendly dragon made of heavy plywood and painted it kelly green. The dragon has become the school's mascot. The ceremony during which the dragon was deemed school mascot consisted of stories and myths about dragons presented by students and faculty; then the high school students carried in the behemoth dragon for placement on campus as the school band trumpeted their march.

For The Lab School's 30th birthday, the students made a 10-foot sculpture of Ganesh—the Hindu god of good fortune and remover of all obstacles—out of old pipes and various tractor parts including fenders for ears and tail lights from an old car for the red eyes. Experiences such as this lead to further discussions about India—its past and present, geography, literature, science, developing countries, and government, in addition to a whole world of subjects.

As new buildings rose on campus during The Lab School's 33rd year, the architectural design class created a fountain for a courtyard depicting a dragon and a child reading a book together, protected and encircled by a steady stream of water.

Pieces made out of wall tile that have drawings on them (done with Craypas and a polyethylene covering that makes them look like they have been fired in a kiln) hang in various locations in the school. Five-year-olds made a wall piece of houses. Ten-year-olds produced masks. Twelve-year-olds used a space theme. Fifteen-year-olds created the signs of the zodiac circling the sun and the moon.

All of these group projects have demanded a great deal of brainstorming, planning, organizing, and decision making—an appreciation of and a respect for each other's work. After all of the planning, the groups have produced works that adorn the walls of the school and continue to bring the students much adulation. Seeing their own work on public display helps build their sense of self-worth and pride.

The Lab School Approach uses projects, life experiences, concrete materials and all art forms to create active learning, enhance sensory motor development, and promote personal, academic, and intellectual development. The curriculum presents students with experiences that they missed in the preschool years in a sophisticated manner that respects the chronological ages and intelligence of the children. The curriculum is designed to teach students what they need to know through what they like to do and can do. Teacher training is the ultimate key to the development of a rich, diverse, intellectual curriculum. The choice of quality human beings to be the teachers and their ability to individualize material in visual, concrete ways produces effective learning.

The Lab School's Visual Arts
Teachers Speak Out

In this chapter, visual arts teachers answer a series of questions regarding their particular craft that tell how their form of art benefits exceptional learners. They describe important routines and procedures in their art classes and then take one project and explain it in great detail, step-by-step, with drawings, to completion. This chapter is designed to encourage other teachers to try these projects in their classrooms and adapt them as needed.

Following most of the steps is an important outcome of the process: using each project as a take-off to help you design other projects is another part of the process. The general attitudes of enthusiasm, acceptance, appreciation of diversity, and optimism also are important ingredients for success. Creativity alone, as wonderful as it is, is not enough. Outstanding art teachers nurture their students through art. This is why so many children, with or without talent, spend time in the art rooms of their school. The art room is a magnet that seems to draw them in and give them comfort. Obviously the students are attracted by the vibrant colors and excitement of art, but I can't help but believe that the human qualities that art teachers often possess also draw them in.

Encouraging students to talk about what they have created is crucial for exceptional learners, who have trouble verbalizing their experiences, organizing projects, and learning sequences. They need to verbalize their experiences in order to internalize them and to help the experiences become part of their being. Explaining to another student how a project is made, sequence by sequence, also helps the student organize another project and increases the student's vocabulary and word fluency. Sometimes it stimulates their critical thinking, so they compare what they have just done with other activities and imagine new possibilities.

The projects described in this chapter can help build cognitive, language, math, science, and socialization skills. How can these skills not have a significant effect on a child's development and knowledge base?

Woodwork
A Conversation with Dieter Zander

What is the special benefit of this art form?

Woodwork has the advantage of teaching academic skills in a real-life, hands-on environment. Whereas some students might not be interested in math and geometry in the classroom, quite a few will respond very differently in a workshop environment where math and geometry are only the means needed to produce something of their own choice and imagination. In contrast to sculpting or other art forms that utilize wood, success with woodwork projects relies heavily on careful planning and good organization. In the hands-on environment of the workshop, a student can learn to predict the outcome of an action from numerous previous trial-and-error experiences. Unlike many classroom situations in which problems must be solved in isolation, woodworking produces the best results when the students can integrate different parts of their internalized knowledge and work together to apply their knowledge simultaneously. In this way, woodworking closely resembles and can help prepare students for real-life situations.

We use pine and fir for woodwork, which are readily available at local lumber yards. As soft woods, they are fairly easy to saw, nail, carve, whittle, shape, drill, sand, and paint. For children who are just learning to use woodworking hand tools, they present an excellent balance of resistance and yield to their efforts. The wood is relatively light, which permits even smaller students to move fairly large pieces. The material also is quite forgiving. Even very visible mistakes can be fixed by either replacing the part or repeating the mistake to keep a symmetry.

Which parts of The Lab School Woodwork Program have proven most helpful to the success of exceptional learners?

Simple, clear procedures are most helpful. Everything, from the beginning idea for a project, to the plan sketch, to the preparation of the work area, to the actual work, is kept as simple and clear as possible. Depending on the students' ability to understand, process, memorize, and follow directions, students are given one step at a time; if necessary, the instructor demonstrates with a concrete example.

To ensure success, all project designs must have been previously tried and tested by the instructor. The entire process of construction, from planning to finishing a completed project, is done with a step-by-step approach. Students are required to verbally recall these construction steps either to the instructor or, better yet, to another student who intends to build a similar project before the finished object can be taken from the shop.

Plan sketches are kept on clipboards that are hung on marked areas on a wall. To plan a project's dimensions, the students either measure an existing model that is of a

The Making of a Box

All students coming to the workshop for the first time must make a simple box. Young students and students with the least skill are provided with precut parts.

Materials:

Glue	Pine or fir lumber of 3/4" thickness
Nails	Flat latex or acrylic paint
Pencils	Measuring squares
Sandpaper	Other typical workshop hand tools
Yardsticks	Handsaws
Hammers	

Steps:

1. All work starts with a simple sketch on paper to record measurements of length, width, and height, which teaches students to use a yardstick.
2. Select a board of appropriate width for the box's height or width. Measure along the board for the desired length. Make a pencil mark. Draw a line across the board at a right angle using a square.
3. Find the correct position for the board and the student's body before starting to saw.
4. Learn to use a handsaw with the instructor's help and cut the board along the pencil line.
5. When all parts have been cut, the instructor marks the spots where nails must be hammered part-way in. The instructor demonstrates how this is done.
6. The instructor demonstrates the gluing process with the first two box parts. He shows the students where and how to apply the glue and how to line up the two parts, then hammer in the nails.
7. The student glues and nails the rest of the box.

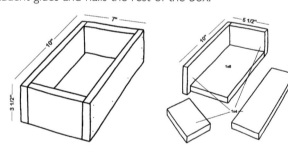

8. The box may now need light sanding to remove splinters.
9. To finish the box, the student chooses between painting it or sanding it more carefully.
10. When painting is the choice, only one color of paint is used each day (to prevent messy color mixes). Because glossy paints tend to accentuate imperfections, latex or acrylic flat wall paint or semi-flat enamel is used.
11. The very last step before the student can take home the box (or any other project) is the student's recall (verbal if possible, otherwise visual) of all the construction steps in their actual order.

size similar to the intended project or measure the material in a mock-up arrangement. Students who have difficulty visualizing shapes in sizes larger than the plan sketch are encouraged to draw the actual intended size on the wall or on the floor. All measurements are for outside dimensions, not for individual parts. For projects that have to fit the student's body size (like chairs, tables, or go-carts) the material to be used is marked around the student whenever possible.

The students take ownership of their completed projects and, therefore, are able to share their success with their friends and family at school and at home. For many students, it is very important that their completed projects get taken home immediately following completion. Very often, when a student's projects, especially first projects, are left in the shop for a long time, students will lose interest in their work.

What guidelines do you use?

Students are strongly encouraged to choose project ideas that match their individual skills and interests. They are encouraged to create their own designs based on their imagination. If necessary, the complexity of a student's original plan can be either decreased or increased.

Students often are unaware that they are learning basic academic skills such as math and geometry during the planning and construction process. Whenever tasks prove too difficult for a student, alternative methods are sought, encouraged, and suggested. For example, to find an exact center, a piece of paper or string measuring the entire length can be folded in half. For the center of a square or rectangle, the crossing point of two straight lines connecting diagonally opposite corners will give the result. To divide an uneven number by two, nails can be divided into two separate piles with the last one to be clipped in half.

Competition is discouraged. The result of a student's work is judged solely on the individual's effort and progress. Because its properties demand careful planning to ensure a successfully constructed, durable project, the wood itself truly is the best teacher.

What is the classroom routine?

Students form a line and are asked to be silent for a few seconds before entering or leaving the workshop. This enables the students to disengage themselves from any previous activity and helps them to "change gears." At the same time, it permits the instructor to look for signs of possible difficulties with focusing and listening to directions.

In the shop the students receive help by taking turns. Their names are posted in alphabetical order clearly visible from anywhere in the room.

Toward the end of a period, 5 minutes before students leave for their next classes, students are asked to store their own project parts and plan drawings. In addition, the students are expected to return all of the tools, regardless of who has used them, to a specific storage place. Each child has a place to store his or her plan drawings and project parts. The larger, frequently used tools, such as handsaws, hammers, squares, and yardsticks, have their shapes outlined on a pegboard on the wall.

Graphic Arts
A Conversation with Karen Hanish

What is the special benefit of this art form?

Many students with learning disabilities already consider themselves failures when they first arrive in the art classroom. Accustomed to their difficulties in traditional academic areas, they expect nothing different of themselves in the arts. However, creating art and experimenting with a variety of media is an easy way to introduce students to the notion that there are many ways to solve a problem.

Which parts of The Lab School Graphic Arts Program have proven most helpful to the success of exceptional learners?

The methods used in the art room can affect the students' ability to solve problems in other classes as well as their everyday lives. By participating in the fine arts, students will learn to

- Take risks: Art by nature is a form of self-expression. As students work with various materials throughout the school year, they will find ways to give form to thoughts or feelings that they might have had difficulty describing previously. This is especially true for children with learning disabilities, who may have problems with writing and language skills. The ability to express their thoughts in this new visual way motivates them to initiate their own ideas when working on projects and to try different approaches in order to solve a problem.

- Learn social skills: Art classes take place in a studio atmosphere in which students must learn to share space and materials. The relaxed atmosphere of the art room also allows for the development of conversational skills while working on projects.

- Hone critical thinking: Encouraging students to talk about their own work as well as the work of others helps students to understand the process of analysis. Teaching students about tools they can use to analyze art, such as the five elements of design (i.e., line, shape, space, color, texture), gives them a way to begin a focused study or discussion of artwork. This idea of parts making up a whole can help to introduce the student to analysis across the academic spectrum. Reviewing the process of a project upon completion helps students appreciate sequencing and prioritization.

Famous Character Linoleum Block Print

Make a linoleum print using a famous character as the subject. The character can be drawn from literature, politics, science, history, or art. Printmaking is an excellent way to explore all of the different elements of art in one project. Older students (ages 11 years and up) can use linoleum blocks and cutters; younger students can use sheets of compressed foam and ballpoint pens or nails to make a print block.

Materials:

Newspaper (under inking and printing work areas)
Piece of glass (or styrofoam tray) for ink
Brayer (hard roller)
Pieces of paper, precut and stacked in a clean area
Water-soluble color ink
Barren (or wooden spoon) for hand printing
Clean area, rack, or table space to put finished
   prints to dry

Steps:

1. *Prepare the block*: Each student must choose a character and find an image of that character or create an image of his or her own. Resources might include picture files, the Internet, graphics from record or CD cases, magazines, or books. A close-up, detailed image of the face of the individual is best. Students also must design the layout of their print and incorporate elements in the design that will convey why their chosen character is famous. The students are creating a visual report and must make choices about what they want to reflect in the print. Once the students have chosen their image, photocopy the image to increase the contrast. This helps to better define the positive and negative spaces as well as the visual balance of the final composition.

2. *Transfer the image to the linoleum block*: To do this, tape a piece of carbon paper, carbon side down, to the linoleum. Place the image of the character on top of the carbon paper. Have students use a red ballpoint pen to trace the image. The red ink helps them to keep track of what they have traced. The students are usually fascinated by this transfer, and it is an excellent way for them to focus on line and shape. When this step is complete, take the carbon paper off the block and have students color the parts of the image that they want to appear on the final print. This also is the time to draw any texture that is desired in the final print. Some students with learning disabilities may have trouble visualizing the outcome of the print and will need assistance in deciding which areas are to be cut out of the printing block. The fun, of course, is watching the "ah ha!" moment when students see their first print completed. If a student is having particular difficulties with the process, you might pair him or her up with another student.

3. *Cut the block*: Before cutting the print block, students must learn how to safely use the linoleum tools. Because students usually feel "grown up" using the sharp tools and special equipment, they likely will be willing to learn the process of setting up their work areas and using safe cutting processes.

Using a bench hook for the linoleum is a good way to keep the block and linoleum cutters from slipping. During the project, students will need to be reminded of how to hold the tools, and it is a good idea to have the students keep one hand on their laps. It might also be useful to offer a prize to those students who do not slip and cut themselves with the sharp tools. (During the last 2 years, only two bandages have been issued in my classroom!)

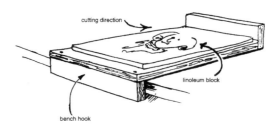

4. *Make the print:* When the students have successfully cut all of the lines, shapes, and textures into their block, they are ready to print.
    *   Begin by rolling out a small amount of ink into a narrow rectangle, approximately the same width as the brayer, onto the piece of glass.

    *   Next, use the brayer to apply an even coat of ink over the entire surface of the linoleum block cut.

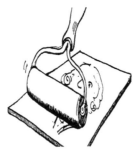

    *   Then, place the inked block onto clean newspaper with the inked side up.
    *   Holding the clean printing paper by two opposite corners, lower it onto the plate and immediately press down a small area to adhere it to the surface. DO NOT allow it to shift.

- Using the barren or spoon, apply pressure evenly from the center to the edges of the paper. If you use a thin paper, students can see the ink as it transfers to the paper. Do not pull up the paper until every inch has been pressed.
- Slowly, starting from one corner, pull the paper up from the linoleum block.

- Place the print on a clean surface away from the printing area to dry.
- Repeat the process for each print of your edition.

5. *Have students present their prints to the class, discussing and recalling the process as well as the content of their prints:* Each student will come away from the project with new skills and problem-solving abilities. They also will have a tangible product that showcases their success.

Plaster Art and Painting
A Conversation with Kelly McVearry

What is the special benefit of these art forms?

Art offers inherent problem-solving activities in an exciting form and makes a bridge to other academic areas. Projects expose children to different modes of organization, as each project requires a different organizational strategy. Art helps to cultivate longer attention spans. Engagement in an intriguing project keeps a student focused.

Art instills a respect for quality. The process of creation, of being fully engaged, is more important than any specific product, but a visible accomplishment can also be a source of pride.

Which parts of The Lab School Plaster Art and Painting Program have proven most helpful to the success of exceptional learners?

Because students with learning disabilities have great difficulty with part–whole relationships, it is helpful to assemble diverse elements into a meaningful whole, such as a sculpture made from found objects or junk. Students with learning disabilities are disorganized and cannot figure out what to do first, next, and last; therefore, projects such as sewing patchwork parts into a wiggly snake can help. Abstract and divergent thinking skills are a hidden layer of learning that an artist can promote through manipulation of concrete objects—or junk! If a child needs to develop imagination and overcome fixed meanings, I present a table of old shoes. I ask the child to transform one shoe into a sculpture using her imagination. I provide fabrics of many textures, paints, Sculpey, string, sand, marbles, wood platforms, and lots of glue. A loafer becomes a frog, a high heel poses as a cactus, a boot is soon a boat.

Art also provides many opportunities for muscle control, such as making pottery on a potter's wheel or making plaster casting sculpture. Fine motor control is aided by tying knots or threading a needle, making jewelry from beads or pasta, using wire, and drawing a self-portrait. The "Art Olympics" places children on teams for events that turn into fun activities; students learn tedious but essential skills, such as cutting accurately along a wavy line, squeezing controlled dabs of glue instead of messy pools of it, and putting tops back on markers and paint tubes.

All of these activities help students develop social skills as they solve problems with their peers, engage in decision making, and work out organizational strategies as part of a team.

What is the classroom routine?

Because each child craves order as much as freedom, it is important to maintain classroom organization. Each child has an assigned seat with a corresponding workspace. Markers, scissors, pencils, and so forth are kept in separate, colored buckets. They

Plaster Casting Sculpture

This project promotes learning on two levels—technical skill through the creation of a no-fail, sophisticated product and the diagnosis/remediation of impulsivity and hyperactivity. The project enlarges attention spans and enhances tactile and visual discrimination. It promotes awareness of the body in space and space management. It serves as a vehicle for the teaching of history (Leonardo da Vinci's ornithopter), science (exothermic reactions), and art history (George Segal).

Materials:

Plastercraft (a brand of plaster-coated surgical gauze)
Plastic trash bags
Vaseline
Water

Steps:

1. Cut the Plastercraft into different size strips (e.g., thin, 2 inches long, 2-inch squares).
2. Cover the work surface with plastic trash bags.
3. Cover one of the child's hands with Vaseline.
4. Dip the strips of Plastercraft in the water.
5. Beginning with the fingers, wrap the strips around the child's hand.
6. Allow the Plastercraft to dry thoroughly, and carefully slide the casting from the child's hand.
7. Paint the casting to finish your project.

always are stored on the same shelf at an appropriate height for the children's age group. Every project is broken down into small steps. Material is provided only for the specific step or process on which the child is working.

We have a visible system for behavior management. A panel with pockets made from colorful felt or card stock hangs on the wall. Each pocket has a child's name on it. A tangible reward related to the current class project is given in recognition of appropriate and desirable behavior. For instance, paper broomsticks were awarded as the group was constructing a life-size sculpture of a witch. A broomstick was placed immediately in a student's pocket, visible to the whole class, when that student exhibited an appropriate behavior.

At the conclusion of each class, all broomsticks were removed from the pockets and counted out loud; then, part of a large drawing of a broom with numbered sections was colored in. When the goal was reached (the whole drawing was colored in), there was a group reward in which all of the students participated. In this case, the reward was experiencing a multisensory haunted house created in the Art Department by the teacher.

Clean-up time can be a war zone. Effective, smooth clean-ups necessitate a keen strategy, and ours is always tied to the behavior management program—typically the thematic panel with individual name pockets on it. In other words, clean-up becomes a game, not a chore; it is an opportunity to be rewarded for responsible behavior rather than a chance to be reprimanded.

Another clean-up strategy is the use of a loud timer. Making the shift from art-making to clean-up into a wordless procedure by setting a timer at the beginning of each class removes the element of clean-up that feels like an arbitrary decision. A timer makes clean-up occur automatically and without debate.

For young elementary children who have art five times per week, the middle of the week is a free-draw day. The class itself remains structured in terms of rules and organization of materials, but the children can dance while they draw, bring in their favorite music, and draw without inhibition. The children look forward to a break from the regular, long-term project, and their motivation is promoted. For the educator, Wednesday can be a diagnostic time—a chance to observe individual cognitive and motor skills, such as how students hold a pencil, organize materials, or make symbols.

Some projects can be taken home when they are completed. But it is often valuable to keep others until the end of the year. A student will know how much he or she has improved when the evidence is there for all to see. Tangible, visible progress is a powerful confidence booster.

Sculpture
A Conversation with Frank Cappello

What are the special benefits of this art form?

This project can be adapted readily to students from ages 10 to adult.

Which parts of The Lab School Sculpture Program have proven most helpful to the success of exceptional learners?

Although the projects we do in the sculpture program use simple and inexpensive materials, they address several common learning difficulties, including organization, attention, and fine motor impairments. In order to build something large and creative, students first must master the basic building concept and manipulative skills required to make a simple tetrahedron out of straws and paper clips. Students are highly motivated to follow the steps in sequence because if they skip steps, large sculptures are easily crushed or fall apart. Students quickly develop a feel for the physical limitations of their constructions, yet they tend to discover their own variations of construction within those limitations. Students who have difficulty drawing or sculpting realistically can succeed in making beautiful abstract objects with this simple technique.

Even though all of the students are using the same building technique, each project is unique. Students take great pride in making an object of their own design. They both create and solve their own particular structural and aesthetic problems as the work progresses. The project can be individual or collaborative, and ideas for building basic shapes can be shared freely, fostering a spirit of collaboration in a population of students that often is self-centered.

What guidelines do you use?

Teachers usually offer a simple basis for introducing the students to the fundamentals of measurement, geometry, architecture, and of course, sculpture. Students not only get to put geometry to practical use, but they also develop efficient sequencing strategies while gaining much-needed motor planning and fine motor skills exercise. Students can produce beautiful objects through the repetition of a simple sequence of skills. Students quickly begin to discover unique ways to solve the design problems that they create, and some find that shared ideas or even collaborative projects are the most productive or interesting.

Geometric Straw Sculpture

This project works best with exceptional learners in grades 6–12.

Materials:

Fine-tip marker   Plastic drinking straws (Dixie brand seem to work best)
Paper   Ruler (12 inches)
Paper clips (#2 steel)   Scissors
Pencil

Steps:

1. The instructor starts by demonstrating that a cube made of 12 linked straws lacks structural integrity and will fall over. This is compared to a tetrahedron that is self-supporting in all directions and is made of only six straws.
2. The teacher uses a pencil and ruler to demonstrate how to make a template that can be used to mark each straw at the midpoint so that it can be cut into equal lengths. Full-length straws can be used for larger projects, but some students with fine motor control problems may find short straws easier to manipulate without bending them. To make a template, the student draws a line the length of the straw on a piece of paper. The paper is cut at both ends of the line, then folded in half. Laying each straw on the paper template, the students mark the center points of the straws with a fine-tip marker.

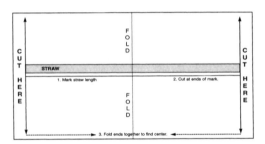

3. Once three straws have been cut to make six segments, the instructor demonstrates how to insert the fat ends of the paper clips into the straws and how to link the clips together. The students then use this system to link three straws into a triangle.

4. Students are highly motivated to find the fastest way to connect straws without pulling apart the existing links. Paper clips are inserted most easily if squeezed and pushed gently but firmly near the insertion point.

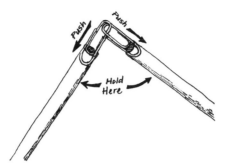

5. The instructor shows how to add three more straws, one to each vertex of the triangle, to form the tetrahedron.

6. Once all of the students have understood the basic principle of adding triangles together to create a tetrahedron, they should be encouraged to experiment freely with the building system to produce original works of art. Advanced students can try experiments with variable length straws or painted finished straws to make representations of real objects or animals.

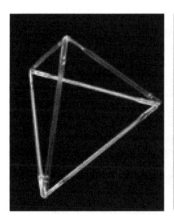
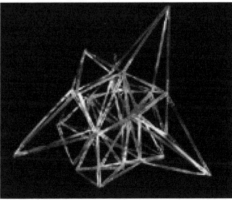

7. Students will create and solve their own particular structural and aesthetic problems as the work progresses. Projects can be individual or collaborative, and ideas for building basic shapes can be shared freely. Students who have difficulty drawing or sculpting realistically can succeed in making beautiful abstract objects with this simple technique.

8. Painted or natural finished sculptures are best displayed by hanging them with 4- to 6-lb. monofilament fishing line. Although larger works can be fragile when handled, they are extremely light for their size and will retain their structural integrity for months if left undisturbed, especially if they have been spray painted.

Architectural Design
A Conversation with Mark Jarvis

What is the special benefit of this art form?

Architectural design gives exceptional learners an opportunity to improve their academic skills through techniques that are more surprising and engaging than they expect. While students work on their projects—designing and building a dream house—they learn about linear and two-point perspective and improve their math and measurement skills. High school students in this class take part in a sophisticated, college-level activity while using simple, readily available material.

Which parts of The Lab School Architectural Design Program have proven most helpful to the success of exceptional learners?

Most people are enchanted by miniaturization. I think everyone can remember at some point in their lives being fascinated with doll houses, model trains, or museum dioramas. Architects use expensively produced models to help their clients visualize their designs. When students take a two-dimensional design and begin to build it three-dimensionally, they begin slowly to visualize what previously were very abstract concepts of scale, proportion, perspective, and geometry. They are solidifying these concepts in a manner that is creative, artistic, and different from previous experiences.

What guidelines do you use?

Organizational skills are enhanced by requiring each student to design his own portfolio, box, folder, or other device that will keep his work organized. Each student will be responsible for a large variety of materials and will need to keep track of when he begins the model. Organization is critical given that it may take as many as four weeks to complete the model. Neatness counts given the precision required to complete the projects.

The students develop teamwork and social skills through team-built models, which provide a less stressful opportunity for success for the occasional student who, given the nature or degree of his or her disability, will have more success when paired with another student. Some students may be more adept at cutting and building, others at drawing and measurement. Learning cooperation and shared success will affect all areas of the students' education.

In the interest of providing students with a nonthreatening, successful experience, we emphasize that mistakes often can be turned into surprising and beautiful additions to the model. Remaining flexible and encouraging is critical with students with learning disabilities.

Model House

All structures are made from cardboard, which can be cut with an X-acto knife and can stand on its own when scored or folded.

Materials:

Mat board

X-acto knives (A thorough lesson in safety should precede any model building. Fresh blades are essential; it is disastrous and dangerous to ask a student to work with a dull blade.)

Balsa wood (This is a very light-weight wood that is easily cut. This is used for architectural details and landscaping. It can be purchased through any art supply catalog or craft/hobby shop.)

One-inch rigid foam insulation (This building material can be found in most large-scale hardware and building supply stores. The student should be provided with a piece large enough to accommodate his model and its surrounding landscape.)

Elmer's glue (Everything in the model is held together with this glue.)

Improvised materials

Steps:

1. The students begin by drawing a design of their dream house. Extravagance and creativity are stressed here. The students are given many source books and magazines to see how architects have expressed themselves and solved design problems. Field trips to study unusual houses and buildings are an excellent adjunct.
2. Once the students have designed their dream houses, they are encouraged to begin to plan the landscape around their houses. Where are the trees, sidewalks, decks, pools, and so forth? Once landscaping has been decided, the students are ready to build.
3. Based on their drawings, the students make a base for their house out of foam insulation. Two or three sheets of insulation can be laminated together with Elmer's glue to create a sandwich that can be carved easily with a serrated blade to create peaks and valleys in the landscape.

4. The students then complete a rigid mat board footprint or floor plan, which is glued to the foam base. Students must focus on measurement and cutting precise right angles using a clear plastic square. This is the most important stage of the process, given that the floor plan template serves as the foundation.

5. Students then cut the walls of their house out of mat board. Glue is sparingly applied to contact sides of two adjoining walls, and they are held in position much as one would build a house of cards. When these first two walls dry, they will be very strong. The house becomes easier to build as each wall goes up.

6. Once the walls and roof have been glued into place, the students can work on the landscape around their houses. This is where the improvised materials come into play. Steel wool can be used for shrubbery, chopsticks for deck supports, and blue cellophane for skylights and swimming pools.

Film Animation
A Conversation with Ruth Schwartz

What is the special benefit of this art form?

In the animation class, students learn the basics of film animation utilizing 16-millimeter motion picture equipment and a variety of animation techniques. Each student completes a series of basic animation exercises, works on a group project with his class as a whole, and then does an individual project.

We teach animation for several reasons. On one level, the skills utilized in the production of a film are analogous to those used in producing an academic research paper. Students must plan their project; create an outline; do research on how scenery should look; create each piece of scenery, character, and prop; film the action according to their plan; then put the pieces together into a coherent whole, adding music, sound effects, and dialogue. In each stage of the process there are problems to be solved and new materials and methods to learn.

Another important piece of the program is the positive feedback that the students get from their work. They are impressed with their own results, and others are impressed, too. Films produced by our animation classes have won various awards and have been featured on PBS and HBO.

A conventional movie camera normally takes 24 images, or frames, per second; video cameras usually record 30 frames per second. Each image differs slightly from the preceding one. A shot of a person waving at the camera would capture one image of the person with arms overhead, the next image with arms slightly lower, and so forth. Because of the phenomenon known as persistence of vision—the human brain retains an image for a fraction of a second, even as a new image is processed—these frames look like fluid motion to the viewer when projected at a rapid speed. To animate an object, the camera is adjusted to take only one frame at a time. The animator takes one or two frames, moves the object, takes one or two more frames, moves the object again, and so forth. When the frames are displayed in rapid succession, the object appears to be in motion. This is the principle at work in all animation.

There is something magical about creating a figure of clay or pencil lines, then watching it come to life on a screen. The allure of animation often provides a powerful motivation for a student who may be reluctant or resistant to conventional classroom activities. Through the creation of an animated film, the student is exercising skills in planning, organization, and research. He is learning specific technical skills. He also is learning that he can surmount a series of problems and obstacles to create a finished product that often surpasses his expectations. His film is concrete evidence of his achievement, and the laughter, applause, and admiration of an audience affirms his success.

Animation Project

Materials:

See section entitled, "How is the classroom equipped?" on page 109.

Steps:

1. *Brainstorming:* The most difficult part of a film often is coming up with an idea. The students involved sit with me, and we toss ideas around. I usually take notes, because writing is an issue for many of my students.
2. *Storyboarding:* When a student or group comes up with an idea, the next step is a storyboard—basically, an outline of what will happen in the film and how the film will look. Again, I usually act as scribe. A storyboard is a series of sketches with captions, resembling a comic strip.

3. *Research and construction:* Students must learn about the elements that will appear in the film. If the main character is a samurai, for example, what does a samurai look like? If the setting is a mountain, how does a mountain really look? What are its colors? What are its shapes? Picture research, using the resources explained previously, helps answer these questions. Once the student has an image of what he'd like to make, construction begins. I help by showing students how to break tasks down into manageable chunks. This can be a particular problem for students with learning disabilities. Sculpting a clay character may seem impossible, but every child can learn to roll a ball of clay, which becomes a head, and so on, piece by piece.

    Sets are made with a variety of materials. For interior scenes, we usually begin with a cardboard box, which is cut down to include only three sides: a "floor" and two "walls." Furniture can be crafted of cardboard, balsa wood, and other materials. Exterior scenes are done on a countertop, and can be as simple as laying down a sheet of green construction paper for grass and thumb-tacking a sheet of blue paper to the wall for sky. Sets can also be quite complex, with papier-mâché mountains and painted sunsets or flowing rivers made of plastic wrap.

4. *Filming:* The actual animation requires a great deal of focus. Because it takes a lot of patience and both the film stock and the processing are quite expensive, I place a high premium on getting it right the first time. Unless a student is quite experienced, I work one-to-one with him to get the camera and lights set up and to watch and advise as he animates.

    Suppose a scene calls for a character to stand on a lonely road waiting for a lift. A 3-foot long countertop is made into a miniature stage set, featuring a road of cut cardboard, a construction paper sky, and a couple of cacti made of clay. A clay animal skull lies by the side of the road. The hitchhiker, also made of clay, has been placed in position with his thumb up.

    Two students, one acting as cameraperson and one as animator, will be working together. The students position the camera and look through the lens to frame their shot. They choose a medium close-up, showing the hitchhiker. They need to check that the camera is focused, which they do by measuring the distance from the character to the camera and setting the camera lens. They use a light meter to measure the light falling on the scene, and set the camera appropriately. Now they are ready to film.

    The cameraperson takes 24 frames to begin—one second of the hitchhiker standing still. Now the animator moves in. She turns the character's head slightly to the right and steps back. The cameraperson takes two frames ($1/12$ second). The animator moves back in and turns the character's head slightly, again to the right. Again she steps out of the way and the cameraperson shoots two frames. Once more the animator turns the character's head slightly to the right and steps back. This time the animator takes 24 frames; the character will be looking to the right for a full second of film.

    Shooting continues in this manner as the hitchhiker waits for a car, then drops his thumb in despair and sighs. (Sound will be added to this scene later, after processing and editing.) In this 45-minute class period, the students will shoot a total of 5 seconds of film.

5. *Editing:* Each roll of film contains about 2 minutes of footage, and because film is costly, we use a full roll before we process it. (Unlike videotape, film is not reusable, and it must be sent to a professional film lab for processing.) Each roll of film will have scenes from multiple productions. After the George Washington scene, for example, a different class will film a scene from its film, "Goldilocks and the Three Rats." Then a third class will film part of its project. When the film comes back to us, the students will need to edit it, physically cutting the various scenes apart from each other and reassembling them in the proper order, using a device called a splicer.

6. *Sound:* Eventually, the entire film is shot, processed, and cut into sequence. The finished product is transferred to video for ease of handling. Now, the film needs music, voices, and sound effects. There are various ways to do this. Sometimes we use a VCR with an "audio dub" feature that enables the user to record sound onto a videotape without erasing the picture. Students assemble what they will need for sound effects: their voices, sound effects CDs, and props to create other sounds. We set up a microphone, run the videotape on the "audio dub" setting, and they perform their soundtrack. It is much like performing a radio play, but it is being recorded onto the video tape of their film. If the students aren't pleased with their results, they can re-record the sound.

    A computer with video editing software is a more sophisticated set-up. Music, voices, and sound effects can be recorded separately and added to the film. The advantage is that the soundtrack can be layered or built: first adding music, going back and adding voices, then adding sound effects. This is a more precise process but sometimes lacks the spontaneous energy of the "radio play" approach.

Which aspects of The Lab School Film Animation Program have proven most helpful to the success of exceptional learners?

Because animation involves specific attention to sequencing and allows complete control of the filmed environment, it is particularly suitable for helping children with learning disabilities who, due to their neurological impairment, have a particular need to practice order and organization. Viewing a small world of his own creation through the lens of a camera can provide needed focus to a student who is often unfocused or distracted. Because a wide variety of materials can be used to create an animated film, the process can be tailored to the needs of individual students. Many students like working with characters made of modeling clay. Depending on the skill level of the student, his clay figure can be anything from a shapeless blob of clay to a highly detailed, realistic rendering of a human. Other students have tactile issues and hate the feel of clay. They might prefer to make paper cut-out figures or even use photos cut from magazines for their animation. Students also can use "found" objects such as chess pieces, buttons, or nuts and bolts as their characters. With planning and imagination, a successful animated film can be made with any of these materials.

Very often, students with learning disabilities can have social issues as well. For this reason, each animation class produces a group project. This provides an opportunity for students to practice skills such as sharing ideas, being flexible, and learning both to rely on others and to be responsible to others. A film done by a group can be much more complex than an individual project. A range of tasks is available for students of any skill level, and the finished product is a source of satisfaction for every participant.

How is the classroom equipped?

The classroom is equipped with standard materials and tools such as rulers, hole punches, scissors, knives, markers, pencils, and paper of all types. In addition, we stock plasticine, papier mâché, and a good collection of miscellaneous junk—buttons, packing materials, paper towel tubes, sand, glitter, and fabric.

An invaluable and inexpensive resource is our picture file. We have a file cabinet filled with labeled, alphabetized folders containing pictures of animals, landscapes, skies, people, buildings, and plants. The pictures are collected from magazines, calendars, and the like. A student who needs to make a bear, for example, can go to the research file to find a reference photo that will help. Basic reference books are also helpful: illustrated books on farm animals, machines, living in the city. Increasingly, the Internet is a valuable tool for picture research, and CDs are now available with photos that are excellent for reference purposes.

Supplies and tools are stored in clearly labeled shoeboxes on open shelves. For student work in progress, we use plastic dishpans (13″ × 16″ × 6″), labeled with students' names, stored in a deep bookcase unit. It is critical for students to have a specific place to keep their own work.

In our animation classes, we use a 16-millimeter camera mounted on a tripod for three-dimensional work and on a camera stand for flat work. We use 500-watt photo lights. We do our preliminary editing manually with a tape splicer. For final editing, a commercial film lab transfers our film to video, which we can then edit and add sound to using a computer video editing program. We concentrate on hands-on animation (e.g., clay, cut-outs) rather than computer-generated images because of the tactile component. Working with physical objects that they can mold, touch, and manipulate can be helpful to students with perceptual and sensory motor issues.

What guidelines do you use?

It is important that the project be simple enough for the student to finish. An excellent idea that is too elaborate to complete will disappoint and frustrate the student. I tell new animation students that they must be able to explain a plot to me in three or four sentences: the set-up, the middle, and the end. If the plot is too complex to describe in this way, it is too complex for a beginner to undertake.

High school students often want to depict scenes that involve spurting blood, severed limbs, and so forth. As a rule I simply don't permit excessive violence; it's easier than arguing with students on a case-by-case basis.

What is the classroom routine?

At The Lab School we offer animation only at the high school level. My classes usually have between five and seven students. However, even very young children can make an animated film with proper guidance, and animation can be done with a larger group as well.

My students work at a large, central table. Students are expected to come into class, take out their projects, and get to work. For the most part, they know where materials are kept and take care of getting their own supplies and materials. I try to move around the large table, answering questions, observing works in progress, and offering suggestions or corrections as needed.

Filming takes place at long counters running along the perimeter of the room. When a student or students are filming, my primary focus is with them; the other students work independently at such times. However, I am always available for questions and can keep an eye on all of the work being done.

The Lab School's Performing Arts Teachers Speak Out

When a student is engaged in a performing art, he is out there, on stage, in front of an audience. Sometimes he is playing a musical instrument; other times he is standing facing the audience or disguised by costume. Perhaps he is dancing or leaping on stage or maneuvering a puppet. Regardless of the particular activity, the student is playing to an audience. Applause is a form of love and approval. It thanks the student for a job well done.

The visual artist may never be seen by an audience; her work, not herself, is on display. She is almost always out of view. The student may watch other people look at her work and may hear acclaim or receive a prize that signifies excellence. The work of a writer or poet speaks for itself; the writer does not have to stand before an audience and read aloud. Visual artists may listen to critiques or read written reviews of their work. Obviously certain personalities do best participating in certain art forms. Whereas the extrovert enjoys playing to audiences, the introvert finds the experience painful.

The different intelligences that thrive within us tend to thrust us in the directions of certain art forms. One expects the student with musical intelligence to find a musical instrument to play or a song to sing. The bodily kinesthetic intelligence leads a person to dance. The student who is comfortable with what Howard Gardner called interaction/interpersonal intelligence and who enjoys speaking may well seek out drama.

As in the visual arts, what the student discovers in the performing arts is that there is a discipline to every art form, that one step leads to another, and that practice is mandatory. Rehearse, rehearse, rehearse—whether it's dance, drama, music, or puppetry. Art does not just happen. One has to work to obtain good results.

Much more teamwork usually is required in the performing arts than in the visual arts. Exceptional learners do not work easily in groups, so it takes extraordinary talent to coach them in the performing arts. The students have to watch, listen to, and react to one another as well as pay attention to timing, where they are supposed to be in space, and how fast or slowly they are moving. Given their disabilities, it is amazing that many of our students turn out to be good thespians, excellent dancers, and gifted musicians.

Some students are so self-conscious that they do best with props. They dance better with a scarf in their hands, demonstrate more dramatic talent when they have masks over their faces or puppets in their hands, and produce high quality music when playing an instrument.

The training involved in working in a performing arts group builds camaraderie. The students and their teacher are all "in it" together. They need each other and must support each other to pull off a first-class performance. The performing arts teacher has to find an inner strength to excite the students and inspire them to reach to higher and higher levels while being thoughtful and supportive of one another. For exceptional learners, the performing arts teacher has to inspire more, excite more, reach higher, and lead all of the students to new heights. The arts prompt almost all of us to climb to new heights and to explore other worlds from the depths of the ocean to the highest clouds in the sky as well as awaken new ideas and feelings within us.

In this chapter, performing arts teachers from The Lab School of Washington answer a series of questions that tell how their form of art benefits exceptional learners. They describe important routines and procedures in their art classes and then take one project and explain it step by step to completion.

Drama

A Conversation with Shaun Miskell

What is the special benefit of this art form?

Participation in the performing arts is not appropriate (or desirable) for every student at every level of development. However, for exceptional learners who are open to the process of rehearsal and performance (and that, in my experience, is the vast majority of them), there are numerous advantages, both obvious and subtle.

What skills are targeted in the study of theatre? Since prehistoric tribes first began to perform around the campfire, the impulse to act has reflected two supremely human needs: to understand and to communicate. This is true at the Royal Shakespeare Company, and it is just as true in drama classes with the very youngest students at The Lab School of Washington. The development of productive rehearsal technique is central to The Lab School Approach to the dramatic arts.

An effective actor is analytical; she strives to identify and anticipate both behavioral and narrative patterns, and she is eager to perceive the cause-and-effect relationship between the actions of a character and the subsequent course of a story. She seeks to understand.

Understanding, she seeks to communicate. An effective actor is organized; she structures the various aspects of her performance (e.g., physical characterization, vocal modulation) to most clearly present her interpretation of the material at hand.

An effective actor is cooperative. Rehearsal and performance constitute an extremely social process. A productive teacher will always seek to create an encouraging, supportive atmosphere in which each member of the class is free, indeed eager, to participate. There is conversation, there is discussion, and, most of all, there is laughter. Finally, there is an awareness that effective actors must work together, encouraging one another's efforts and sharing one another's triumphs.

Which parts of The Lab School Drama Program have proven most helpful to the success of exceptional learners?

An organized, compartmentalized approach to the production process is the most crucial to success. Each class session is structured to facilitate the completion of the production at hand. Students approach all types of projects, from *The Three Little Pigs* to *Hamlet*, employing the same rehearsal technique. The entire process is completed step by step, always with the goal of a finished performance.

Initially, a student must master, at some level, an understanding of narrative structure. He must be able to articulate what happens and why. In elementary level classes, this generally is accomplished by having the instructor relate a story at least two or three times. Then, the class, round robin style, verbally presents the story to the instructor. Discussion ensues as the instructor seeks to deepen the class's grasp of

Production of a 3- or 4-Minute Silent Video

Each class develops a brief "silent movie" as its first video production. Completion of this process generally requires 20–25
class sessions.

Materials:

A notebook for storyboards and production notes
A simple home video camera with a tape
Costumes and props as required by scenario
A computer with video production software (we use Power Macintosh G4s and
    Adobe Premiere version 5.0)

Steps:

1. *Introduction:* The instructor introduces the project by showing the class examples of classic silent films. I am especially partial to the works of Buster
Keaton for his innovative approach to dramatic construction, his brilliant
work as a performer, and his films' general lack of sentimentality.
2. *Scenario development:* The class, under the guidance of the instructor, develops a logical, workable scenario.
3. *Preproduction:* A storyboard is drawn. The panels of the storyboard can be
drawn very simply. Even diagrams with stick figures can be very useful. In
preparing a storyboard, the class frequently will walk around and study a
sequence's location while working through problems and ideas concerning
camera angles. These drawings and diagrams will be referred to throughout
the production process.
4. *Casting:* The instructor casts the project, taking care to consider each student's strengths, weaknesses, and enthusiasm. The instructor must constantly
balance the needs of the group with the needs of the individual. There is a
saying in the theatre that the most important responsibility of a director is
assembling a cast. That is certainly true in this circumstance.
5. *Production:* Using the storyboard as a guide, the project is videotaped. This is
accomplished in small sections, or clips, usually lasting no more than 10 or 15
seconds each. The duties of the camera operator are shared by the class.
Each student learns to operate the camera.
6. *Postproduction editing:* The videotaped clips are loaded individually into the
computer where they are assembled in the correct sequence and trimmed.
One real advantage to using computers for this process is the ability to view
any number of versions of a sequence before the class is satisfied.
7. *Credits:* Credit sequences, including the project's title and a cast list, are created on the computer and added to the assembled project.
8. *Scoring:* Once the project has been assembled, the class chooses recorded
music to provide appropriate accompaniment. This material is captured onto
the computer and added to the project.
9. *Fine tuning:* The project essentially is completed. The class will now view the
video repeatedly and critically, fine tuning it until they are satisfied.
10. *Copying the project:* The completed project is exported onto videotape or
burned onto a CD-ROM. One copy is stored by the instructor for archival
purposes. Multiple copies are made for the members of the class.

the story. A similar approach is used with older students: The instructor initially presents dramatic material by reading dialogue to the class. As the first phase of the process unfolds, the instructor frequently interrupts the reading in order to engage the class in a discussion of narrative structure.

Following the preproduction period, the class begins the process of rehearsal. In elementary school, dialogue is mastered through repetition and drill. Each student echoes the instructor through a technique similar to chamber or story theater. More advanced students work with texts, supported, to varying degrees, by the instructor. As this process continues, the instructor's direct participation becomes less central to the performance. The students gradually come to own and control the presentation.

The basis of most theatrical productions at the elementary school level is folk tales from a wide variety of cultures and historical events. The preparation of these presentations immerses the involved students in the material in a most experiential manner. Accordingly, the student's awareness of the world around him is broad and embracing.

At the junior high and high school levels, theatrical productions are generally drawn from world literature (short stories are especially appropriate here) or from dramatic scripts, both contemporary and classic. In addition to developing the problem-solving, critical thinking, and organizational skills described above, The Lab School's junior high and high school students also acquire a familiarity with and passion for Greek and Roman plays and, most especially, for the works of Shakespeare.

The ability to present oneself before a group of strangers comfortably and without anxiety is an extremely valuable skill. The most effective way to develop this skill is through the performing arts.

In addition to live theatrical performances, every level of drama class at The Lab School conceives, develops, and produces original videotaped films. Initially, the students, with the guidance of the instructor, create a scenario. This original scenario is developed through the standards that are employed for live productions—dramatic structure, problem solving, and narrative logic. When the basic shape of the scenario has been established, a storyboard is constructed. A storyboard is similar to a newspaper comic, with each frame representing a new camera angle. This storyboard then becomes the guide for videotaping.

It is worth mentioning that video projects have several real advantages over live presentations, especially for students with learning disabilities. First, because a video project usually is completed over a number of weeks, a student is required to master dialogue only in small sections. Once a sequence has been successfully committed to tape, a student no longer needs to recall the lines for that scene. This can, of course, be especially helpful for students with serious language and/or memory difficulties. Second, a videotape can be perfected endlessly in the security of the class environment. If a student makes a mistake or forgets a line, that "take" is simply discarded and reshot. This process can be repeated as often as required. This goes a long way toward eliminating performance anxiety. Also, a student can watch and appreciate his own participation in a completed videotape. Third, videotapes generally are recorded out of sequence. The process of reassembling these clips of material in the proper narrative sequence can be of enormous value for students with learning disabilities, because it helps them to organize their oral and written work.

What is the classroom routine?

The entire drama curriculum revolves around the process of rehearsal and performance. The class functions much as an acting company, each member accepting a variety of roles throughout the year. Every project requires the participation of every student. The concepts of cooperation and community are central.

Each session's plans are designed to advance the progress of the class project at hand, be it a live production or a videotaped "movie." Through these projects, each student's weaknesses and strengths are identified and addressed.

At the elementary school level, students line up at the door of the classroom and are required to be quiet before entering the room. In doing so, each student has the opportunity to focus his energy on the tasks ahead. When the group is quiet, each student is greeted individually by the instructor and welcomed into the classroom. Once inside, the students sit in a circle on the floor. The instructor reviews the current status of the project at hand and outlines the task at hand. The entire class then participates in a physical and vocal warm-up designed to further focus the class.

Following the warm-up, the class proceeds with the session's primary task. If the current project is a live production, the class will be a rehearsal. If the project is a movie, the day's shooting schedule is rehearsed and executed.

Just before the conclusion of the session, the group reassembles in the circle as the instructor discusses with the class what has been accomplished and what will be accomplished at the next meeting. It is worth mentioning that, especially when working with students with disabilities, the instructor *must* remain flexible in terms of daily expectations. Due to the vagaries of individual mood and group dynamics, some sessions are extremely productive and others are not. Following this discussion, the class lines up at the classroom door and is dismissed by the instructor.

The routine at the junior high and senior high school level is quite similar. The students are expected to enter the room quietly, take a seat, and wait for the session to begin. The instructor makes a point of greeting and welcoming each student. Participating in the informal "small talk" that develops is a valuable social skill, which often is a serious challenge for many Lab School students. For many students, simply being able to comfortably and appropriately converse in a group is a major success.

As with the elementary school classes, when the session begins, the instructor engages the class in a discussion evaluating the status of the current project and outlining the day's task.

Following this discussion, the class proceeds with the session's primary task. If the current project is a live production, the task will be a rehearsal. If the project is a movie, the day's shooting schedule will be rehearsed and accomplished.

As the session winds down, the instructor discusses with the class what has been accomplished and what will be accomplished at the next meeting. Following this discussion, the class is dismissed by the instructor.

Dance
A Conversation with Stephen Johnson

What is the special benefit of this art form?

The most important benefit of dance is its ability to organize students' bodies. Students need to determine which parts of the body they will have to use for the tasks they will perform, students have to have the muscle tone and development to maintain their posture and attend without being tired out, and students have to learn how to balance and be connected with gravity and the earth so they can move in the space without falling or tripping. Students also need to know how to channel energy so they know how much energy to use for each task.

Which part of The Lab School Dance Program has proven most helpful to the success of exceptional learners?

I find gymnastics training to be the most beneficial aspect of the dance program; it uses all parts of the body, and each muscle must be isolated and exercised before students use it so that they are aware of what specific muscles can do for them. The balance skills and training needed are built into the exercises. It helps to involve all of the dance forms: modern, jazz, and ballet. In ballet, students have to point their toes and have straight legs for some positions. They have to have muscle tone to hold themselves up in some positions, particularly when they have to hold themselves on one leg or when they are upside-down.

Modern dance and jazz dance help students with learning disabilities who are very disorganized because they have trouble with what comes first, next, and last. Dance helps build organization.

Talk about gymnastics in terms of sequences, particularly learning sequences.

First, students have to move their bodies in sequence. They have to know that, in some activities, they will start with their hands; then, their arms, shoulders, and other body parts will join in. To move the body in sequence, students have to know the sequence of skills and from where to start and how to finish. Then I can take it a step further. If students are moving across the floor, I give them sequences of movements: first skip, then jump, then chassé. Then, they have to remember how to perform the movements for the different activities in their proper sequences and to make a transition from one form of movement to another. Following sequences is very, very difficult for children with learning disabilities. To get them to do sequences and transitions smoothly is my most difficult task.

Cane Dance

A simple project to try with a class of beginners is the Cane Dance. The Cane Dance involves eight different movements, I teach only one movement at a time. Only when the students have learned the first movement do we move onto the second rhythm. That means that if there are 3 months in a semester and it takes 1 month to learn the first movement, it is possible that the students will only learn three movements that semester. It is up to the teacher to assess the ability of the group and program to the group dynamic. The dance can be dressed up by adding hats and scarves or taping the canes with colored tape.

Materials:

Cane (one for each student)
Masking tape

Steps:

1. Because many students with learning disabilities do not have a sense of how close or far away from others to stand, I put tape on the floor to teach the students floor patterns. A circle is taped on the floor as a starting point for each child, who stands in the center of the circle. When the students enter a performance area, the first thing I do is place them on the stage and tell them to find something visual (e.g., a picture, a pillar, a sign) on which they can focus. That way, they know where to stand, and I don't have to put tape on the floor. They need to know that every time they come out on the stage, they should be right in front of that point.
2. The students learn how to do each movement of the Cane Dance first without a cane. The students begin by walking through the steps so they can see where their weight should be—where their body will be in space. I often ask the students, "Where is your weight?" In a dance, you must always know which foot the weight is on; is it on the right foot, is it on the left foot, is it in the middle? I ask them, "What position is your body in?" I will put my hand on them and actually guide their bodies. This is done for each step.
3. Once the students have learned the steps, they each are given a cane. I have found that when the students have props in their hands, it gives their hands and upper torso something to do, and they can all be together on something. Also, using a prop helps them concentrate on the prop and not on their self-consciousness. Initially, they learn to swing the canes without any other movements because they can lose control of them if they are not careful.
4. Once the students have learned the steps and have learned how to control the canes, they learn how to incorporate the cane movements into the steps. Often, it is difficult for the students to look at the person on either side of them and still remain in sync. Because of this, I give the students a pattern for their feet and, again, show them where their weight should be with every beat of the music. I use counts that are based on the rhythm of the music. I yell the rhythm out, and the students' feet have to come down when I say; they have to kick when I say kick until they can perform the movements without cues.

What else do you think helps them organize themselves?

Constant regimen. They need to have the same set of movements every day in which they are using every part of their body. The warm-up is so important. They have to do the same movement every day with a particular muscle. The warm-up is another form of a sequence, and once the students learn it, I never have to say a word. I start the music and they can warm themselves up and never miss a part. It becomes part of their kinesthetic memory. They do it every day when they come in, and they always remember it.

What guidelines do you use?

I try to find their strengths and weaknesses, and then I choreograph to their strengths. By repeating a sequence over and over again and sandwiching their weaknesses between their strengths, their weaknesses rise and come to the level of their strengths.

If a student is clumsy and afraid of falling and failing, I must build his trust to get him to dare to try. I move with him to get him moving. We laugh at movements that come out wrong. When the student can laugh, the movements are no longer a threat; consequently, he will try the movements again and can succeed; however, if he is made to feel bad about what he is doing, he will not try again. Once the student can repeat the sequences with confidence, the whole class gets excited about his accomplishments and joins in the learning process. If the class supports the student who has difficulties with dance, it helps the student conquer the difficulty. As the student succeeds, we give him as much praise as possible. The next time the child comes into the class, he is waiting to get that same praise.

Children with learning disabilities are notorious for not being able to work in groups. Therefore, we make the class alluring, exciting, and special, so the students want to be a part of the group. We also have very strict structure. If a student breaks the rules, she automatically has "time out"; the students know they have three chances and then they are out. Because the students do not want to miss the fun and the opportunity to learn, they get very upset when they are sent out of the class. When they come back, they usually will not misbehave again. Luckily, I very seldom send children out.

When I have a child who is far more talented than the others, I make that person an assistant, and the assistant must demonstrate and help those who are experiencing difficulties. That makes the assistant feel a sense of responsibility to the other students and gives him an added ego boost.

What is the classroom routine?

The children enter the room in a line and display appropriate behavior: They stand up straight and do not lean on the wall, and they are serious and focused. If they lose their focus before they get to their chair, they go back outside the room and reenter appropriately—no skipping, no jumping, no running, and no goofing off on the way to their chairs. Each part of the class is done that way. We wait until all of the students are in their chairs with their shoes off and are ready to go to the mats. If the students cannot behave appropriately, they do not go to the mats; they go back to their chairs and start over again. Each section of the dance is a separate piece, and each child must be appropriate before we proceed to the next section. After the warm-up, we work on the current project, be it gymnastics, ballet, or jazz dance. At the end of the class, as a reward, I give the students a free activity. However, if the students do not finish their work, they do not get the free activity; instead, they return to their chairs and put on their shoes, and they are upset because they did not get a reward. The next time they come to class, they usually work harder so they can get the free activity.

How much do you use drama during dance?

I use drama all the way through dance. I might be a character from a drama or imitate the students through comedy, showing them how funny it looks when they make mistakes; then they can see how their mistakes look so they can correct them. I use their part and overdramatize it so they will laugh at themselves. When I want serious dance and I want it to look a certain way, I use drama to show them what they are doing wrong so they can correct their mistakes. They can see that their movements do not fit into the particular dance and that they need to be focused. They love to correct their instructors, so I will make mistakes on purpose so they can critique what I did.

Elementary and Intermediate Music
A Conversation with Susan Mebane Carter

What is the special benefit of this art form?

Music is the language of the soul. This performing art is universally profound in its ability to stimulate feelings and to provide a foundation for a sense of belonging to something greater than one's own individual existence. Participation in making music is a whole-body experience; consequently, the benefits for students with learning disabilities are far-reaching.

Group music activities can have a stunning impact on improving and enhancing a child's problem-solving abilities, coordination, auditory and visual memory skills, teamwork, goal setting, self-expression, self-confidence and self-esteem, poise, and much, much more! These abilities can be accomplished on the most basic musical level as well; for example, singing a simple song such as *Row, Row, Row Your Boat* provides an effective vehicle for connecting sound to symbol while developing phrasing in language with the song's ascending and descending melody. The overwhelming effectiveness of music also is seen in the required and usually automatic commitment to focusing during participation. Take our song again—inevitably, images of a "stream" and "life is but a dream" rather than other images and distractions prevail during song practice. The therapeutic nature of learning to play an instrument also is seen on many levels; playing an instrument requires repetitive physical movement in addition to cognitive, auditory, and visual participation, all of which also assist in sensory integration.

The unique and possibly one of the most beneficial elements to musical involvement is the repetition necessary in practicing songs and/or instruments. This art form requires skill building achieved only through extensive and focused practicing, which enforces the underlying physical and cognitive learning that is subsequently achieved.

The beauty of this art form is best expressed in ensemble and individual performances, which provide students with a forum for sharing their accomplishments with audiences. The success of well-planned and well-executed performances encourages the student to continue her work in this extensive skill-building endeavor. There is no greater reward and motivator than the genuine applause of an entertained audience!

Which parts of The Lab School Music Program have proven most helpful to the success of exceptional learners?

One of the most rewarding aspects for our music students is performing, and The Lab School offers many opportunities throughout the year. The preparations for performances commence early in the year and require students to pay tedious and painstaking attention to detail as they develop the necessary vocal and instrumental

Bell/Chime Choir

This activity is best suited for elementary students. In this activity, students play the harmony indicated on the musical score arranged from the well known children's song, "Yankee Doodle," in rhythm. The "magic" for students with learning disabilities is that, while they attain a beginning understanding of reading music notation and participate in making music as a group, they discover the similarities of chord progressions used in so many different melodies.

Materials:

Bells/chimes (one bell or chime for each student in class)
Small round stickers in a variety of colors

Steps:

1. Each student is assigned a different colored dot, which is placed on their bell/chime and also corresponds to a note on a musical scale.

2. The students then practice using the instruments to strengthen their coordination skills.
3. Students are then asked to memorize their colored dot and the note that their chime plays.
4. After the students have successfully mastered playing their individual chimes (please note that this may require several lessons for students who have difficulties with motor skills), review the music chart, which can be displayed on poster board. (Note: Music educators are advised to "abandon" traditional music notation in many elementary general music classes. Accurate note values will be introduced in subsequent more advanced chime choir exercises.) In this particular song, each note in the chord has the value of two counts. The idea is to create unison playing of each chord while the teacher plays the melody. A student conductor is required to point to each chord as the music is played; students can share this task throughout the learning of the song.

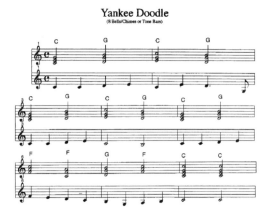

Yankee Doodle
(8 Bells/Chimes or Tone Bars)

5. When the chord progression has been mastered, discuss the concept of melody. I have found that not introducing the corresponding melody until after sufficient practice time on the chords provides an anticipation and even some rather good guesses about the song's name. Popular songs have made wonderful chime and bell choir additions in our class projects. Students will be amused when they identify the simplest melodies that were hidden in the unknown harmony. At times, students studying instruments privately have played the melodies in my class.

6. Ultimately, students playing bells/chimes also will be asked to sing along if the accompanying lyrics are simple and mastery of the melody is possible. Drums and other percussive nonmelodic instruments add wonderful layers to this ensemble. Repetitive practice is necessary for the beginning bell/chime choir. Sometimes, when the work become tedious, students exchange bells/chimes to generate new enthusiasm for the same song.

skills. This requires each student to develop awareness of others and the ability to cooperate with their fellow performers while concentrating on individual musical development. Because, in many ways, this type of work parallels life, the skills that students with learning disabilities develop are of great benefit to them. Little needs to be said about the self-esteem and confidence that students achieve with successful performances; these performances create a stronger individual student and team member and add to the student's realization that the best results are achieved when the whole ensemble works up to its potential because of individual efforts.

What guidelines do you use?

Every child who enters my class has the capacity to be musical. My endeavor is to excite children into wanting to be productive members of musical projects. Armed with the knowledge that rhythm—from heartbeats to physical and verbal communication—is the mainstay of life, the curriculum for music classes uses this invaluable tool in most activities. All young children love to sing and play percussive instruments, satisfying their cognitive need for imagination and physical need for repetitive movement and auditory processing. Children with learning disabilities are no different; the objective is to tailor projects according to each individual's need. Students are able to work on auditory, language, and motor skills in a nurturing, creative environment where the ultimate goal is to enrich the students' experience and thereby reinforce the students' desire to be musical. What a privilege it is to teach a subject that is inherently enjoyed by students. My primary responsibility is to use this to benefit the student's development regardless of his musical ability.

What is the classroom routine?

Each elementary school general music class has a special identity, which is developed through the fall of each year. Curricula are designed for these classes to fit the personality and ability potential of each group with the understanding that, because varying disabilities will hinder individual participation, constant nurturing encouragement will be necessary.

Although singing is a major component in the music curriculum, some classes evolve to actively playing melodic percussion instruments, such as bells, tone bars, and xylophones, which provide excellent development for hand–eye coordination, decoding, motor skills, rhythm, left-to-right discrimination, and auditory processing. More advanced elementary classes are introduced to the recorder, which requires the students to read treble clef music. This wind instrument provides an excellent opportunity to enhance sound and symbol association for reading as well as the previously mentioned skills. With students who have varying degrees of ability and potential, at times it is necessary to create an eclectic instrumental ensemble to facilitate the class's success. Visual cues are critical when learning a musical instrument. Written music is not introduced until the student has mastered playing the instrument, which addresses motor skills and auditory processing.

When a class exhibits good beginning ability to sing on pitch as a group, the teacher can emphasize movement and song and eventually develop a show group. To achieve a good beginning show chorus, it is important to make the key and rhythm in the chosen songs suit the group's vocal ability rather than "fit" the children's voices into the original key signature. With training, the children's vocal ability will improve, and songs that require a more complex vocal range can be introduced. When teaching new songs, remember that students learn by repeating the teacher's pitches and lyrics. Written vocal music is not introduced until the intermediate and junior high music classes. Singing is a very personal endeavor, and care must be taken to never embarrass a student by forcing solo work until the student is ready. This is especially true for students with learning disabilities. Generally speaking, a child will much more readily play a solo on an instrument than sing a solo until she is confident about the results of her efforts. Again, a nurturing and supportive class works wonders in stimulating the confidence and risk taking that can be so difficult for children.

The intermediate and junior high classes are designed to identify and teach students who have serious interests in music. Developing a musical ensemble in which students can participate through high school is one of my major goals. Flexibility becomes crucial when working with students of this age. The training necessary for learning an instrument is expansive, and discouragement can be minimized by revising the curriculum as needed. Of course, because fostering and promoting talents in our students remain foremost in our plan, the identification of talented students begins with the first elementary music class at The Lab School.

High School Music
A Conversation with Sean Rozsics

What is the special benefit of this art form?

A student's involvement in music can be beneficial in many ways. Student musicians develop a sense of accomplishment and achievement as they develop their abilities to express themselves musically. Many of the basic skills—decoding, sequencing, problem solving, and task analysis—that are used on a daily basis in music class also can help students succeed in other areas. For example, mathematically inclined students will be able to recognize and appreciate the logical and symmetrical patterns and relationships that are inherent in music.

Students also learn many social skills in music class, such as the value of teamwork, mutual respect, tolerance, and appreciation as they work together to achieve common goals. As the practicing student musician improves, she experiences the rewards of diligence and commitment in the form of increased ability and becomes more able to incorporate these values into her own work ethic. When student musicians are able to give form to their energies, they develop a feeling of empowerment that many nonartists could not begin to imagine. The creative student artist develops a sense of self-esteem and self-awareness that allows him to have increased confidence in other areas of endeavor. The student who learns music is forever enriched with a vivid, lasting, and exciting form of self-expression.

What parts of The Lab School Music Program have proven the most beneficial to the success of exceptional learners?

Two important facets of the music program have enabled students to become successful musicians. First, there is a relaxed and supportive atmosphere in the music class. If a student is to be creative, he must have a daily forum to freely discuss, explore, and experiment with any and all forms of musical ideas without any external expectations or considerations. Student musicians working together learn the necessity of mutual support and respect as they share and exchange musical ideas. Whereas poets and painters can create their art in solitude, musicians must work with others during the process of creation. As this process often can be painstaking and soul baring, student musicians must feel secure, respected, and appreciated. It is the teacher's responsibility and goal to make every class a working environment in which students recognize the importance of their own contributions but develop a strong connection to the collective will of the group.

The second important facet of the music program that has enabled students to become successful musicians is the emphasis on structure and theory at every level. Student musicians must learn to choose their own notes, and to do this, they must have an understanding of musical principle and theory. Scales, intervals, triads, and

Improvisation and Experimentation

This small project would be appropriate for the first few weeks of a class of beginners. The purpose of this lesson is to introduce students in a fun and challenging way to some of the simple principles and methods of musical improvisation and experimentation. Students will be presented with a few simple rules and guidelines and will then have the chance to hear what sounds good and, just as important, what does not.

Materials:

Two keyboards (although one will suffice)
Various other instruments, including drums and a bass guitar

Steps:

1. On the keys of the keyboards, make or attach small, red markings (a dry erase marker will clean off of most plastic keys, or small stickers also will work) on the A, C, and E keys. These notes comprise the A minor chord. Make or attach small blue markings on the A, C, and F keys. These notes comprise the F major chord.

2. This lesson can be presented like a game, not unlike musical chairs, in which the students have to react to musical cues. Have one student sit at each keyboard. These two students will be playing the melodic ideas (whether they know it or not), and other students will be playing rhythm. Whichever students are available can contribute rhythmically; a bass player and drummer are preferable. A coordinated student with no experience often can play the electric bass for this exercise. Organize these players to play two measures of A minor followed by two measures of F major over a slow tempo beat. Once a simple rhythm has been established, the keyboard players are ready to begin. The first keyboard player will play red notes during the first two measures, or eight counts, and the second keyboard player will play blue notes over the third and fourth measures. The three rules they need to follow are 1) they can only play one note at a time, 2) they must hit a correctly colored note on the first beat of each measure, and 3) they can only use white notes to complete phrases.

3. The music teacher will recognize this as a simple two-chord progression in the key of A minor, utilizing the A minor scale. Although it may take a few minutes to explain various fine points to certain students, most classes should be able to generate something musical with this approach, and this, along with countless similar and related exercises, can help implant the genesis of musical understanding.

A few notes of caution regarding this exercise: Make sure none of the involved students are colorblind; and, because the visual cues will not be on the keyboard forever, do not let students get too used to them. This exercise is meant to demonstrate the simple idea that landing on the right note at the right time is what choosing notes, or improvising, is all about.

components of chord construction and composition continually are emphasized so that students can understand how music is made and be able to organize their own musical thoughts and ideas. Student who develop this musical knowledge and awareness will be able to better appreciate and understand music for the rest of their lives.

What is the classroom routine?

Each music class develops a distinct personality of its own as time passes, and the students develop bonds of understanding and commitment. A good music class is one in which the students' different degrees of talent, taste, and temperament have been taken into account in the planning stages and grouped with respect to these differences. Different classes will have different goals for the year and will vary their functions accordingly. More experienced classes may spend more time than less experienced classes rehearsing detailed pieces for the purposes of public performance, whereas less experienced classes would be more likely to focus on simple improvisational techniques and ideas.

On a daily basis, students arrive to class and are expected to set up their instruments, tune up, and prepare to play in a reasonably short amount of time. Each class usually starts with soft improvising over a simple musical idea while each student prepares her own workspace in preparation for the day's musical activity. Once the students are prepared and the class seems ready, the instructor summarizes the status of the current class project and discusses both short- and long-term plans for the class. All students are encouraged to verbalize their assessments of the ideas in progress and to diplomatically contribute their own suggestions at every step of the creative process. When the class works on long-term musical projects, it is important that all of the students enjoy the selected material and are able to make significant musical contributions to the piece. Each class will work on a few projects concurrently so that no project becomes too boring through daily repetition. As the year goes on, students become familiar with the working process and each student develops an important role within the class. At the end of the year, most students are involved in performances that allow them to exhibit many of the skills that they have learned in class throughout the year.

With regard to the improvisation exercise you described, are there any possible variations or extensions to this activity?

This project is easy to modify. For example, the two keyboard players can exchange chords or play four measures at a time. Or, on the newer electric keyboards that have hundreds of easily accessed sounds, the student keyboard players can be encouraged to change sounds before each turn. Also, at some point during the exercise, the students should be encouraged to experiment with the black notes on the keyboard. Because these notes are not in the key of A minor, they will stand out in stark contrast to the notes in the scale of A minor. It is important to demonstrate the notes that do not work in this exercise; students usually can hear these differences easily.

Putting It All Together

One of the main problems with our culture is that we are all in such a hurry. All of this rushing is part of what is driving us away from our beginnings—times when the arts cradled our civilization, when discoveries were encouraged so questions could be asked, and when contemplation and reflection in the outdoors were part of growing up. It used to be that making things out of objects found in neighborhood garages or on the street or building a secret clubhouse brought children together as part of the same team. Through these experiences, the children could see how talented Malcolm was at putting things together, what great ideas Margo had, how daring Chris was, how much they loved to be with Mary Jo, and how Patsy made them all laugh.

Today, we do not allow children to be children for very long. However, my experience is that if we rush our children into adulthood, they become adult children for interminable periods of time, not assuming responsibility for themselves or for anyone else. We put infants into jeans and bikinis. We hurry preschoolers to grow up. We hurry children to achieve early in their schooling. We pack their afternoons with activity after activity: studies, athletics, arts, and organized groups and clubs. We want instant results, much the same way as we demand instant answers and instant cures and devour so many instant breakfasts, lunches, dinners, and snacks. Many people are so rushed today that they live on take-out food and instant products. Where is all of this rushing taking us?

Something is wrong with our values in America. We are losing sight of children. They are not miniature adults or puppets but young human beings who need time to develop and become their unique selves. They need schools that are attuned to their needs and that prize diversity.

Endless pressure speeds children into experiences for which they are not ready and cheats them of experiences they need for their total development. Infants undergo a great deal of motor development; they learn to organize their bodies, which in turn will eventually help them organize their minds. They learn to use both sides of the body and then learn to use one side at a time. Their eye–hand coordination requires innumerable opportunities to coordinate their eyes and hands together.

At midnight, on a network television show, I witnessed a class video with infants crawling toward their mothers when they saw a card with the word "come" on it; a group of professionals was guiding parents to teach reading in infancy so the children would become good readers. I wonder who says they will become good readers; where's the proof? Some of us learn to walk sooner than others; does that mean we are better walkers? Preschools in our competitive, hurried culture are advertising themselves to parents today as academic centers. It seems as though we want our tiny children to skip childhood, wear academic robes, and spout academic material. Some preschools literally have preschoolers wearing academic robes for their graduation to kindergarten. Why is there a graduation ceremony anyway? Why can't preschools advertise the great play opportunities they offer? What's wrong with children playing? Play is children's work. Play should not be belittled.

The ancient Greeks knew that the body and the mind had to be developed as fully as possible to produce an educated person. Today, many do not understand this vital connection. Today, people are in a hurry and want to skip necessary steps; they want infants to read even though they have little experience to understand what they are reading. Sounding out letters is not reading. Reading involves breaking down the code, sounding out graphic symbols, and integrating those symbols to have meaning so that words link with experiences and lead the reader to new worlds.

When a child is rushed into reading before he is ready—when he has to endure the pressure of being "the best" on tests, in class achievement, and, sometimes, in athletics, too—how much attention is being paid to what is best for this particular child? Parents often feel the need to compete with other parents; they fear that their child will not make it to the best of schools. High standards are good. Unreasonable goals, however, hurt children and often do not achieve their objectives in the end.

Children with special needs who are pressured often "shut down"; then it becomes clear that pressure slows their learning: For example, Andrea's parents pressured her to such a degree that, although she enrolled in an outstanding university, she left after 2 years and was embittered toward her parents who thought they had been doing the right thing for her. It took years before she was ready to return to higher education. When she did, it was to study social work, not prelaw. Andrea's friend Lynn also dropped out and became a massage therapist even though she achieved a 3.8 grade point average despite her moderate learning disabilities. Lynn's cousin Fred left school because he felt such failure and moved abroad to "find himself."

TRAINING THE MIND THROUGH PLAY

Curiosity is an outstanding trait of infants. As they grow older, they are constantly exploring the unknown and trying to find out why and how things work. Their minds and critical thinking skills are trained by following their curiosity. They build their knowledge through play. They link experiences and relationships through play.

Exceptional learners need even more time to play because they have inordinate difficulty in accurately and consistently perceiving, processing, and retrieving information. This is part of the neurological immaturity and disorganization that, along with difficulties with memory and paying attention, is the nature of their disability. Many of them do not know how to play. Because they have considerable language disabilities, motor difficulties, and sequencing issues, they do not play and, therefore, do not have the opportunities to practice skills and develop schemas for many processes and relationships. Play and the use of the arts give these students a chance to develop these skills and schemas at any age. Through play and the arts, children fill in the missing pieces of their understanding of relationships that many children learn at age 3 or 4. Exceptional learners need to build their mental filing and reference systems anew and, in sophisticated ways, must be presented with preschool experiences so they can begin to categorize incoming information correctly. They need to be exposed to more concrete, hands-on learning, more play, and more arts than other children their age. All of the art forms can help ignite the whole learning process. The arts are motivators. They demand involvement. They produce tangible results that evoke praise from audiences. They bring with them the civilization that human beings have been able to create on earth—the wonder, the beauty, the joy, the sorrow, the anger, and the originality of expression.

Parents whose children have failed in regular school experience a hurt that travels to every part of their being. When a child suffers, the parents usually suffer, too. Conversely, when parents see their child eager to go to school, excitedly showing off the serpentine lamp she made out of wood, practicing the rap she made up about "Australopithecus" in Cave Club, or teaching swing dancing to her siblings, they usually are overjoyed. It is then that parents see the value of the program.

The arts help foster friendships among students as well. When a child who had no friends suddenly has a best friend, parents—whose attention previously focused only on academic achievements—suddenly realize that there is a fourth "R" that also is part of schooling: relationships. When parents see and hear active involvement in school activities, they realize that their child has a chance to succeed in school. In my experience, it is then that parents and schools become partners.

Developmental psychologists (e.g., Piaget) have proven over the years that children require sensory motor experiences to lead them into symbolic learning. However, school systems, in their haste to achieve high test scores, tend to cut out play and the arts. For example, the title of an article in *The Washington Post* in mid-December 1999, was "Kindergarten Gets Tougher." The Board of Education of one of the foremost school districts in the country unanimously approved changes to "beef up kindergarten academics. Quiet time, music time, art time, and exercise time are out. Reading, math, and social studies are in."

OBJECT-CENTERED LEARNING

When 8-year-old Charlie was studying inventions, he created a wheel out of toddler-sized plastic hoops. The spokes of the wheel were made out of tinker toys attached to a wad of clay. He had seen wheels all his life. He had even pored over photographs of wheels, but he did not question their existence. However, when he made his own wheel, a wheel that worked, he desired all kinds of information as to why wheels work the way they do. His teacher prodded his curiosity further by asking him, "Why do you think human beings created wheels? Why were they built during the Stone Age? What previous inventions led to the creation of the wheel? How did the wheel change people's lives? Which of our modern inventions use wheels? Could we have built computers without the invention of the wheel?" Charlie's wheel encouraged an exploration of history, geography, and a whole host of social sciences.

Hands-on learning promotes the exploration of a variety of subjects. It is multi-disciplinary. It is concrete and visual. The child making an object looks at it keenly and develops a clear a sense of its shape in his mind. The object then triggers memories of similar objects and leads to comprehension of the role of that object in human life. One primitive tool can lead a child into a variety of worlds of knowledge. The act of touching the object leads to a comprehension that merely hearing about it cannot bring. Making the object may also lead to vocabulary development. For exceptional learners, who need plenty of time to process information, particularly verbal knowledge, object-centered learning is an effective teaching practice.

Hands-on museums are attractive to all children but are a real bonus to exceptional learners. Chapter 1 mentions neurologist Frank Wilson's book, *The Hand: How Its Use Shapes the Brain, Language, and Human Culture*. Wilson believes, "It is a virtual certainty that complex social structures and language developed gradually in association with the spread of more highly elaborated tool design, manufacture, and use (p. 30)." He states that human beings are different from the highest functioning animals because of our tool development and use as well as our language, reasoning, and self-consciousness. People tend to look down on object-centered learning, feeling that children who are taught this way are being trained to be gas station attendants or garage mechanics. But, according to Wilson's research and data, hands-on learning seems to contribute to a higher order of thinking and to the highest ranges of intelligence.

TESTIMONIALS

Perhaps the best endorsement for The Lab School Approach comes from the voices and experiences of the children who attend The Lab School of Washington Day School and the adults who attend The Lab School of Washington Night School.

VOICES AND EXPERIENCES OF CHILDREN

Hard-to-teach learners who spent years sitting in classroom chairs trying unsuccessfully to listen to instructions, failing to make sense of what the teacher was saying, and painfully attempting to write something comprehensible often cannot believe a school environment exists in which they can move around, use their hands, and make things.

Derek, age 9, told a visitor to The Lab School most compellingly, "You won't believe it. I didn't believe it, I actually feel smart here!" Half the battle is won with that statement.

Sofia told her counselor that since she has been able to learn this new way, she wants to come to school in the morning. She said, "I have so much more energy. Every morning is a leaping morning." Sadé just smiles and says she's a "happy pumpkin" because she can do music and dance and woodwork and Gods Club. Roderick is eager to show a visitor that he can read and sound out letters, can clap the parts of music phrases, and can discuss what he's learned.

Yvette wants everyone to see the child-size pyramid she and her classmates built with burial chambers inside it covered with murals of everyday life in Egypt. Jendayl cannot wait until people will listen to her play the flute that she constructed in woodworking shop; she can also tell you the scientific principles on which she based the making of the flute. Jarraur wants to show the film he made about brains and the role they play in learning. Meaghan, Ben, Andrew, James, and Amber want to sing and clap the song, "How We Learn Rap," which they composed together. These 14- and 15-year-olds who were very attached to their boom boxes, and particularly to rap music, had heard an example of rap produced by Pam Knudson, The Lab School's primary teacher, and decided to make up their own version.

HOW WE LEARN RAP

(* represents one hand clap; ** represents two claps)

How do I learn best, I wonder?
How do I learn best?**
Can I know?* Can you know?*
Lemme tell you.
Come on, let's go.

I hear** I speak**
It's information that I seek.
I speak** I hear**
The sound will make it clear.

It's my ears** my ears*
It's my ears that work for me!

If I learn it in a poem,
Chant it, sing it in a song,
The lesson that you teach me
Will stay with me for long.
Coz it's my ears** my ears*
It's my ears that work for me!

I look** I see**
It all comes clear to me.
I see** I look**
A map, a graph, a book
They offer me a hook
Coz it's my eyes** my eyes*
It's my eyes that work for me!

I see patterns and designs
Chart it, graph it, then it's mine.
Add some color, shape, and line
It's in my brain a long, long time

Coz it's my eyes** my eyes*
It's my eyes that work for me!

I move, I act, I bounce, I touch;
By moving I can learn so much
If I can dance* or make a mask*
You'll see me handle any task
Or make a model* I'll explain
That's how things stay inside my brain.

Coz it's my feet and hands** feet and hands*
It's my feet and hands that work for me!

What works for me** don't work for you**
What works for you** don't work for me**
Both ways are good, you will agree
It's just that we learn DIFFERENTLY!

TESTIMONIALS OF ADULTS

Many of the adults who attend The Lab School of Washington Night School also recall their positive experiences with the arts.

"The only time I understood stuff at school was when I drew it or constructed it. Then it made sense to me."

"When I made things or did projects, the learning got into my bones and I had it with me forever."

"When they let me do graphics on the computer, I felt as though I was on a magic carpet, designing new worlds."

"Photography let everybody, including me, know that I was alive."

"I showed everybody at school that I could act. The Drama Club was my savior. Taking on the role of somebody else took me out of my world and put me into new situations where I learned so much. I, who couldn't remember my telephone number, remembered my lines in drama."

"They had no dance in my school. I danced every afternoon. I could learn anything through dance. My mother taught me multiplication through dance. My aunt taught me geometry through dancing. I wish my school had used my ability in dance to help me feel smarter."

"I sang my heart out with joy. I never sang at school."

"Rhythm and melody helped me learn. I learned my telephone number by stomping out the rhythm. My teachers kept trying to make me memorize by saying or writing it over. I simply failed."

"The art teachers sheltered me. I was safe in their rooms and I produced my best work for them, and guess what? They appreciated it."

"I sculpted faces. They called me Leonardo, but it was with respect."

"The movie camera was my ego. I did great making films. I'm in that field today."

"You know, there's a whole lot of us out there who wasted 13 or 14 years in school. We never learned to read right. We never came out with much wherewithall or skills. We're the losers. Society is the loser. There were ways to teach us but they weren't used."

"Schools need to be smaller, more personal with more movement and laughter—more hands-on stuff to make sure kids learn."

RAUSCHENBERG DAY

In 1985, when The Lab School of Washington decided to demonstrate formally to its students and parents that there was light at the end of the tunnel, we began to honor well-known achievers who are outstanding in their fields of endeavor and who have severe learning disabilities. We honored six celebrities during the first year that we celebrated, the first of whom was Robert Rauschenberg, Master of Modern Art. When he came to The Lab School of Washington to visit with the students, he said, "It can make your life absolutely miserable when you can't keep up with the other people in the school. Your whole social life is based on it, and, you know, it took me years to realize that I wasn't stupid. If anyone with learning disabilities can learn that when they are still young, they can be saved from an awful lot of pain and disturbing memories." A visual thinker who sketched in all of his textbooks and immersed himself in nature, Rauschenberg wishes he could have had a hands-on education in which he learned through color, movement, and objects.

In 1994, Robert Rauschenberg and The Lab School of Washington began a dynamic collaboration funded by the Rauschenberg Foundation. A contest was set up for art teachers from all over the United States to come to Washington to celebrate the Power of Art. Teachers from mainstream schools, special schools, and public and private schools were encouraged to apply. To do so, they had to explain their philosophy of teaching and describe specific ways that art helps children, particularly children with special needs, to learn academic skills. Examples of children's art were requested in the contest application.

Each year since then, the winners—usually 25–30 of hundreds of applications, from 22 to 25 states in the nation—come to Washington, D.C., for an extremely busy, exciting day. The winners become acquainted with one another at a reception on Thursday evening; then, on Friday, they begin at The Lab School with an early breakfast meeting followed by my workshop on the characteristics of children with learning disabilities, attention-deficit/hyperactivity disorder (ADHD), and language impairments. We discuss how specific art forms can help students who have particular learning problems, and we do some role-playing activities. An extensive tour of The Lab School follows. Robert Rauschenberg arrives at lunch time and meets with all of the winners.

Lab School students then put on a multimedia presentation, "Rauschenberg style," in honor of the great artist, who thoroughly enjoys being with the students. In May 2000, the children's presentation began with the unveiling of an 8-foot-high bas relief sculpture of a gryphon—a mythological beast that is half eagle and half lion. The sculpture handsomely adorns the façade of a new building on campus. The sculpture was a result of a 2-month-long project by senior high students in the studio arts class. They began the project by designing the gryphon on a computer using graphics software. Then they projected the outline onto a large block of foam building insulation; carved it using a power saw, knives, rasps, and various power tools; and coated it with latex theatrical plaster for the detailed carving. Finally, the students applied two coats of bronze dust and clear acrylic to produce a realistic metallic sheen.

The "gryphon" theme threaded through the whole performance that followed the unveiling of the sculpture. Lab School students of all ages presented aspects of the gryphon myth in story, dance, song, drama, and pantomime. Weeks of imagination and preparation—stimulated primarily by Lab School English classes, during which words were mustered and compiled into scripts and poems—went into creating the event. Subsequently, music was selected, and costumes, scenery, and panels for a set were constructed and painted; these events were spurred on by the visual and performing arts teachers. Students throughout the school learned about gryphons. Because the arts tend to draw people together, the students also learned much about teamwork as they carried their big projects to completion.

The hour-long program culminated with the reading of a poem written by a 14-year-old student and read by a high school student. The poet told a story of lost children searching for they knew not what, drawn to the gryphon's nest in which they discovered a courageous, wise mentor. As they dared to spread their own wings they found that they were supported not by the wind but by one another and that they, themselves, were the gryphon.

The poem was interpreted in dance by a graduating senior who is pursuing a professional dancing career. Poignant in his eagle mask and winged costume made by art students, he was accompanied by the high school band, which played original music composed by yet another student. The dancer's sensitive portrayal of the magical creature moving bravely from hopelessness to triumph served as a metaphor for many students at the school and was a fitting conclusion to the show.

Following the student's presentation, Rauschenberg discussed his work, techniques, and methods with the award winners. When an artist asked Rauschenberg, "What is the most important thing an art teacher can do for a student?" he quickly responded that it is vital to foster curiosity. Then he discussed art materials and approaches. Robert Rauschenberg usually pays for and hosts an evening dinner reception at the National Gallery of Art, during which the art teachers and school guests can see a sampling of Rauschenberg's work and hear him talk about his philosophy of art and life.

Most of the art teachers say, "It's a day in my life that's like the most wonderful dream I could have," or "From feeling like the low man on the totem pole in my school, to going to the National Gallery of Art to feel honored and treasured, I am flying...." Robert Rauschenberg gives each winner a hand-painted certificate that he has created especially for the day as well as a present to each of the art teachers' schools of $500 to $1,000 worth of art supplies. The whole day is a gift that keeps on giving.

Great artists need to be invited into schools to inspire children and teachers and to encourage everyone to reach a little higher, a bit wider, and in new directions. As Joanie, age 14, said, "That great man thinks we're important enough to give us a moment of his time. I wonder if he truly knows how much it means to all of us." He cares deeply and once said, "The possibility always exists to nourish an important new genius in learning disabled children, if their spirit is not broken and creative dreams are allowed to develop" (Rauschenberg Day, 1997).

EXCEPTIONAL LEARNERS CAN SUCCEED THROUGH THE ARTS

We see the magic daily; for example, Aviva, Blair, Will, and Ariel bring visitors to see the life-size model of a space ship rocket they have just built in science, and they excitedly describe its powers. Owen and Daniel show me the old telephone that they have transformed into a frightening mask, which will hang on the wall outside of my office. Ian fences in the school's rendition of *Hamlet*. Nica and Stephen jitterbug as part of their report on the 1940s. Angus sculpts the faces of Aristotle, Plato, and Socrates on bookends while Brian does a brass rubbing to place on his clay Gothic cathedral. These children are deeply involved in what they are doing. They are having fun, they are enthusiastic, and they are learning science, literature, history, philosophy, and a whole host of academic subjects. Here are the children that some experts have condemned to lives of total failure, some of whom were in four schools before they were even 6 years old, and one who had given up on life and schooling but was cajoled back to school. These students are going to achieve high school diplomas. More than 90% will go on to colleges, and a few of them will continue on to graduate school.

These children are our future. They are walking into the uncertainties of the 21st century capable of problem solving, able to do critical thinking, and able to communicate ideas through technology, pictures, charts, models, and other means. For exceptional learners, education indeed can make the difference between a productive life or a life full of failure. The arts, taught properly, can impart academic learning. The arts bring a sense of awe and wonder back into education, building vigorous minds. The arts foster connections, relationships, bridges between the old and the new. Arts education is the best teacher of what a civilization *is* and *can be*. The power of the arts can, in fact, empower exceptional learners. The arts of tomorrow, like the arts of ancient times, need to prevail to educate and civilize all of us.

A Clarion Call

THE GOOD NEWS[1]

New York City's Project Arts provides classroom resources and gives teachers access to arts organizations; in addition, they have begun to teach teachers through the arts. It claims persuasively that the arts help students measure up to solid academic standards in all subjects.

A prominent researcher from the University of California, Los Angeles, analyzed data on more than 25,000 students from the U.S. Department of Education's National Educational Longitudinal Study and discovered that students who participated extensively in the arts did better on a number of academic measures, regardless of socioeconomic status, than did those who were not involved in the arts. He also discovered that prolonged participation in music and theater was reflected in students' success in math and reading.

Fifty of the Los Angeles district's 540 elementary schools signed on to a voluntary arts education program in the year 2000. These districts are trying to thread the

---

[1]Adapted from Manzo, K.K. (2000). Classroom renaissance. *Education Week, 19*(35), 36–41.

arts deep in the curriculum. Fifty more districts are planning to begin an arts program in 2001.

Of the 127 public schools in Minneapolis, 40 have added arts-related strategies to their curricula.

In 2000, Boston hired 65 new arts specialists and constructed its first arts high school.

Florida's Miami-Dade County System won acclaim from the Getty Foundation as the county most supportive of arts education in the nation.

THE BAD NEWS

In many states, arts programs have been cut to free money for reducing class size, buying computers, strengthening athletic programs, employing more psychologists, or adding security personnel.

In many communities, it is believed that purely academic standards must be made more rigorous; and therefore, the amount of time students spend in arts classes must be drastically reduced or eliminated.

THE TEST SCORE FETISH

Educators place a high value on tests, which are believed to measure intellectual success; however, tests are not pro-child and do not consider children's best interests! It is simple to measure whether test scores have gone up or down or stayed the same. It is less simple to measure a student's reasoning, ability to compare ideas, and original thinking. It is difficult to determine the effect of the arts on academic achievement even though assessment tools have been devised to do so. There is an inherent value of the arts to body, soul, spirit, and intellect that cannot be quantified easily. Exceptional learners often are not administered tests because they bring down the school or district's scores.

Exceptional learners are the real victims in a climate of competing assessment. The constant pressure of legislators all over this country to raise the bar and to force more testing tends to produce the one-size-fits-all approach to teaching and assessment. When schooling becomes all about passing tests, it is a passive, certainly not an intellectual, journey.

The dendrites (or "magic trees of the mind") to which Dr. Marian Diamond refers (see Chapter 3) do not develop when schooling becomes one long drill. Many practices designed to prepare students to score well on state assessments are not sound education practice; thinking on a higher level suffers. Rote memorization becomes the basis of the score sheet.

As Howard Gardner says in *The Disciplined Mind,*

> The ultimate success of a school depends on the quality of its personnel, the thoughtfulness of the programs, the sustained involvement of parents and the larger community and the willingness to make mistakes and to learn from them. None of these is susceptible to a quick fix...high-quality school and high-performing students have not achieved this status overnight. Rather, they have devoted years to articulating a program and making sure that it is carried out systematically, thoroughly, and reflectively. (1999, p. 235)

Amen. Those of us who have been active in the field of education for many years know well that there are no quick fixes, no miraculous cures, no panaceas, and no easy answers. There are certain camouflages that can give the appearance of instant achievement; however, these fixes usually are due to manipulation of results. Many of us have shared the experience of studying night and day for a test and then not being able to remember the material a week later. We discover that cramming is a short-term memory exercise; unlike the participation in the arts, it does not result in life-time learning.

ARTS TEACHERS

Often, arts teachers are the hidden treasures of our schools. We must bring them forth into the central hallways where they can enrich learning in all subjects and bring out the glorious creativity of the other teachers in our schools. Arts teachers can help our schools to flourish and help our students learn even more effectively.

Traditionally, arts classrooms and teachers have provided refuge for "different" students, solace for the wounded, and a comfort zone for almost all students, as well as a training ground for the talented. The arts help the brain to develop and to become more available for learning. As Norman Cousins, a theorist who believes in the power of the human mind over the body, said so eloquently, "The growth of the human mind is still high adventure, in many ways the highest adventure on earth." Artists, art teachers, and general education teachers are all needed to help children use and enjoy the ride.

SPECIAL EDUCATION

Very little research has taken place on the role of the arts in special education and with exceptional learners. The Lab School experience is that, in many cases, the arts are the lifeline, the savior, the generator of success. It is within one art form or another that students demonstrate deep interest or talent, which can serve as a hook for further learning.

Teaching through the arts is a creative solution to new mandates in education, such as the Individuals with Disabilities Education Act (IDEA) of 1990 (PL 101-476), which grew out of the most humane legislation ever created in America: the Education for All Handicapped Children Act of 1975 (PL 94-142). These laws sup-port a free and appropriate public education (FAPE) in the least restrictive environ-ment (LRE) for all children of all abilities.

The IDEA Amendments of 1997 (PL 105-17) challenge educators to provide stu-dents with learning differences with access to the core curriculum. It mandates that ed-ucators use alternative assessments (e.g., portfolios) in the classroom and in large-scale assessments (e.g., achievement testing) to evaluate the strengths of students who learn differently. Much of this activity is expected to take place in general education class-rooms that contain diverse populations. In order to produce viable results, educators must know how to modify curricula to help these students acquire the same concepts as their higher achieving peers without disabilities. The goal is to "raise the bar" for all students by raising expectations and facilitating achievement. The arts can serve as a vehicle to excellence and equity in education. The arts can be life empowering for exceptional learners.

This is why, particularly for children whose lives are on the line, the arts need to be on a par with math, science, social studies, and athletics. All of these subjects are vital to a quality education, but to achieve the goal of excellence and equity, administrators, teachers, parents, and children need to adopt new attitudes. Politicians and school board members must come to see the intrinsic value of the arts to all children and the overwhelming need of exceptional students for a chance to flourish, to find their routes to learning, and to build their sense of themselves.

This is school reform at its best! It is very American in that it crosses new frontiers to achieve an independence of spirit and the opportunity to develop potential in new and spectacular ways.

Americans have a history of breaking with tradition. In order to empower our millions of children with exceptional learning needs, we must break with the educational tradition that has existed since our school system began. All of us have to change on behalf of our exceptional students to offer them the future they deserve and to help them to participate more effectively in society. We must revolutionize our thinking about teacher education and about curricula so that the arts can permeate school experience and so that concrete, visual, object-centered learning becomes the norm.

References

Allen, A., & Allen, G. (1998). *Everyone can win*. McLean, VA: EPM Publications.

American Psychiatric Association. (1994). *Diagnostic and statistical manual of mental disorders* (4th ed.). Washington, DC: Author.

Ames, K., & Peyser, M. (1990, Fall/Winter). Why Jane can't draw (or sing, or dance...). *Newsweek Special Edition*, 40–49.

Armstrong, T. (1994). *Multiple intelligences and the child*. Alexandria, VA: Association for Supervision and Curriculum Development.

Ayres, J. (1979). *Sensory integration and the child*. Los Angeles: Western Psychological Services.

Bartlett, F.C. (1932). *Remembering*. United Kingdom: Cambridge University Press.

Bos, C., & Vaughn, S. (1988). *Strategies for teaching students with learning and behavior problems*. Needham Heights, MA: Allyn & Bacon.

Bryan, T.H., & Bryan, J.H. (1986). *Understanding learning disabilities*. Palo Alto, CA: Mayfield Publishing.

Carter, R. (1998). *Mapping the mind*. Berkeley: University of California Press.

Csikszentmihalyi, M. (1996). *Creativity: Flow and the psychology of invention*. New York: HarperPerennial.

Damasio, A.R. (1995). *Descartes' error: Emotion, reason and the human brain*. New York: Avon Books, Inc.

Denckla, M. (1996). A theory and model of executive function: A neuropsychological perspective. In G.R. Lyon & N. Krasnegor (Eds.), *Attention, memory, and executive function* (pp. 263–278). Baltimore: Paul H. Brookes Publishing Co.

Deschler, D., & Ellis, E. (1995). *Teaching adolescents with learning disabilities strategies and methods*. Denver, CO: Love Publishing Co.

Dewey, J. (1939). *Education and experience*. New York: Collier Books.

Dewey, J. (1954). *Art and education: A collection of essays* (3rd ed.). Merion, PA: Barns Foundation Press.

Diamond, M., & Hopson, J. (1998). *Magic trees of the mind: How to nurture your child's intelligence, creativity, and healthy emotions*. New York: Penguin Books.

DuPont, S. (1992). The effectiveness of creative drama as an instructional strategy to enhance the reading comprehension skills of fifth-grade remedial readers. *Reading Research and Instruction, 31*(3), 41–52.

Education for All Handicapped Children Act of 1975, PL 94-142, 20 U.S.C. §§ 1400 *et seq.*

Eisner, E. (1997). The roots of art in schools: An historical view from a comtemporary perspective. *Educating artistic vision*. Reston, VA: The National Art Education Association.

Fein, S. (1984). *Heidi's horse*. Pleasant Hill, CA: Exelrod Press.

Fiske, E. (1991). *Smart schools, smart kids: Why do some schools work?* New York: Touchstone.

Fowler, C. (1996). *Strong arts, strong schools: The promising potential and shortsighted disregard of the arts in American schools*. New York: Oxford University Press.

Galdwell, M. (1999, August 2). The physical genius: What do Wayne Gretsky, Yo-Yo Ma, and a brain surgeon named Charlie Wilson have in common? *The New Yorker*, 57-65.

Gardner, H. (1984). *Art, mind, and brain: A cognitive approach to creativity*. New York: Basic Books.

Gardner, H. (1984). Artistry after brain damage. In H. Gardner, *Art, mind, and brain: A cognitive approach to creativity* (pp. 318–335). New York: Basic Books.

Gardner, H. (1991). *The unschooled mind: How children think and how schools should teach them*. New York: Basic Books.

Gardner, H. (1993). *Creating minds: An anatomy of creativity seen through the lives of Freud, Einstein, Picasso, Stravinksy, Eliot, Graham, and Ghandi.* New York: Basic Books.

Gardner, H. (1999). *The disciplined mind: What all students should understand.* New York: Simon & Schuster.

Goleman, D. (1995). *Emotional intelligence.* New York: Bantam Books.

Goodlad, J.I. (1984). *A place called school: Promise for the future.* New York: McGraw-Hill.

Grandin, T. (1995). *Thinking in pictures: And other reports from my life with autism.* New York: Vintage Books.

Greene, M. (1995). *Releasing the imagination: Essays on education, the arts, and social change.* New York: Jossey-Bass Publishers.

Hammill, D.D., & Bartel, N.R. (1995). *Teaching students with learning and behavior problems: Managing mild-to-moderate difficulties in resource and inclusive settings* (6th ed). Austin, TX: PRO-ED.

Healy, J.M. (1991). *Endangered minds.* New York: Simon and Schuster.

Hudspeth, C.C. (1987). The cognitive and behavioral consequences of using music and poetry in a fourth grade language arts classroom. *Dissertation Abstracts International, 47*(8-A), 2884.

Individuals with Disabilities Education Act (IDEA) of 1990, PL 101-476, 20 U.S.C. §§ 1400 *et seq.*

Individuals with Disabilities Education Act Amendments of 1997, PL 105-17, 20 U.S.C. §§ 1400 *et seq.*

Ivey, B. (1999, March). *Coming together around common concerns: The arts are our future.* Keynote address to the National Art Education Association, Washington, D.C.

Jensen, E. (1998). *Teaching with the brain in mind.* Alexandria, VA: Association for Supervision and Curriculum Development (ASCD).

Johnson, D., & Myklebust, H. (1967). *Learning disabilities: Educational principles and practices.* New York: Grune & Stratton.

Kafai, Y., & Resnick, M. (1996). *Constructionism in practice: Designing, thinking and learning in a digital world.* Mahwah, NJ: Laurence Erlbaum Associates.

Kilpatrick, W.H. (1925). *Foundations of method: Informal talks on teaching.* New York: Macmillan Publishing.

Kranowitz, C. (1998). *The out-of-sync child.* New York: Penguin Putnam.

Lerner, J. (2000). *Learning disabilities: Theories, diagnosis, and teaching strategies* (8th ed.). Boston: Houghton Mifflin.

Lyon, G.R. (1994). *Frames of reference for the assessment of learning disabilities.* Baltimore: Paul H. Brookes Publishing Co.

Mabry, L. (1991). Alexander Dumas Elementary School, Chicago, Illinois. In R. Stake, L. Bresler, & L. Mabry, *Custom and cherishing: The arts in elementary schools.* Urbana, IL: Council for Research in Music Education.

Manzo, K.K. (2000). Classroom Renaissance. *Education Week, 19*(35), 36–41.

McGuigan, C. (1999, November 22). The man who designed Bilbao: An interview with Frank Gehry. *Newsweek,* 92.

Miller, L.K. (1989). *Musical savants: Exceptional skill in the mentally retarded.* Mahwah, NJ: Lawrence Erlbaum Associates.

Moore, B.H., & Caldwell, H. (1993). Drama and drawing for narrative writing in primary grades. *Journal of Education Research, 87*(2), 100–110.

National Institutes of Health. (1998, November 16–18). Diagnosis and treatment of attention deficit hyperactivity disorder. *National Institutes of Health Consensus Development Conference Statement Online, 16*(2), 1–37.

Nonmonovitch, S. (1990). *Free play: Improvisation in life and art.* New York: Jeremy P. Tarcher.

O'Farrell, L. (1993). Enhancing the practice of drama in education through research. *Youth Theatre Journal, 7*(4), 25–30.

Paley, N. (1995). *Finding arts place: Experiments in contemporary education and culture.* London: Routledge.

Peters, T. (1982). *In search of excellence.* New York: Harper and Row.

Pinker, S. (1997). *How the mind works.* New York: Norton.

Reed, E.S. (1996). *The necessity of experience.* New York: Yale University Press.

Sacks, O. (1996). Prodigies. In O. Sacks, *An anthropologist on mars* (pp. 188–243). New York: Vintage Books.

Sacks, O. (1996). A surgeon's life. In O. Sacks, *An anthropologist on mars* (pp. 77–107). New York: Vintage Books.

Schulte, B. (1999, December 15). Kindergarten gets tougher: New Montgomery curriculum favors academics over naps. *The Washington Post*, p. B01.

Silver, L.B. (1984). *The misunderstood child.* New York: McGraw Hill.

Smith, S.L. (1993). *Succeeding against the odds: How the learning-disabled can realize their promise.* New York: Jeremy P. Tarcher.

Smith, S.L. (1994). *Different is not bad, different is the world: A book about disabilities.* Longmont, CO: Sopris West.

Smith, S.L. (1995). *No easy answers: The learning disabled child at home and at school.* New York: Bantam.

Smith, S.L. (1996/1997). Succeeding through the arts. In *Their world* (pp. 34–39). New York: National Council for Learning Disabilities.

Smith, S.L. (1998, October/November). Teaching academic skills through the visual arts. *Momentum, 29*(4) 19–22.

Smith, S.L., & Irvine, S.E. (1999). Technology the Lab School way: A multisensory empowering experience for students with severe learning disabilities and ADHD. *Learning Disabilities: A Multidisciplinary Journal, 9*(3).

Spitzer, M. (1999). *The mind within the net.* Cambridge, MA: The MIT Press.

Stenzel, M. (1994, December). Kids did it!: He digs history. *National Geographic World, 232,* 21.

Storr, R. (1998). *Chuck Close.* New York: Harry N Abrams.

Timpe, A.D. (1987). *Creativity: The art and science of business management.* New York: Kend Publishing.

Trusty, J., & Oliva, G.M. (1994). The effects of arts and music education on students' self-concept. *Update: Applications of Research in Music Education, 13*(1), 23–28.

U.S. Department of Labor. (1993). *The Secretary's Commission on Achieving Necessary Skills (SCANS) executive summary.* Washington, DC: Author.

Van Witsen, B. (1979). *Perceptual training activities handbook.* New York: Harper & Row.

Vygotsky, L. (1978). *Mind in society: The interaction between learning and development.* Cambridge, MA: Harvard University Press.

Wadsworth, B.J. (1995). *Piaget's theory of cognitive and affective development* (5th ed.). New York: Longman.

Weil, S.W., & McGill, I. (1989). *Making sense of experiential learning.* Philadelphia: The Society for Research into Higher Education and Open University Press.

West, T.G. (1997). *In the mind's eye: Visual thinkers, gifted people with dyslexia and other learning difficulties, computer images and the ironies of creativity.* Amherst, NY: Prometheus Books.

Wilson, B. (1993). *Popular art and school art: Comic books and Japanese children's graphic narrative constructions of reality.* Paper presented at the meeting of the Jean Piaget Society, Philadelphia.

Wilson, F.R. (1999). *The hand.* New York: Vintage Books.

Wingert, P., & Kantrowitz, B. (1997, October 27). Why Andy couldn't read. *Newsweek,* 56–64.

Winner, E. (1982). *Invented worlds: The psychology of the arts.* Cambridge, MA: Harvard University Press.

Winner, E. (1998). *Gifted children: Myths and realities.* New York: Basic Books.

Wolk, S. (1994). Project-based learning: Pursuits with a purpose. *Educational Leadership, 52*(3), 42–45.

Yanow-Schwartz, J. (1994). Experimenting wih the arts in education. In *American artist* (pp. 70–74). New York: BPI Communications.

Zeki, S. (1999). *Inner vision: An exploration of art and the brain.* Oxford, England: Oxford University Press.

Appendixes

THE ARTS
A way of life for some
THE ARTS
A lifeline for others
THE ARTS
Help children feel smart, not dumb

THE ARTS
Provide a refuge, even some solace
THE ARTS
Profice excitement and adventure
THE ARTS
Energize those who have run out of gas

THE ARTS
Civilize students and can develop wit
THE ARTS
Make history, math, and science come alive
THE ARTS
Awaken and feed the human spirit

THE ARTS
Teach the exceptional student
THE ARTS
Teach the child more than traditional learning
THE ARTS
Teach what is implied and what is meant

THE ARTS
Are often Heaven sent
THE ARTS
Stimulate the exceptional child to learn
THE ARTS
Awaken the child who is different

We need THE ARTS
to be more prominent
in our schools
in our schooling,
particularly
with children
who learn differently

Task Analyses

In order to teach students with moderate to severe learning disabilities effectively, a teacher must isolate and build on a child's strengths and then work on the child's weak areas through his strengths. Equally as important is the teacher's ability to break into smaller units the task that the child is being asked to do. This job, which is called *task analysis*, requires analytical thinking. It helps to do the task first and then break it down. The greater the amount of detail, the more useful the task analysis is. At The Lab School, artists as well as teachers must do task analyses.

TASK ANALYSIS FOR READING AND UNDERSTANDING THE CALENDAR

Reading a calendar requires the ability to decode words and numbers. Understanding a calendar requires the ability to comprehend the concept of time, the representation of symbols, and the knowledge that the names of months, the days of the week, and individual dates relate to each other. To fully grasp the idea of how a calendar works, the student must recognize that it tells about the past, the present, and the future. Once the student comprehends the concrete units of years, months, and days, the teacher can explain the more advanced scientific theories of the sun, moon, and stars and how the solar system relates to the calendar.

Vision is the primary perceptual skill required for reading a calendar. The visual elements include

- *Figure–ground* to distinguish the calendar from its background in space and to distinguish specific signs on the calendar page
- *Spacing* to comprehend the grid structure representing the month and days and to comprehend how to group words and numbers in their correct space

- *Form constancy* to recognize that although a calendar might appear in a different format, such as a week at a time, month at a time, or entire year on one page, it still represents the same concept

- *Directional constancy* to differentiate horizontal from vertical and understand the significance of each on the calendar

- *Laterality* to know right from left

- *Eye tracking* to be able to accurately follow horizontal, vertical, right, and left directions

In order to comprehend the calendar, students also must know

- How to count from 1 to 31

- The names of the months and the order in which they always occur

- The names of the days of the week and the order in which they always occur

- The abbreviations of the months of the year and the days of the week

- How to recognize holidays that are noted on the calendar

- How to personalize a calendar by transcribing important personal dates, such as birthdays, vacation dates, and special family dates onto the calendar

Specific facts must be known in order for the student to conceptualize the way in which a calendar functions. These facts include the following:

- Time can be measured and organized into units of a day, a month, and a year, and these units are what comprise a calendar.

- The year is generally written using four numbers representing century, decade, and exact year.

- There are 12 months in a year.

- The months have 30 or 31 days with the exception of February.

- There are seven days in a week.

- Yesterday is the day before, and tomorrow is the day after.

- On most calendars, a week starts with Sunday and ends with Saturday.

- Each number on the calendar page represents a day, and if there is a space on the page without a number, it is not to be counted as a day in that month.

- A month can start and end on any day of the week.

- If a month or year ends on a Tuesday, the next month or year will begin on Wednesday, which is true for any sequence of days in the week.

- On some calendars if the number of days in the month exceeds the spaces allowed for that number, a diagonal line is used with the top number representing the fourth week and the bottom number representing the fifth week—23/30.

- The date always is given with the day first, then the month, then the date, and finally the year.

Whereas the sequential names of the days of the week and months of the year must be memorized in order to use a calendar, the concept of how the days and the months relate to one another must be understood in order to apply this information effectively and make it meaningful.

TASK ANALYSIS FOR TEACHING A CHILD TO USE A YO-YO

Using a yo-yo is not as easy as it looks; in fact, it requires mastery of many fundamental skills. The qualitative components of using a yo-yo are

- *Preparation phase:* The elbow is flexed at 90 degrees, the forearm is internally rotated, and the dominant hand is in front of the body holding the yo-yo with the loop at the end of the string placed on the middle finger.
- *Movement:* Movements include the following:

  1. The elbow flexes tightly to about 45 degrees.
  2. The arm extends rapidly while quickly extending the wrist.
  3. The fingers release the yo-yo just as the wrist flicks upward quickly.
  4. The eyes observe the drop and track the yo-yo.
  5. The arm extends as the shoulder flexes for the yo-yo to reach end of string.
  6. Just as the yo-yo reaches the end of the line, the wrist must again extend with a quick movement, using just the right amount of upward pull to cause the yo-yo to roll back up the string. Some experienced yo-yo players report that they can tell when the moment is right by the changing sound of the yo-yo string as it unwinds.
  7. The elbow bends to absorb force.
  8. The hand grips the yo-yo as it returns.
  9. At the moment the hand grasps the yo-yo again, the child must decide quickly whether to throw the yo-yo again, which would require a rapid redeployment of the yo-yo, or to hold on to the yo-yo and stop playing.

As those who have tried to use a yo-yo know, timing and movements are not learned easily. The potential yo-yo master has to be able to withstand the frustration of not learning right away and of having to rewind the yo-yo by hand for unsuccessful launches and must not get discouraged if the return is accompanied by getting hit by the hard end of the yo-yo. Frustration tolerance, perseverance, and the ability to adjust motor planning to fine-tune the skill all are involved in this seemingly simple act.

STEP 1: EXPLAINING TO THE CHILD HOW TO USE THE YO-YO

Attention

- *Coming to attention:* The child must be able to focus his attention on the task being taught.

- *Selective attention:* The child must be able to concentrate on the task of using the yo-yo. He must be able to follow directions and not be distracted by outside stimuli.

- *Sustained attention:* The student must be able to focus throughout the drop AND the pull of the yo-yo.

- *Body image:* The child must be aware of his body in space.

- *Directionality:* The child must face the teacher and make eye contact

- *Vestibular control:* The child must be able to sit or stand long enough to hear the directions.

- *Selective listening:* The child must choose to focus on the voice of the teacher and block out other distracting noises.

- *Sustained listening:* The child must concentrate on the teacher showing him how to use the yo-yo. He must hear the words and remain focused until the drop and pull are complete. This child must continue to concentrate after the demonstration is completed, until cognition and comprehension are achieved.

Auditory Perception

- *Auditory acuity:* The child must *hear* the directions.

- *Auditory discrimination:* The child must distinguish the teacher's voice from surrounding sounds. The child must hear the difference between the individual phonemes and hear these phonemes blended into words.

- *Auditory sequencing:* The child must hear the phonemes in the appropriate order, forming morphemes. These morphemes must be heard in the correct order, forming meaningful words. The child must hear the words in the correct syntactic order to understand the process of using a yo-yo.

Receptive Language

The child must understand several aspects of language:

- Phonemes are blended to form morphemes, and morphemes carry meaning.
- Morphemes make up words and therefore have meaning.
- The vocabulary of the words must be understood.
- The words of the sentence are syntactically ordered in the sentence for the purpose of conveying intended specific meanings.

STEP 2: ORIENTING THE BODY IN PREPARATION FOR USE
Gross Motor Skills

Although throwing a yo-yo primarily is a fine motor skill, there are some aspects of the task that involve the larger muscle groups (i.e., gross motor skills).

- *Directionality:* Conceptually, the child must be able to understand what it means to move forward, drop the yo-yo down, move his wrist up, and so forth.

- *Flexibility:* The position of the body must be flexible in relation to the yo-yo. The child must be able to bend and twist to accommodate a bad drop or eventually to perform more elaborate yo-yo moves.

- *Body awareness:* The child must be aware of his entire body. He needs to know and understand that his arms contribute to his balance and movement.

- *Postural stability:* The trunk must provide a stable base for arm and hand movement. Likewise, the position of the feet and legs add to that stable base and are placed just far enough apart to balance the movement of the arms and hands.

- *Ability to isolate movement:* The child must be able to isolate movement of different parts of the body, such as the separate movement of the elbow from the shoulder and the forearm from the elbow.

- *Ability to control force exerted by large muscles:* This is very important. If the shoulder movement is too forceful, when the yo-yo is released, it may shoot upward instead of down. If the elbow flexes too hard, the yo-yo will likely hit the child.

The child with learning disabilities is *unable* to function if territory is not defined and he is unsure of where he is in space. Sometimes, there is also difficulty in isolating movements so, for example, when the elbow extends, the whole arm and fingers extend, making any motor planning difficult. Frequently, children with learning disabilities have what is referred to as *low tone*, meaning that their muscles tend not to give sufficient support to the body to maintain postural stability. It is an effort for them just to maintain an erect posture. These combined factors can severely limit gross motor activities.

Spatial Perception

- *Touch:* The child realizes where he is in space: "I am here." This is necessary for eye tracking and eye–hand coordination.

- *Position in space:* The child must understand extensions of space and perspectives from different spaces. "The yo-yo is [position]." The child must understand this so he can hold his hand at an appropriate distance from the floor for the drop.

- *Contrasts:* "Okay, the yo-yo will start there; let it go down to the bottom, then pull up." Prepositional distinctives abound.

- *Directional contrasts:* "I extend my arm like this in front of me" (versus retract or behind).

- *Size of space:* "The string is long. How far will it drop? How fast?" The child must understand concepts of *far, fast, close*, and *distant*.

STEP 3: THE YO-YO IS DROPPED AND PULLED UP

Eyes observe the drop and track the yo-yo to the bottom of the string; then, the child pulls the yo-yo back up to the hands.

Visual Perception

The child must have a good sense of body laterality and spatial judgment to achieve accurate visual perception.

- *Observation skills:* The child must be able to concentrate through the entire drop and use sequencing skills to know when to pull.
- *Discrimination:* The child must have fast visual analysis and synthesis. The child must also understand and visualize the curve of a drop.
- *Form constancy:* The child must recognize that the yo-yo is the same size and weight even when it is in the air and looks much smaller.
- *Figure-ground:* The child must distinguish the yo-yo from the background. He must isolate the yo-yo moving through the background and not be distracted by external stimuli.

Space

- *Watching space:* The child must move and focus his eyes accurately and smoothly on the yo-yo. The eyes should be able to smoothly track the yo-yo while the head maintains a stable position. The child must also be able to judge the shorter distances as the yo-yo approaches the bottom of the string.
- *Moving in space:* The child has to plan his arm and hand movements through space in relationship to the yo-yo and his environment. He must be able to judge whether there is room to sail the yo-yo through space without bumping into anything.

Time

- *Informal measures of time/intervals of time:* The child must be able to estimate the time it will take for that yo-yo to get from his hand to the end of the string. The child also must estimate the time it takes to go through the sequence (of getting arms up and ready) to pull up the yo-yo. As the yo-yo is approaching his hands, the child must coordinate these time intervals so they both cease at precisely the time that his hands grasp the yo-yo.
- *Sequence of time:* Yo-yo is dropped; extend arm; yo-yo is almost there; pull; yo-yo is almost here.
- *Speeds of time:* The child must understand the difference between a fast drop and a slow drop and make the interval changes accordingly. This is very necessary for eye tracking.
- *Timing:* The child must sense the relationship between the drop and the pull and must simultaneously sense the rhythm of the drop and pull to estimate an accurate arrival (catch) time.

STEP 4: THE YO-YO IS CAUGHT

Contact with the yo-yo is made, hands grip the yo-yo, and elbows bend to absorb the force.

Fine Motor Skills

- *Sensory integration:* The child needs sensory integration to understand the cues from within his body and from the environment. Part of sensory integration is the ability of the brain to interpret the input from touch, or tactile, discrimination. The feel of the yo-yo in the hand and the feel of the string looped over the finger tell the child that the yo-yo is held properly. When the round yo-yo returns to the hand, the child senses by the feel of the object whether it is in the right position.

- *Coordination:* The child must first have his hands and fingers at the appropriate angle for the yo-yo to fit into his grip. Then he must know where his fingers are. These same fingers must be able to smoothly translate (move) the yo-yo from the palm of the hand to the fingertips and then quickly release the yo-yo without releasing the loop of the string. Finally, the child must be able to move his fingers to grip the yo-yo with the right amount of pressure when it returns. Holding too tightly will mean stopping. Holding it loosely enables a rapid redeployment, and play can continue. This skill also requires eye–hand coordination to coordinate the grip with the time of impact. Visual-motor coordination is needed to coordinate movement with what the eyes are seeing. This includes the visual signal to the muscles in the arm to contract and brace the elbow and hand to absorb the impact of the returning yo-yo simultaneously with gripping the returning orb.

Time

- *Remember temporal sequences:* The child must remember what to do first. If he releases the yo-yo without first positioning the hand and extending the wrist, the yo-yo will not return properly.

- *Focus:* The child needs to be able to focus through this entire task in order for to use the yo-yo successfully. The child must be able to maintain attention while other children are playing nearby or a lawn mower is running next door. Children with attention-deficit/hyperactivity disorder may experience difficulty maintaining focus.

From this task analysis, a lesson plan is created.

Lesson Plan

To create a successful lesson plan, the teacher must put a detailed task analysis together with a profile of the child's strengths and weaknesses. Add a dose of creativity to build on the student's interest and talents, and the teacher has a lesson plan that can serve the needs of the child, hold her attention, and help the child achieve. Detailed planning is required for successful arts activities, too.

LESSON PLAN FOR TELLING TIME

Short-range goals for telling time include the following:

- Read the clock, and tell the time.
- Read the clock, and write the time.
- Set the clock according to a time that has been stated orally to the student.
- Set the clock according to a time that has been written down for the student.
- Write down a time that has been stated orally.

Long-range goals for telling time include the following:

- Student should be able to use the many different expressions for telling time.
- Student should understand time as a concept, especially in relation to space.
- Student should be able to use a variety of time pieces including digital clocks, watches, Roman numerals, clocks with no numbers, and so forth.
- Student should be able to estimate time intervals with some accuracy.

This lesson plan is designed to cover only immediate short-range goals. Some aspects of the long-range goals will begin to be taught within the teaching of the short-range goals. Other aspects, in primitive form (e.g., understanding time as a concept), are of necessity already present in elemental form to allow the child to begin to tell time.

The following list is an example of further analysis of a child's strengths and weaknesses to determine appropriate and inappropriate methods of teaching him to tell time:

- He is old enough to understand basic space/time interval.
- Written matter on time will not be of much use to him by himself.
- He can probably do his best work in some form of discovery method.
- His good verbal skills can be used for providing him with feedback regarding his problems and reinforcement for what he learns (by repeated feedback).
- The logic of a clock appeals to him.
- He already has a comprehension of time as an abstract.
- His poor auditory skills suggest use of a kinesthetic approach.
- His poor visual skills reinforce the idea of a kinesthetic approach.
- Misbehavior is less likely if he actively is involved in the task.
- Role play can be used for teaching some concepts.
- Gross motor skills can be utilized.
- His drawing skills can be used, but writing should be limited.
- He can work out the math of a clock (e.g., a quarter hour, half an hour) in his head.
- He is given support with writing numbers, perhaps by using stencils.

SETTING CONDITIONS

This child should have access to a wide variety of timepieces to play with, take apart, and simply fool around with at times other than the specific time set aside for teaching time. Because of his age, real clocks and watches minus faces will be more appealing than "babyish" toy clocks and paper plate clocks.

There are some clock songs (e.g., Grandfather's Clock) that reinforce the rhythm of time. Other number sequence songs may also be useful.

BASIC TEACHING TECHNIQUE

The basic teaching technique is the development of a "body clock." The student will participate actively in the construction of the clock. The body clock also will be the device for helping the student transition to the use of a regular clock. The body clock typically will be secured to the floor, but during the transition phase, it will be pinned up on a wall.

The fundamental idea is to make the diameter of the clock equal to the height of the student to give him maximum identification with his body and the clock.

Step 1

Secure a large, sturdy piece of paper to a double thickness of wallboard on the floor. Find the center of the paper, and drive a nail into that spot. Secure a piece of string (fastened so that it moves freely on the nail) to the nail, and at the end of the string, put a large magic marker that easily can be held. The length of the string from the nail to pen should be half the height of the boy. Show the child how to hold the string out tight and have him draw a circle. There may have to be a couple of retakes on this, but try to get a clean circle. This will begin to give the student the concrete experience of the form of a clock. *It is important that the child draw the circle in a clockwise direction, even if it requires him to get down on the floor to do so.* Note to the student that the reason he has to draw the circle in a clockwise direction is because this is the direction in which the clock moves.

Step 2

Designate the point at the top of the circle where the child began to draw, and write the number 12 in magic marker in large, easily read numbers outside of the circle. Then give the student sturdy stencils and a wide magic marker and tell him where he should add the rest of the numbers outside of the circle. Make sure the student knows that these numbers represent hours. Do not use half or quarter hour or minutes in talking about the task. That will come later.

Step 3

Have the child walk clockwise around the clock face calling off the hours (e.g., "1 o'clock") as he comes to them. When he can sequence this correctly, have him lie face down on the clock. (This is the "body" view he will use in telling time when he is upright). As he supports himself on his left arm, have him point to the hours (beginning with one) with his right hand, saying the hour as he comes to each number in sequence. At the 6 (or 5, whichever seems best for him) have him roll over and with the other hand continue to 12— always saying the hour out loud as he comes to it.

All directions at this point and at any other point during the activity must be simple, direct, and given only when the student clearly is attending. Use correct prepositions to accustom him to thinking in terms of *moving away from* or *moving to* on the face of the clock.

When the student can do this succession of numbers and movements and statements of hours successfully, reward him with a rousing record of "Rock Around the Clock!"

Step 4

Continue to practice the sequence both on foot and face down until no mistakes are made. Meanwhile, discuss the fact that clocks are made up of 60 minutes. Have him work out in his head what half, one quarter, and three quarters of 60 minutes would be (explain that 1/4 and quarter mean the same). If the students needs a concrete form of counting, give him counters. Have him lay the 60 counters out in a ring, and help mark the ring at 5-minute intervals and write the number.

Step 5

Repeat Step 1, only this time, draw the circle on a large piece of sturdy, clear plastic and number the circle *inside* with the minutes at five minute intervals. The teacher may have to help with this part of the activity if stencils are too hard for the child to use on this.

Repeat Steps 2 and 3, only this time the child will simply say, "5 minutes" or, "10 minutes." When the sequence is correct, have the child add at 15-minute intervals,

"15 minutes or one quarter of an hour" and, "30 minutes or one half of an hour," until that is well fixed.

Step 6

Now combine the two clock faces (plastic on top), and add two lightweight pieces of plastic (fixed to swing easily from the center nail) as clock hands. Be sure the short hand is much shorter. Now have the student push the shorter hour hand around, calling off the hours. He will soon find out that he cannot move the hour hand without moving the minute hand. Have him walk the minute hand around. Then have him sequence the hour and the minute hand: "This is 6 o'clock and 5 minutes," "6 o'clock and 10 minutes," and so forth.

Step 7

While continuing to practice on the clock faces (vary it by having the student set the hands with his toes, nose, and so forth) have the student role play a journey by walking between two chairs. Ask him when is he walking *to* the chair? When is he walking *from* the chair? When is he after, when before? When he understands how these terms can be used either way, return to the clock and begin to add "after" and "to." Gradually add the other time phrases as he becomes completely clear about the first ones.

Step 8

Pin the "body clock" on a wall next to a conventional school clock and begin setting sequential and, later, nonsequential times on the school clock for him to copy if he can write. When he can copy the times, ask him to write down the time. Eventually, move to writing down some times and having the student set the school clock hands—always in clockwise direction. If the student has not grasped the idea of substituting hour numbers for minutes, show him the logic behind it.

By now, the student probably is able to use other clocks and watches. Let him play with these all that he can. To provide the student with a final check, cover a digital clock face with a flap. At intervals during the day, ask the student to look at the school clock, to say and write down the time, and then to compare it with what the digital clock says.

When the student truly comprehends a 12-hour segment, explain to him that there is a twelve-hour segment for the day and an identical repeat for the night. Then introduce the terms *noon* and *midnight*. Tell the student that the day segment is called AM and the night segment PM and that AM starts at midnight and PM starts at noon. (Initially you can teach AM to mean "after midnight" and PM to mean "past morning." The correct terms can come later in the long-range goals.)

Although long-range goals are not addressed in this lesson plan, some of them are logical next steps for the student. Long-range goals might include

- Learning to use an alarm clock
- Learning to use a timer
- Trying to guess when an alarm will ring when he knows the time for which it is set but cannot see the alarm clock
- Doing language experience stories on "feelings" of time, such as when he was sick, in an accident, on vacation, at the movies, at school, with a friend, with a parent, or taking a test

The Outstanding Learning Disabled Achiever Awards

Each year The Lab School of Washington honors leaders of excellence who also have learning disablties. The awardees, who visit with Lab School students, show that people with learning disabilities can soar to any height! The following is a list of awardees and their occupations at the time of the award:

1985

G. Chris Andersen, *Investment Banker*
Cher, *Actress*
Tom Cruise, *Actor*
Bruce Jenner, *Olympic Decathlon Champion*
Robert Rauschenberg, *Artist*
Richard C. Strauss, *Real Estate Financier*

1986

Harry Anderson, *Comedian, Actor, Magician*
Ann Bancroft, *Arctic Explorer*
Frank Dunkle, *Head of U.S. Fish and Wildlife Service (deceased)*
Greg Louganis, *Olympic Diving Champion*
Henry Winkler, *Producer, Director, Actor*

1987

Marina B, *Jewelry Designer*
Chuck Close, *Artist*
Richard Cohen, *Syndicated Columnist*
Mark Torrance, *Corporation Executive*
Margaret Whitton, *Actress*
Roger W. Wilkins, *Scholar, Author, Professor*

1988

Tracey Gold, *Actress*
Malcolm Goodridge III, *Vice President, American Express*
Magic Johnson, *Basketball Star*
Thomas H. Kean, *Governor of New Jersey*
Emily Fisher Landau, *Foundation President*
Daniel Stern, *Actor*

1989

Harry Belafonte, *Singer, Actor, Humanitarian*

Gaston Caperton, *Governor of West Virginia*

William J. Doyle, *Antiques Expert, Auctioneer (deceased)*

Fred W. Friendly, *Broadcast Journalist, Scholar (deceased)*

Dexter Manley, *Football Star*

Paul J. Orfalea, *CEO, Kinko's*

1990

Donald S. Coffey, Ph.D., *Distinguished Professor, Johns Hopkins University Medical School*

Marc Flanagan, *Producer, Writer*

John R. Horner, Ph.D., *Paleontologist*

Hugh Newell Jacobsen, *FAIA, Architect*

1991

Susan Butcher, *Alaska Iditarod Dog Sled Race Winner*

Charles Guggenheim, *Documentary Filmmaker*

Wendy Wasserstein, *Prize-Winning Playwright*

Wallace Westfeldt, *Television Producer*

1992

Sir John Sway, *Premier of Bermuda*

1993

Elaine Heumann Gurian, *Deputy Director, U.S. Holocaust Memorial Museum*

Florence Haseltine, M.D., Ph.D., *Director, National Institutes of Health Center for Population Research*

J. Serward Johnson, Jr., *Sculptor*

Victor Villaseñor, *Author*

1994

Richard Avedon, *Photographer*

Fannie Flagg, *Actress, Author, Comedienne*

General Joseph Hoar, *Retired Chief of U.S. Central Command*

Raymond Smith, *CEO, Bell Atlantic*

1995

Robert Benton, *Director, Writer*

Fred J. Epstein, M.D., *Pediatric Neurosurgeon*

Neil Smith, *Football Star*

Humanitarian Award—David Copperfield, *Illusionist*

1996

James Earl Jones, *Actor*

Nell Minow, *Lawyer, Corporate Turnaround Specialist, Author*

Robert Nixon, *Filmmaker, Conservationist*

Dan O'Brien, *Olympic Decathlon Champion*

1997

Honorable Carolyn McCarthy, *Democratic Congresswoman, New York*

Steven M. Stanley, Ph.D., *Paleobiologist*

Jonathan Pendragon, *Magician, llusionist*

1998

John McDaniel, *CEO, Helix/Medlantic Healthcare*

Dianne Pilgrim, *Director, Cooper-Hewitt National Design Museum*

Vince Vaughn, *Actor*

David Yurman, *Jewelry Designer*

1999

Billy Blanks, *World Martial Arts Champion, Tae-Bo Creator*

Don Coryell, *Head Coach San Diego Chargers (Retired), College Football Hall of Fame*

Honorable Sam Gejdenson, *Democratic Congressman from Connecticut*

2000

James Carville, *Political Consultant, Senior Political Advisor, President Bill Clinton*

Kelly McGillis, *Movie Star, Shakespeare Theater Actress*

Clarence Page, *Chicago Tribune Essayist, The Newshour with Jim Lehrer*

Don Winkler, *Chairman and CEO, Ford Motor Credit Company*

The Lab School
of Washington Fact Sheet

For many years, The Lab School of Washington has been a national resource for all those concerned with the needs of the nation's 8 to 10 million children and adults with learning disabilities. This role was underscored in 1995, when The Lab School was identified by the U.S. Department of Education as a National Diffusion Network Model Education Program and public school systems were encouraged to use The Lab School as a resource and to replicate its programs. The Lab School was the only independent special education school for learning disabilities in the country to receive this distinction. In 1994–1996 and in 1996–1997, The Lab School was one of only two private special education schools in the country to receive the National Blue Ribbon Award of Excellence for both the elementary and secondary school programs.

Professor Smith is one of the nation's leading authors on learning disabilities. Her books *No Easy Answers: The Learning Disabled Child at Home and at School* (Bantam Books, 1995) and *Succeeding Against the Odds: How the Learning-Disabled Can Realize Their Promise* (Jeffrey B. Tarcher, 1993) have brought inspiration and guidance to millions of parents, teachers, and adults with learning disabilities. Her colorful children's picture book, *Different Is Not Bad, Different Is the World: A Book About Disabilities* (Sopris West, 1994) looks at the *abilities* in disabilities.

As Director of the American University Graduate Program in Learning Disabilities since 1976, Professor Smith has trained thousands of teachers in Lab School methods. Each year most of her graduate students serve their practicums under Master Teachers at The Lab School. George Washington University and Howard University also use the school as a training site for Day School practicums as well as Night School internships.

In September, 2000, The Lab School opened a campus in Baltimore for children 7 to 10 years old. It is located in Port Discovery, the Kid-Powered Museum in

Baltimore's Inner Harbor. It continues The Lab School's tradition of high quality, information centered, project learning education.

The Lab School of Washington serves as a national and international resource on learning disabilities. In addition to its Day School, The Lab School offers intensive tutoring services for children and adults, diagnostic assessment and psychotherapy for children and adults, college and career counseling, an After-School program, a 1-year training program for tutors, and speech-language and occupational therapy. The Lab School's Night School serves adults with learning disabilities. The Outreach Department offers professional development workshops for educators and mental health professionals, lectures for parents, and products including videotapes, audiotapes, books, and articles.

Index

Academic Clubs, 69–72
  Cave Club, 71
  goals of, 70
  Gods Club, 71
  Industrialists Club, 72
  Knights and Ladies Club, 71–72
  methods used in, 70–71
  Museum Club, 72
  Renaissance Club, 72
ADHD, *see* Attention-deficit/hyperactivity
  disorder
African Heritage Day, 58–59
Anxiety, 43
Apprenticeship program, 81
Archaeological dig, 59–60
Architectural design, 10, 23, 46, 78, 102–104
  designing a model house, 103–104
  helpfulness to exceptional learners, 102
  special benefit of, 102
  teaching guidelines for, 102
Art history, 78
Artists as teachers, 57–58, 141
Arts
  building confidence through, 13–14
  diagnostic clues through, 11
  exceptional learners' success through,
    136–137
  as learning tools, 5
  as organizers, 12–13, 32–33
  for people with disabilities, 3–4
  physical experience of, 6
  in preschool and kindergarten, 5
  respect for diversity and, 7–10
  symbolic meaning of, 5
  teachers of, 141
  teaching staff about the power of the,
    56–57
Arts curriculum, 3, 10–11, 139–140
  elimination of, 140
  special education and, 141–142
  test score fetish and, 140–141
  at The Lab School of Washington
    elementary school program, 67–69
    high school program, 78–81
    junior high program, 76–78
    primary program, 66–67
Arts education research, 2–3
Arts pamphlet, 81
Attention-deficit/hyperactivity disorder
  (ADHD), 3, 15, 18–19, 21, 23

prevalence of, 18
subtypes of, 18–19

Behaviors
  of children with learning disabilities, 25–26
  positive attributes of negative behaviors,
    21–24
  positive reinforcement for, 43–44
Brain circuitry and hand movements, 6–7
Bruner, Jerome, 35, 36

California Achievement Tests, 2
Cane Dance, 118
Cave Club, 71
Collages, 10, 33
Computers
  staff comfort with, 54
  Writer's Lab and, 74–75
Concrete learning, 20–21
Confidence, 13–14
"Core competencies" for workplace, 3
Critical thinking, 38–39
Curiosity, 131
Curriculum and the arts, 3, 10–11,
  139–140
Curriculum of The Lab School of
  Washington, 63–85
  elementary school program, 67–75
    Academic Clubs, 69–72
    arts, 67–69
    geography, 73–74
    science, 73
    technology/Writer's Lab, 74–75
  group projects and productions, 46–47,
    83–85, 112
  high school program, 78–83
    arts, 78–81
    general curriculum, 83
    language, 82–83
    school store/business, 82
    Senior Seminar/Ethics, 81–82
  junior high program, 75–78
    arts, 76–78
    science, 76
    social studies, 75–76
  math, 65
  primary program, 65–67
  reading and language arts, 64–65

Dance, 8–9, 117–120
  Cane Dance, 118
  classroom routine for, 119
  drama and, 120
  in elementary school program, 68
  helpfulness to exceptional learners, 117
  in junior high program, 77
  for learning sequences, 117
  as organizer, 117–119
  in primary program, 66
  special benefit of, 117
  teaching guidelines for, 119
DC Area Artists, 81
Democracy class, 75–76
Depression, 43
Development, 129–130
  motor, 130
  rushing of, 129–130
  stages of, 35
  theories of, 35–36
  training the mind through play, 131
Dewey, John, 35–36
Diagnostic clues through arts, 11
Different intelligences, 24–25, 111–112
Discipline, 12, 33
Disciplined Mind, The, 140
Disorganized children, 28, 31
  arts as organizers for, 12–13, 32–33
  establishing order in time and space,
    33–34
  neurological immaturity and, 32
Drama, 2, 9, 113–116
  classroom routine for, 115–116
  dance and, 120
  in elementary school program, 68–69
  helpfulness to exceptional learners,
    113–115
  in high school program, 79–80
  in junior high program, 77–78
  in primary program, 66
  production of silent video, 114
  special benefit of, 113
Drawing, 2, 23, 79
Dropping out of school, 17, 130
Dyslexia, 22, 24

Education for All Handicapped Children Act
  of 1975 (PL 94-142), 141
Egocentricity, 24–25
Elementary school program, 67–75
  Academic Clubs, 69–72
    Cave Club, 71
    goals of, 70
    Gods Club, 71
    Industrialists Club, 72
    Knights and Ladies Club, 71–72
    methods used in, 70–71

    Museum Club, 72
    Renaissance Club, 72
  arts, 67–69
    dance, 68
    drama, 68–69
    music, 69, 121–124
    woodwork, 68
  geography, 73–74
  science, 73
  technology/Writer's Lab, 74–75
Emotional difficulties, 41–43
Empowerment through the arts, 48
English as a second language, 2, 18, 20
Ethics class, 81–82
Eurythmics, 66
Exceptional learners, 4, 18–19
  concrete relationships and, 20–21
  difficulties experienced by, 41–43
  evaluation of, 19–20
  neurological immaturity of, 12, 19, 32
  providing order and focus through arts for,
    31–39
  success through arts, 136–137
  total involvement of, 36–37, 50
  training the mind through play, 131
  see also Learning disabilities
Experiential learning, 6, 7, 32–34, 132
Explosive children, 26
Extroverts, 111

Feuerstein, Reuven, 36
Film animation, 79, 105–110
  classroom routine for, 110
  equipping classroom for, 109
  helpfulness to exceptional learners, 109
  project for, 106–108
  special benefit of, 105
  teaching guidelines for, 110
Filmmaking, 9–10, 15
Foreign language instruction, 82–83
Free and appropriate public education, 141
Friendless children, 26
Friendships, 131

Gardner, Howard, 24, 35, 36, 140
Geography, 73–74
Goal setting, 15
Gods Club, 71
Graphic arts, 92–95
  helpfulness to exceptional learners, 92
  making a linoleum block print, 93–95
  special benefit of, 92
Graphics Squad, 77
Group projects and productions, 46–47,
  83–85, 112
Gymnastics training, 117, *see also* Dance

Hand, The: How Its Use Shapes the Brain, Language, and Human Culture, 132
Hand movements and brain circuitry, 6–7
Hands-on learning, 6, 7, 32–34, 132
High school program, 78–83
    arts, 78–81
        apprenticeship program, 81
        architectural design, 78
        art history, 78
        arts pamphlet, 81
        drama, 79–80
        drawing, 79
        film animation, 79
        music, 80, 125–127
        music perspectives, 80–81
        stage design, 79
    general curriculum, 83
    language, 82–83
    school store/business, 82
    Senior Seminar/Ethics, 81–82
Historical perspectives, 1–2
Humanities class, 75
Humor, 14

IDEA, *see* Individuals with Disabilities
        Education Act of 1990 (PL 101-476)
Identity problems, 42
Idiosyncratic solutions, 45–46
Imagination, 32
Improvisation, musical, 126, 127
Impulsive children, 27
In Search of Excellence, 57
Individualized instruction, 53
Individuals with Disabilities Education Act
        Amendments of 1997 (PL 105-17),
        141
Individuals with Disabilities Education Act
        (IDEA) of 1990 (PL 101-476), 17, 141
Industrialists Club, 72
Inquiry, 2, 55–56
Insatiable children, 27–28
Instrumental music, 121–123, 125–127, *see
        also* Music
Intellectual development, 35
Interdisciplinary teaching teams, 55
Introverts, 111

Junior high program, 75–78
    arts, 76–78
        dance, 77
        drama, 77–78
        music, 78, 121–124
        studio art, 76–77
        three-dimensional art, 77
    science, 76
    social studies, 75–76

Kindergarten arts programs, 5
Knights and Ladies Club, 71–72
Kreeger Museum, 60–61

Lab School of Washington, The
    art forms taught at, 7–10
        dance, 8–9
        drama, 9
        filmmaking, 9–10
        music, 8
        other, 10
        woodwork, 7–8
    artists as teachers at, 57–58
    arts-rich environment of, 49–50
    community involvement of, 58–61
        African Heritage Day, 58–59
        archaeological dig, 59–60
        Kreeger Museum, 60–61
        U.S. Botanical Garden, 60
    curriculum of, 63–85
        elementary school program, 67–75
        group projects and productions, 46–47,
            83–85, 112
        high school program, 78–83
        junior high program, 75–78
        math, 65
        primary program, 65–67
        reading and language arts, 64–65
    educative process at, 49–61
    goals of, 64
    parents and teachers as partners at, 14–15
    philosophy of, 7, 50
    Rauschenberg Day at, 135–136
    staff of, 51–57
        comfort with technology, 54
        commitment to inquiry, 55–56
        description of, 51
        interdisciplinary teams of, 55
        nurturing of, 53–54
        teaching about the power of the arts,
            56–57
        teaching concretely, 52
        teaching task analysis, 52–53
        teaching through problem solving, 52
        teaching through simulations, 51–52
        teaching to individualize instruction, 53
    students of, 63–64
        testimonials of, 132–135
    teaching method of, 49
    theoretical framework of, 64
Language arts curriculum at The Lab School
        of Washington, 64–65
Language impairments, 3, 11, 32
Learning
    active, 7, 21
    art forms as tools for, 5
    critical thinking and, 38–39

Learning—*continued*
  developmental theories and, 35–36
  exceptional learners, 4, 18–19
  experiential, 6, 7, 32–34, 132
  How We Learn Rap, 133–134
  lack of organizational skills for, 32
  object-centered, 21, 132
  in preschool and kindergarten, 5
  reflection and, 2
  schema theory and, 37–38
  symbolic, 131
  through total involvement, 36–37, 50
Learning disabilities, 3–4
  arts as organizers for children with, 12–13
  different intelligences and, 24–25
  different personality styles and behavior
      and, 25–28
  limiting environment of children with,
      13
  neurological immaturity and, 12, 19
  prevalence of, 17–18
  role of arts in diagnosis of, 11
  school dropout and, 17, 130
  see also Exceptional learners
Least restrictive environment, 141
Literal thinking, 20
Loners, 26

Magic Trees of the Mind, 64
Manipulative behavior, 28
Math curriculum at The Lab School of
      Washington, 64–65
Math skills, 32
  hands-on activities and, 6
  music training and, 3
Metropolitan Reading Comprehension Test,
      22
Mischief makers, 23
Motor development, 130
Museum Club, 72
Museums, 20, 21, 132
Music, 2, 8, 121–127
  elementary and intermediate, 69, 78,
      121–124
    classroom routine for, 122–123
    helpfulness to exceptional learners,
      121–122
    special benefit of, 121
    teaching guidelines for, 122
  in high school program, 80, 125–127
    classroom routine for, 127
    helpfulness to exceptional learners,
      125–127
    improvisation and experimentation
      exercise, 126, 127

  special benefit of, 125
  mathematical functioning and, 3
  in primary program, 66
Music perspectives, 80–81

National Educational Longitudinal Study,
      139
National Gallery of Art, 136
National Institute of Child Health and
      Human Development, 18
Neurological circuitry, 36
  hand movements and, 6–7
Neurological immaturity, 12, 19, 32
Nurturing of staff, 53–54

Object-centered learning, 21, 132
Organizational skills, 31–39
  arts as organizers, 12–13, 32–33
  discovering relationships, sequence, and
      logic, 34
  establishing order in time and space,
      33–34

Parents
  effect of children's success/failure on, 131
  as partners with teachers, 14–15
  pressure on children from, 130
Passion, cultivation of, 44
Perfectionists, 27
Performing arts groups, 112
Perseveration, 22, 28
Personality traits, 25–26, 111
Piaget, Jean, 35, 131
Plaster art and painting, 96–98
  classroom routine for, 96–98
  helpfulness to exceptional learners, 96
  making plaster casting sculpture, 97
  special benefit of, 96
Play, 5, 130
  training the mind through, 131
Poetry, 2
Positive reinforcement, 43–44
Preschool programs, 5, 130
Preschool skills, 37–38
Primary program, 65–67
Printmaking, 10, 33–34
Problem-solving skills, 6, 7, 22–23
  finding idiosyncratic solutions, 45–46
  teaching to staff, 52
Project Arts (New York City), 139
Project learning, 47
PL 94-142, *see* Education for All
      Handicapped Children Act of 1975

PL 101-476, *see* Individuals with Disabilities Education Act (IDEA) of 1990
PL 105-17, *see* Individuals with Disabilities Education Act Amendments of 1997
Puppetry, 10

Questioning, 2, 55–56

Reading, 130
    curriculum at The Lab School of Washington, 64–65
    difficulties with, 2, 4, 18, 31–32
Reasoning skills, 32
Rebellious children, 26
Reflection, 2
Reinforcement, positive, 43–44
Renaissance Club, 72
Research on arts education, 2–3
Rigidity, 22

SATs, *see* Scholastic Aptitude Tests
Schema theory, 37–38
Scholastic Aptitude Tests (SATs), 3
School dropout, 17, 130
School store, 82
Schooled Society, The, 36
Science
    in elementary school program, 73
    in junior high program, 76
Sculpture, 99–101
    helpfulness to exceptional learners, 99
    making geometric straw sculpture, 100–101
    special benefit of, 99
    teaching guidelines for, 99
Self-absorption, 25
Self-esteem, 3, 4, 41–48
    empowerment through the arts, 48
    low, 42
    strategies for building, 43–47
        cultivate passion and uncover talents, 44
        employ project learning, 47
        find idiosyncratic solutions, 45–46
        foster sense of group, 46–47
        make something out of nothing, 46
        provide positive reinforcement, 43–44
Senior Seminar/Ethics, 81–82
Sensitive children, 26
Sequencing skills, 31–34
    gymnastics training and, 117
Simulations for teachers, 51–52
Singing, 122–123, *see also* Music
Spanish class, 82–83

Special education, 141–142
Stage design, 79
Storytelling, 74
Stress, 42–43
Stubbornness, 22
Studio art, 76–77
Symbolic learning, 131

Task analysis, 52–53
Teachers of art, 57–58, 141
    at The Lab School of Washington, 51–57
        comfort with technology, 54
        commitment to inquiry, 55–56
        description of, 51
        interdisciplinary teams of, 55
        nurturing of, 53–54
        teaching about the power of the arts, 56–57
        teaching concretely, 52
        teaching task analysis, 52–53
        teaching through problem solving, 52
        teaching through simulations, 51–52
        teaching to individualize instruction, 53
Teamwork, 46
Technology
    staff comfort with, 54
    Writer's Lab, 74–75
Theatrical productions, *see* Drama
Three-dimensional art, 77
Time management, 34

Uncovering talents, 44
Unschooled Mind, The: How Children Think and How School Should Teach, 21
U.S. Botanical Gardens, 60

Values, 130
Visual thinkers, 23
Vocabulary, 32, 35
Vocal music, 122–123, *see also* Music

Willfulness, 22
Woodwork, 7–8, 89–91
    classroom routine for, 91
    in elementary school program, 68
    helpfulness to exceptional learners, 89–91
    instructions for making a box, 90
    special benefit of, 89
    teaching guidelines for, 91
Writer's Lab, 74–75
Writing difficulties, 24

Live It, Learn It

The Academic Club Methodology
for Students with LD and ADHD

By Sally L. Smith

Live It
Learn It

The Academic Club
Methodology for
Students with
Learning Disabilities
and ADHD

Sally L. Smith

"Awakens and enhances student learning by evoking and integrating the magical powers of exploration, art, play, and imagination."
–Nancy Mather, Ph.D., Professor, University of Arizona

Improve school success for students with learning disabilities and ADHD through the Academic Club Methodology, the proven learning-by-doing approach presented in this energizing guidebook. Sally Smith–the highly respected founder of the Lab Schools, where over 90% of students with learning disabilities go on to college–reveals how educators can immerse students in any subject using the arts. To help teachers use this multisensory teaching technique to motivate students, this handbook gives them easy-to-follow guidelines for establishing an Academic Club, suggested activities, profiles of Academic Clubs, details on how the Clubs promote positive behavior, insightful interviews with teachers, and advice on adapting the approach in different settings. With Sally Smith's infectious energy, humor, and creativity, teachers will transform their classrooms into clubs where each student belongs and learns.

Price: US$29.95 • Stock Number: 6830 • 2005 • 232 pages • 7 x 10 • paperback • ISBN 1-55766-683-0
